THE OAKWOOD PRESS

The Barry Railway Steamers

by

M.A. Tedstone

THE OAKWOOD PRESS

British Library Cataloguing in Publication Data
A Record for this book is available from the British Library
ISBN 0 85361 635 3

Typeset by Oakwood Graphics.
Repro by Ford Graphics, Ringwood, Hants.
Printed by Cambrian Printers, Aberystwyth, Ceredigion.

Paddlebox details, *Gwalia*. *Richard Clammer Collection*

Title page: A boat-train has arrived at Barry Pier and the passengers are heading for the pontoon alongside which *Westonia* is berthed, possibly late-1907 or later, after the ban on Red Funnel Line vessels trading at Cardiff. *Brian Luxton Collection*

Front cover: The new order at the Pier Head, Cardiff - the Red Funnel Line steamers *Westonia* and *Gwalia* in 1905, at what has become the waterfront of Cardiff Bay.
Rear cover, top: *Devonia* boarding passengers at Weston 'Old Pier', otherwise known as Birnbeck Pier, during the era of the Red Funnel Line between 1906-1911.
Rear cover, bottom: A 1907 advertisement for the new paddle-steamer *Barry* to promote rail-connected sailings via the Barry Railway Company services from Cardiff (Riverside) via Barry Pier to Weston-super-Mare and elsewhere. *(All) Lionel Vaughan Collection*

Published by The Oakwood Press (Usk), P.O. Box 13, Usk, Mon., NP15 1YS.
E-mail: sales@oakwoodpress.co.uk
Website: www.oakwoodpress.co.uk

Contents

An undated view which nicely illustrates the detail of embarkation arrangements at Barry Pier, the station platform (*to the right*) being reached via the walkway from the pontoon.
Lionel Vaughan Collection

Introduction

Almost a century has elapsed since the Barry 'Red Funnel Line' steamers disappeared from the Bristol Channel excursion scene, and although Barry Pier has gone, as has the railway that served it, the remains are yet visible, and so the memory of the handsome fleet of paddle-steamers that were based there lingers on. The recollections of those that travelled on the former Barry vessels that survived until World War II, albeit handed down over six decades later, have been the stimulus to ask why it was that the White Funnel Fleet of Bristol was so challenged, at a key time of the evolution of the British paddle-steamer, by the upstart South Walian Barry Railway Company.

To understand the story of the so-called 'Barry & Bristol Channel Steamship Company', which had such a brief life after being launched in 1905, it is necessary to consider - on the one hand - the origins of the parent Barry Railway Company and - on the other - how P. & A. Campbell Ltd of Bristol with its 'White Funnel Fleet' became the dominant excursion-steamer operator in the Bristol Channel by the 1890s, the era in which this story starts. But first, to get an idea of how those railway entrepreneurs may have viewed their future, all one has to do is stand at Friars Point at Barry Island or on the pebble beach at Porthkerry, on a clear day, and gaze across the Channel at the not so distant shores of Somerset and the lofty cliffs of North Devon, and the inspiration is all too clear. A more down-to-earth reason was of course readily apparent if one looked at the increasing numbers of passengers who passed through the gates at Cardiff's Pier Head to embark upon the steamers that awaited, and who represented a rapidly growing market for excursion steamer sailings.

The Barry Railway Company could trace its roots to early Parliamentary openings in the 1860s, being very much a railway company created to serve a docks complex for the export of coal. Here, passenger train operations were somewhat secondary to the primary purpose of moving minerals traffic down from the various valleys, and through the substantial Barry Docks complex out to virtually anywhere in the world. The Barry network grew fairly rapidly in the 1880s, and was substantially complete by 1897 when the route to the west - the nominally separate Vale of Glamorgan Railway - opened. To cut a long story short, the Barry Railway Company had succeeded in gaining access to numerous valleys already served by other railways in order to tap the abundant minerals traffics of the South Wales coalfield for export through its large new Barry Docks, which rivalled the nearby ports of Cardiff, Penarth and Newport and, rather further afield, Swansea.

On the other hand the White Funnel Fleet of the Bristol-based company of P. & A. Campbell Ltd had its origins as a purely excursion-steamer business trading in the Bristol Channel, which had commenced after the charter of the first *Waverley* in 1887, without any particular railway interests or involvement. The expansion of the Bristol company was gradual at first, but became more rapid in the mid-1890s. The Campbell brothers saw how their rival Cardiff-based company Edwards, Robertson developed valuable links between its 'Yellow Funnel Fleet' and the powerful Taff Vale Railway for through ticketing between South Wales valleys towns such as Pontypridd and resorts in Devon and Somerset, via Cardiff and Penarth. But by the late 1890s the White Funnel Fleet of P. & A. Campbell Ltd had taken over the vessels of its Cardiff-based competitors, and the supremacy of the Bristol ships was clear for all to see.

Either *Gwalia* or *Devonia* coming in to pick up passengers at Barry Pier on the 'Railway Run' from Cardiff and Penarth to Lynmouth and Ilfracombe, North Devon.
Brian Luxton Collection

From the viewpoint of the Barry Railway Company, then, seeking to expand its empire, a Bristol-based company had established a dominance in the lucrative and fast-growing excursion-steamer traffic then being generated in South Wales. Perhaps it was only natural that the Barry interests should seek to challenge those that were perceived as threatening, or even monopolistic. As the Barry Docks complex had taken shape, it was a relatively straightforward matter to extend passenger railway operations from Barry across to Barry Island for leisure traffic, and then to push further through tunnel to what was to become Barry Pier station, immediately adjacent to the main entrance lock to Barry Docks. Here was deep water, sufficient for much of the shipping of the day to be able to enter Barry Docks, irrespective of tidal constraints. Extreme tidal patterns in the Bristol Channel were of major significance to shipping, and a passenger steamer pontoon-berth, with an adjacent railway station for easy interchange of passengers at any state of the tide, seemed an obvious adjunct to this prosperous railway network in the late-1890s.

Although the Barry Railway Company thought in terms of controlling its own steamship operations from the outset, it was realised that this would meet with opposition from the established P. & A. Campbell Ltd company at Bristol with its large fleet, and so the Barry company initially settled for an alliance whereby the White Funnel Fleet of steamers served Barry Pier when it opened in 1899. But it was to be an uneasy alliance, and so inevitably the point was soon reached where the Barry company would feel obliged to go it alone. The struggle that followed was to be both litigious and complicated and the structure of this book is thus based on four distinct periods in the life of Barry Pier, in order to present a comprehensive picture of the passenger shipping activities of the Barry Railway Company. The first period covers the years up until 1904, before the railway company opted to purchase its own fleet. The second period, which comprises the larger part of this account, spanned the years 1905-1909 when this new fleet was operated directly in connection with the Barry Railway Company, and when the head-on competition between red and white funnel interests was intense, and the legal battles were high-profile.

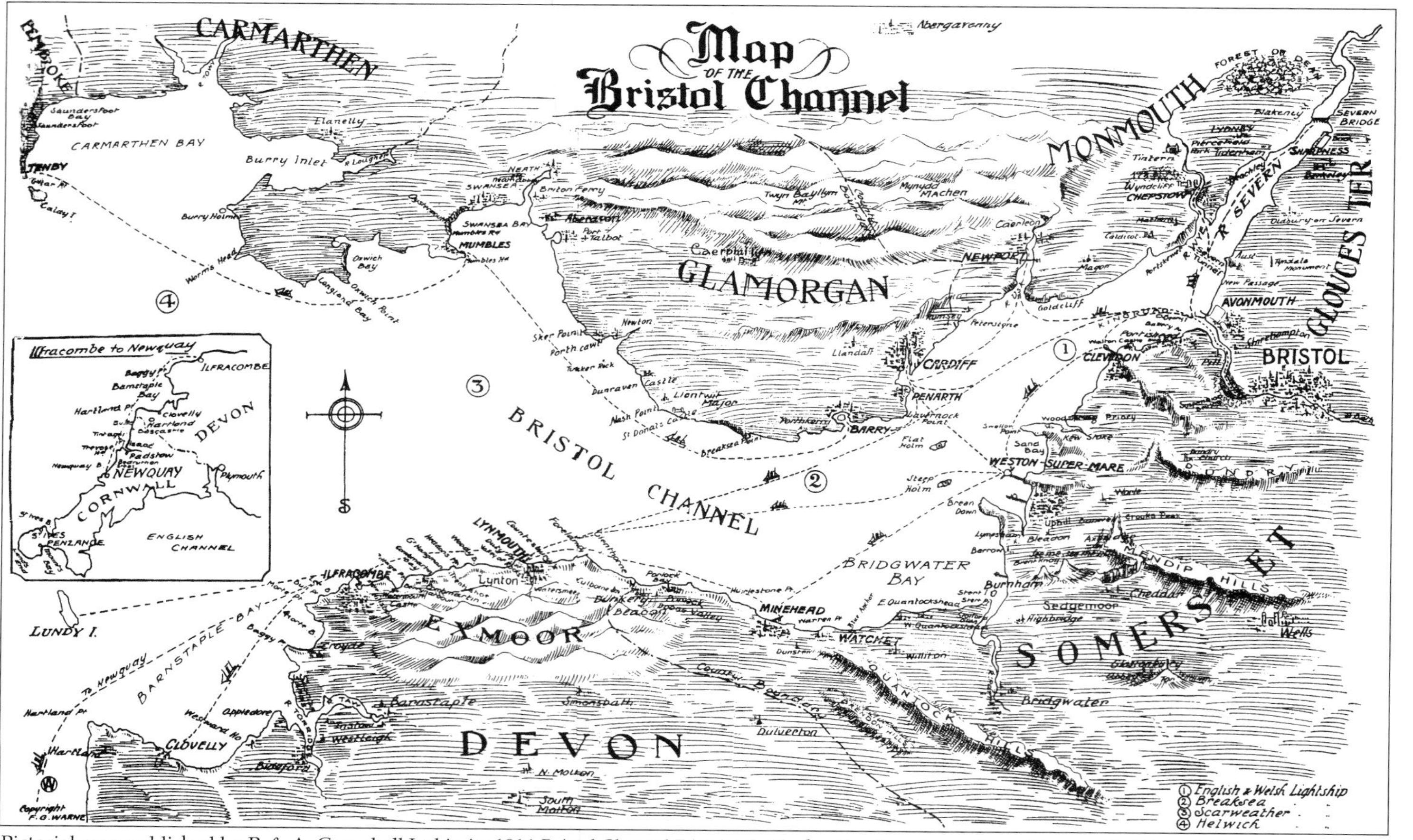

Pictorial map published by P. & A. Campbell Ltd in its 1914 *Bristol Channel District Guide* shortly after absorption of former Red Funnel Line services. Barry is included but only in an indicative sense as a calling-point on Cardiff to Mumbles & Tenby excursions, although there were still Barry-Weston services operated as well as Barry calls in primary Cardiff & Penarth to Lynmouth & Ilfracombe runs.

Author's Collection

Three of the Barry steamers seen together at Barry Pier, and the fourth at sea in an attractive publicity postcard view probably dating from 1907. *Brian Luxton Collection*

A third, brief period came after the railway sold its three remaining vessels to a wholly separate undertaking who operated in the two seasons, 1910 and 1911. After this the red funnel disappeared from the Bristol Channel excursion passenger scene and the fourth and final period takes the story forward from 1912. This was when P. & A. Campbell Ltd took control, and ended in the 1970s, after services at Barry Pier had dwindled and were finally given up, and the pontoon dismantled.

It was the late H.G. Owen of Swansea, well known for his research and knowledge of many aspects of Bristol Channel maritime matters, who inspired me to tackle this subject. Having got to know George in the early-1990s, I took the article he wrote in 1957 on the Barry Railway Company steamers for the journal *Ship Ahoy* as the starting point for my study. He wrote then that '. . . the history of the Barry Railway Company's ownership of excursion steamers is a lengthy and confused one. It would require a whole volume to deal adequately with this subject . . .' Puffing away on his pipe at his home in the Uplands at Swansea, looking down over Swansea Bay, George's wry recollections of the welcome afforded to a few hundred, thirsty Swansea folk seeking refreshment at genteel Minehead on a Sunday in the 1920s after arriving on *Lady Moyra* - taking contemporary Welsh licensing restrictions into account - led me to ask more questions. It is a matter of great regret that George died in 2003 before this book was finalised but his input into its content cannot be understated. His memory of events from the 1920s and 1930s was remarkable, and our extensive correspondence and friendship led me to seek to find the answers to the issues that arose when discussing just how it must have been at the beginning, when the Barry Railway Company embarked upon its costly and short-lived adventure into shipping.

Mike Tedstone
Purton, Wiltshire
August 2004

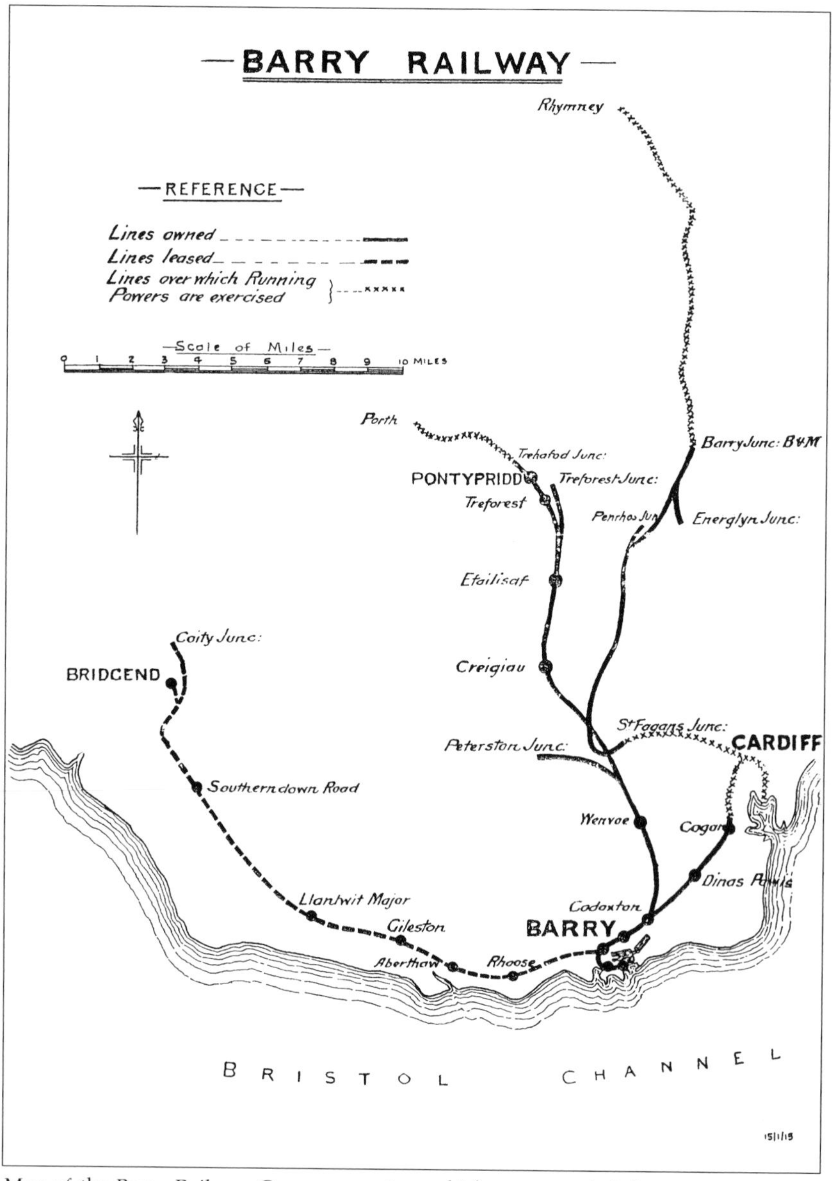

Map of the Barry Railway Company system which accompanied the 1915 Report and Accounts, showing the full extent of lines built plus adjacent lines. Passenger trains were operated from Barry to Bridgend, Porth and Cardiff (Riverside and Clarence Road stations) as well as between Cardiff and Pontypridd (Graig) partly over the Great Western Railway (GWR) main line from London to Cardiff and Fishguard. *Cardiff Library*

Chapter One

Development of Barry Pier 1895-1904

Once on the Glamorgan seashore, people felt the lure of the deep, whether or not they had essential business in great waters. The islands of the Channel and the sunny hills of the further side were a perpetual invitation to travel. The Barry Railway Company saw an opportunity for another enterprise - getting people into ships - after getting coal into ships.

Iorwerth W. Prothero, *Barry: The Centenary Book*

The Barry Railway Company vision

The term 'vision statement' was very much in vogue in the 1990s, yet a century before it must have been the case that it was partly 'vision' which impelled the promoters of public undertakings onwards to successfully raise large amounts of capital for huge construction projects. If we accept that, by the early 1890s, the Barry Railway Company was an established fact in South Wales, despite the opposition it had received from the Taff Vale Railway and others, then the notion of looking across the Bristol Channel to the not very distant shores of Somerset and Devon was an obvious one. From the Minutes of Meetings of the Directors of the Barry Railway Company in February 1895 we can trace the probable beginnings of the Barry excursion steamers as John Wolfe Barry, Consulting Engineer, submitted plans for a 'landing stage for steamers'. Perusal of a map of Barry No. 1 Dock, and its associated railway sidings, is sufficient to show that such a facility was a relatively straightforward affair to conceive of, although at this time the railway to Barry Island had not yet been completed. But the intention to extend the railway beyond Barry Island station, through tunnel, was soon clearly defined and an Act promoted accordingly for the requisite powers then necessary to build such a line to gain access to what was to become Barry Pier.

The year 1895 was an interesting one in tracing the history of the Bristol Channel excursion steamer businesses, as the rate of expansion of the White Funnel Fleet had then become distinctly rapid. The first *Waverley* was operated from Bristol in 1887 by Messrs P. & A. Campbell, primarily on excursion services to Ilfracombe, and expansion occurred with a second ship, *Ravenswood,* joining *Waverley* for the 1891 season. The transition to becoming a limited company with substantial equity occurred in 1893 and P.& A. Campbell Ltd, as they became known, had in that year experimented on the Cardiff to Weston-super-Mare 'ferry' run with the chartered *Sea Breeze.* After putting their own *Waverley* on the run in 1894 after the new *Westward Ho* entered service alongside *Ravenswood,* a stronger White Funnel Fleet presence was firmly established at Cardiff by 1895 with more calls there from the growing Bristol company, in straight competition with Edwards, Robertson and its local Yellow Funnel Fleet. Another new paddle-steamer *Cambria* joined the fleet in 1895, the same year that Penarth Pier was opened, and provided additional revenue sources. Over at Weston, Birnbeck Pier was busy and, although wholly tidally-constrained, its

Treharne Pier at Whitmore Bay, Barry Island, was occasionally used by smaller paddle-tug excursion steamers in the early 1890s. *Brian Luxton Collection*

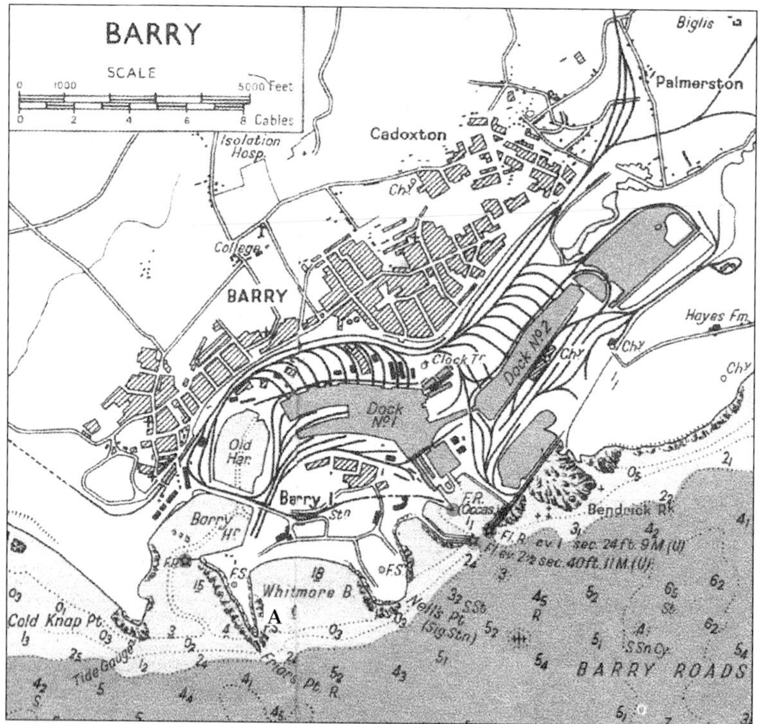

Map of Barry Dock and Old Harbour area, showing the relative locations of the early Treharne Pier (A) and the rail-linked Barry Pier, reached through tunnel beyond Barry Island station. *Stanford Colour Chart/Author's Collection*

management harboured their own vision for a low-water extension to attract more visitors if only the steamers could be able to call at any time of day rather than as the tides so inconveniently dictated. Yet another new purpose-built vessel was to join the White Funnel Fleet in 1896, the celebrated *Britannia.* Finally, this was supplemented by *Lady Margaret,* then only one year old, and which had run in association with the Edwards, Robertson concern, before succumbing to Campbell pressures. We should note that in the early 1890s the smaller paddle-tug members of the so-called 'Yellow Funnel Fleet' of Edwards, Robertson, such as *Earl of Dunraven,* would call occasionally as tides permitted at Treharne Pier at Barry Island, although this privately-owned structure had but a short life.

This then was the situation which obtained prior to the half-yearly Barry Railway Company shareholders' meeting held in August 1896, at which the intention to link Barry with Weston-super-Mare by sea became publicly apparent. The Directors of the Barry Railway Company now revealed their hand in terms of a stated belief in the superiority of their potential Barry Pier facility compared to that at nearby Cardiff:

> . . . for some time their Directors had been doing all they possibly could to promote the construction of a deep water pier at Weston and when it was completed boats could be run from Barry to Weston at fixed hours without being dependent upon the tides.

Behind the scenes, discussions had already taken place between the respective officials of the Barry Railway Company and of P. & A. Campbell Ltd. The Directors of the latter company had been notified of the intention of the Barry interests to seek the essential Parliamentary Powers required by a railway undertaking to run its own passenger ships, in October 1895. This was bound to alarm the Campbells whose own investment was now of substantial proportions, and they would have felt threatened by a nearby new steamship company on a parallel route. Opposition to any application by the Barry Railway Company for Steamship Powers was thus inevitable. Discussions took place over the next few months, and by March 1896 it had in effect been agreed, albeit informally, that the Barry Railway Company would give P. & A. Campbell Ltd 'first refusal' to run a cross-channel steamer service from Barry Pier if and when this facility was constructed. By October 1896, the Chairman of P. & A. Campbell Ltd, Alfred Deedes, had made it plain to Thomas Roe Thompson, a Director of the Barry Railway Company and of whom we shall hear much more, that P. & A. Campbell Ltd opposition to a Bill promoted by the Barry would be such that the railway company would almost certainly fail if it pursued such an attempt.

This alliance was to prove an uneasy one, as well as being short-lived, but it set the tone for subsequent relationships between the two undertakings. A few years were to elapse before Barry Pier was actually constructed and ready for passenger use. In the meantime, the new railway line from Barry to Barry Island finally opened on the August Bank Holiday Monday, 3rd August, 1896, and it is clear from reports of that occasion that work on the extension of the branch railway through to Barry Pier had already commenced. Also of interest is that the Campbell steamers had in fact already made occasional local appearances with calls at the Barry Dock entrance-lock, one such being taken by *Westward Ho* on Wednesday 15th July, 1896 to convey a Barry Chamber of Trade party of around 300 souls on a trip to Cheddar via Weston. As the railway to the island had not then been opened, brakes conveyed the party to the dock from Island Road, Barry over the causeway. Described in the *Barry Dock News* as a great success, occasions such as this arguably established the dilemma that ultimately was to cause the Barry Railway Company management such grief: on the one hand, the splendid new White Funnel Fleet of steamers was clearly quite capable of handling Barry Pier calls within their Bristol-based empire, but on the other, local pride and mistrust of what some came to see as a monopoly power eventually drove them to procure their own fleet, under their own control, irrespective of the cost.

Progress on the short Pier Railway extension and pontoon pier itself clearly became prolonged after the commencement of works in 1896, and scrutiny of Minutes of the meetings of the Directors of P. & A. Campbell Ltd makes it clear that the Bristol company thought that the new Barry Pier passenger facility would be ready in 1898, but this proved to be a false alarm. At the half-yearly meeting of the Barry Railway Company in January 1897 it had been reported that:

> . . . contractors will be able very shortly to commence putting in the foundations of the low-water landing stage. The contract for the construction of the pontoons and landing bridge has been let, and operations have begun . . .

At that stage the Deep Lock had just commenced to be used, and a 10 per cent dividend was declared on Ordinary Stock. Perhaps those responsible were over-optimistic, but as 1897 progressed there was no sign that things were going to be ready that year. In early 1898 shareholders were told that works on the low-water stage and pontoon were proceeding satisfactorily, and the *Barry Dock News* in June 1898 was able to report that:

> . . . two pontoons for the landing-stage were delivered this week to Barry Dock from Lysaght's, Bristol, both 90 ft in length, 24 ft beam, 10 ft depth. A third, of like dimensions, was launched at the builders yard on Monday, also the small pontoon was on the blocks at works . . .

Another attempt by the Barry Railway Company to gain its own powers to operate steamships in 1898 failed, and a second truce period was established in late 1898 when the Barry Directors resolved that:

> . . . if an independent steamship company provided the necessary service of steamers from Barry Dock with a view to developing the undertaking of the Barry Co. assistance should be given to such independent company by agreeing to make such allowances and rebates out of through bookings of passengers and goods as might be agreed from time to time . . .

Thus the scene was set for the situation that was to obtain when Barry Pier and its associated extension railway from Barry Island finally opened for traffic in 1899, and the first steamer to call was the White Funnel Fleet paddle-steamer *Lady Margaret*. The deal had eventually been hammered out between the Welsh railway company and the English excursion steamer operator for vessels operated by the latter - seemingly at their risk as there is no recorded evidence to suggest a contractual or payment agreement - to service the smart new pier belonging to the former. This deal was something of a gamble for P. & A. Campbell Ltd, which had enlarged its fleet in order to be able to provide the required level of service at Barry over and above the already established commitments at Bristol, Newport and Cardiff. Not just one extra vessel would be required but two, as this extract from a Barry Railway Company Directors' meeting on 2nd December, 1898 made clear: '. . . Messrs Campbell were to station one boat at Barry for cross-channel traffic, and to start a boat from Cardiff every day, so as to leave Barry at fixed times for Ilfracombe . . .'

Before describing how Barry Pier and its associated railway were brought into use in 1899, it is worth briefly considering how the network of passenger train services operated by the Barry Railway Company had evolved, as well as looking at how the excursion steamer market in the Bristol Channel had developed so quickly in the preceding decade. Both parties had committed very sizeable amounts of capital to their respective undertakings, by way of many miles of expensively-engineered railway lines and a large number of newly laid-down paddle-steamers. Each had clearly to protect its own commercial interests, but crucially there was already a degree of distrust and the two undertakings were somewhat wary of one another.

Barry Railway Company passenger services

Railways around Barry were first mooted in the mid-1860s, but nothing came of these first stirrings. A attempt to deposit a Bill in 1882 for incorporation of a Barry Dock and Railways Company was defeated, but success was achieved at another attempt in 1884. Primarily intended as a means of getting coal down from the Welsh valleys for export through a dock at Barry that would compete with the busy nearby port of Cardiff, a first stretch of the main route of the Barry Railway Company - as it was to officially become in 1891 - opened between Cogan and Barry in 1888, feeding off the Taff Vale Railway. Barry (No. 1) Dock opened in 1889, and by 1893 passenger trains were running between Cardiff and Barry, from the GWR Riverside station adjacent to Cardiff General (latterly Cardiff Central) station. In 1894 these services were extended beyond Riverside into the heart of Cardiff's dockland area, at Clarence Road, just a short step away from the Pier Head where the excursion and packet steamer services were concentrated.

The Cardiff-Barry services were to remain the most important part of the Barry Railway network used by passenger trains, but an important link with the Rhondda valley saw the introduction of passenger services in 1896, between Barry and Porth via Creigiau. By means of running powers over the Great Western Railway main line through South Wales and a connecting spur at St Fagans, west of Cardiff, the Barry Railway Company was also able to run an alternative service (i.e., to that primarily provided by the Taff Vale Railway) between Cardiff and Pontypridd, to its own Graig station rather higher up above Pontypridd than the larger Taff Vale station at Pontypridd set high up on arched structures above the populous Glamorganshire town.

A third 'flank' of the Barry Railway Company was that to the west, nominally promoted and built by a separate Vale of Glamorgan Railway Company, but in reality a Barry subsidiary. The line between Barry and Bridgend opened in 1897, but setbacks in construction meant that it was not until 1900 that passenger services from Bridgend and Llantwit Major to Barry really settled down. In the meantime the short branch from Barry to Barry Island had opened in 1896, effectively wholly for passenger use. The Pier branch was then authorised in 1896, opening in 1899. Other sections of the Barry Railway, to tap into the Rhymney valley and elsewhere, did not attract scheduled passenger traffic. So at the time excursion steamers were concentrating the minds of the Barry Directors, they effectively had three corridors over which it was envisaged that passenger traffic could be channelled via Barry and the Barry Island branch to their new pier and thence across or down the Bristol Channel: eastwards from Cardiff, northwards from the Rhondda, and westwards from the Vale of Glamorgan. The first was by far the most significant, and the only axis on which dedicated boat-trains were to run.

The rapid growth of Barry itself was notable, and census details quoted by Mr Lake, the General Manager of the Barry Railway Company in an interview published in *The Railway Magazine* in 1906 were revealing: from a level of about 100 in the early 19th century before the railway arrived, by 1891 the population had risen to almost 5,000. Just a decade later the figure in 1901 was over 27,000, and still growing. Barry was not now merely a dock, Mr Lake observed, but a seaside resort and an increasingly important residential suburb of Cardiff.

The Bristol Channel excursion steamer scene

By the late 1890s the White Funnel Fleet of P. & A. Campbell Ltd had established its supremacy in the Bristol Channel once the local Cardiff operator Edwards, Robertson, gave up the operation of its Yellow Funnel Fleet after 1896. John Gunn of Cardiff ran some of the former Yellow Funnel vessels for a couple of seasons, 1897/98, but then also gave up, as a result of which P. & A. Campbell Ltd decided to buy two of his steamers *Bonnie Doon* and *Scotia* for operation in 1899. The White Funnel Fleet had rapidly expanded to six vessels by 1896 - these were *Waverley, Ravenswood, Westward Ho, Cambria, Britannia* and *Lady Margaret.* A seventh had been added in 1897, *Glen Rosa.* As if this was not enough to satisfy a rapidly growing market another vessel which became available from Belfast, *Slieve Donard,* was also acquired for the 1899 season, duly renamed *Albion* to give a more local nomenclature. It is clear from Campbell records that they were buying up steamships at this time to ensure they did not fall into the hands of others, whilst at the same time they were attempting to sell certain of their fleet to the Turks! At this time, the Campbell brothers were commencing to experiment with operations on the South Coast of England too.

Another explanation for this build-up of the White Funnel Fleet to 10 vessels was, of course, the anticipation of the opening of the newly-constructed Barry Pier in 1899. But a virtual monopoly had been created at Cardiff, a fact which had not gone unnoticed by the Barry Railway Directors. Another local passenger steamer presence at Cardiff was offered by *The Marchioness,* on the surviving daily Bristol 'packet' run operated by W.T. Lewis to serve the interests of the Bute Docks Company Ltd, which carried cargo and only a modest number of passengers, and could scarcely be said to have really competed with the Campbell steamers.

The English side of the Bristol Channel

At this time it was very much the case that the larger part of the revenues earned by the P. & A. Campbell Ltd White Funnel Fleet was generated from South Wales traffic sources, at Newport, Cardiff and Penarth. The fleet was unequivocally Bristol-based for maintenance, and its winter quarters and its roots were there alongside the company HQ at Britannia Buildings. These were located close to the Cumberland Basin, in sight of the famous Clifton Suspension Bridge and the dramatic, winding Avon Gorge. Nevertheless, it was South Wales traffic sources which largely influenced the way in which the steamers were actually deployed: although there would be daily sailings from Bristol, much mileage was accumulated on the core 'ferry' run between Cardiff, Penarth and Weston, as well as between Cardiff and the Somerset & Devon resorts of Minehead, Lynmouth, Ilfracombe and Clovelly, and also on sundry other runs which took in Chepstow, Mumbles and latterly Tenby.

Birnbeck Pier at Weston-super-Mare had opened for traffic in 1867. Clevedon Pier had opened for traffic in 1869, and after a difficult period had undergone reconstruction and re-opened in 1893, whereupon its importance to the burgeoning excursion steamer market grew. To a lesser degree, a pier at Burnham had also been in use since the 1860s, and so Somerset was able to offer three destinations to satisfy the demands of the South Wales folk who looked upon the steamers as the means of getting away on day-excursions with plentiful fresh sea air as well as the means of going away on holidays to the numerous hotels in Weston as well as the Devon resorts further afield. Although there was still no pier at Minehead, the steamers called there and landed their passengers either by launch, or at the ancient harbour if the tide served. Whilst of limited significance, at Burnham the adjacent Somerset & Dorset Railway offered a passenger interchange facility which, in a sense, mirrored what was to be provided at Barry. Indeed occasional combined steamer and rail day-excursions from Cardiff to Bournemouth and elsewhere via Burnham were promoted by the White Funnel Fleet, which took advantage of this link, and which was to become a factor in the outlook of the Barry interests in due course.

Weston-super-Mare was clearly the prominent coastal resort in Somerset, the steamer crossing from Cardiff taking around three-quarters of an hour. At the time we are concerned with, the late-1890s, the Weston-super-Mare Pier Company which owned Birnbeck Pier aspired to a low-water extension in order that steamers could arrive there without the tidal restrictions that applied to the original North Jetty. Such was the rate of growth of Weston as a resort that another company had been formed to build an alternative promenade pier right at the centre of the town. The Grand Pier, as it became, did not open until 1904, initially with no steamer Landing Stage extension. Construction of this addition was severely delayed, with consequences for the Barry interests, and which will also be described in due course. But, in July 1898, the *Bristol Observer* newspaper carried a very lengthy article on the prospects which then faced the owners of the older-established Birnbeck Pier, and which arguably shed light on why a railway company in South Wales might then have felt justified in seeking a share of the growing excursion steamer market between Cardiff and Weston. A fire in December 1897 had caused enormous destruction to the principal pierhead buildings at Birnbeck and, rather than a rebuild programme based on like-for-like, expansion was optimistically planned:

> . . . there were many who looked on the calamity as terrific but, as is so often the case, out of evil came good, and the Directors of the Pier Company, though hardly welcoming the devastation that the conflagration caused in its strictest sense, have turned it to good account, so that now the Pier buildings have been made thoroughly up to date, and they will therefore be in thorough keeping with the new Pier, which soon will be ready for the reception of passengers and traffic at low water . . .

The anticipation of the low-water extension at Birnbeck Pier, as it was to eventually become over a decade later, was somewhat premature, but its significance in 1898 was the way in which it would have been seen to fit in with the expansionist aims of the Barry Railway Company, just a few miles away across the Bristol Channel. Given the promotion of the Grand Pier as well as Birnbeck's low-water extension, it was perfectly reasonable to assume in Barry that one or other of these would actually materialise, and that if a reasonable proportion of South Wales folk could be induced to travel by Barry Railway Company services via Barry Pier, at fixed times daily - not unlike the practices which then prevailed on the Clyde - in order to cross to Weston without being tidally constrained at that end, then prosperity would ensue. But the reality was a few years away and, at the point that Barry Pier opened in 1899, the initial links were with the original Birnbeck Pier at Weston, and with Lynmouth and Ilfracombe in Devon.

One might, for the sake of completeness, mention Wooda Bay pier, also in North Devon and which opened in 1897, but this was destined to be distinctly short-lived and of little consequence to this story.

The Welsh side of the Bristol Channel

To complete this snapshot of excursion steamship operations in the Bristol Channel at the time of the imminent opening of Barry Pier and its associated railway in 1899, it is worth mentioning that the growing size and importance of Barry and its docks had not gone unnoticed as a possible destination for White Funnel travellers from the English side. A first trip to Barry from Ilfracombe was offered in 1896, at around the time the new *Britannia* had been delivered, and more trips ran in 1897. Further west another Welsh destination for travellers from England (as well as from Cardiff) was then on offer - this was at the Mumbles, just a few minutes steaming time away from Swansea, which itself was not then part of the P. & A. Campbell Ltd empire. As with Minehead, landing was effected by small boat at Mumbles until - in 1898 - a smart new promenade pier opened. Swansea was then the demesne of Pockett's, a relatively old-established concern who offered excursion sailings with *Brighton*, and which had replaced the older *Velindra* after 1894. The normal Swansea excursion operation then was a morning crossing to Ilfracombe and thence a cruise to Lynmouth, Clovelly or Lundy before a late-afternoon or evening return across the Channel back to Swansea: the new Mumbles Pier fitted in very well with this well-ordered pattern.

Finally, after a faltering start in 1897, the new Victoria Pier at Tenby fully opened in 1899, and became an additional destination on the excursion steamers' map, albeit a relatively far-flung one. All in all, there was a lot going on for Bristol Channel excursionists as the opening of Barry Pier grew closer.

1899 - The opening of Barry Pier

Agreement had eventually been reached between the Barry Railway Company and P. & A. Campbell Ltd that their steamers would provide the daily services at the new pier, all of which would have railway connections. This involved a degree of risk on the part of the Bristol company which, as we saw earlier, had taken steps to expand its fleet in 1897 and again in 1899 and was now poised to incur greater operating expenses by making available two vessels at Barry Pier, in the expectation that its share of takings - basically the steamer element of through railway bookings from Cardiff Riverside station and elsewhere to Weston or Ilfracombe via Barry Railway Company trains to Barry Pier, and thence by steamer - would be commercially advantageous.

Much of the detail of the next few years that follow have been extracted from the two primary South Wales newspaper sources, the *Western Mail* and the more locally circulated *Barry Dock News*, alongside information gleaned from official P. & A. Campbell Ltd and Barry Railway Company records. In November 1898 it was reported that Barry Pier would be ready to open by Easter 1899 and whilst the contractors Messrs Price & Wills were being pressed to complete the job, it was also made apparent that a renewed attempt by the Barry Railway Company was being made to secure Parliamentary Powers to operate its own steamers, and that a Bill would be in Parliament by December 1899. This must have been seen by the Campbells as a threat. They were expecting to conclude an agreement for their White Funnel Fleet steamers to service the new pier, in order to utilise their own capital resources as they had planned. However, by the end of December the Bill was abandoned, as an understanding with the Bristol company was finally agreed.

The role of a certain Mrs Grundy must now be introduced and explained, for it was she that supplied a chatty yet informative column known as *Mrs Grundy's*

The Barry Railway Company locomotive fleet was largely made up of a wide variety of goods-types. Out of a total of 148 locomotives which passed to the GWR at the grouping in 1922, only 17 were passenger-tank types, comprising two class 'C' 2-4-0T, four class 'G' 0-4-4T and 11 class 'J' 2-4-2T. Of smart, purposeful appearance No. 66, one of the class 'G' types built in 1892 by the Vulcan Foundry, is seen under the care of driver Makepeace.

National Museums & Galleries of Wales

Jottings in the weekly editions of the *Barry Dock News*. Written under an editorial *nom de plume*, this column documented various goings-on in the newly-created Barry and Barry Dock community which had evolved as the docks had been constructed, and whose early members then stayed on, as it were, to occupy jobs as dockers and railwaymen *et al.* A certain parochial style of conservatism characterised the tone of these jottings but, over the years, much of value was recorded of the activities of the Barry steamers and how these events touched upon the lives of the local residents. The original Mrs Grundy, in literature, was evidently a lady whose views epitomised 'conventional propriety', as will become clear.

Her first utterances on the new enterprise at Barry Pier were to the effect that it was expected that Barry Pier would open on 17th July, 1899, and not 12th July as had evidently been reported elsewhere. Regrettably this proved to be premature, and Barry Railway Company records make it plain that the Inspecting Officer, Col Yorke, R.E, found a number of matters requiring attention on the Barry Pier railway line before permission to open could be granted. On 16th June, 1899, this notice appeared in the *Barry Dock News*:

BARRY NEW PIER AND PASSENGER BOAT SERVICE
OFFICIAL DATE OF OPENING
INTENTIONS OF THE BARRY COMPANY

The announcement made elsewhere last week of the date of opening of the new Landing Stage at Barry Docks, and the commencement of a regular service of Passenger Boats therewith, was both inaccurate and unauthorised. We are officially informed that the date fixed upon by the Barry Railway Company for the dual event is Monday, the 17th July, and not the previous Wednesday. As we announced a fortnight ago, there will not only be a regular service of passenger boats between Barry and the various watering-places on the opposite coast of the Bristol Channel, but the boats will call at Barry several times a day and trains will be run in connection therewith from Cardiff, the Rhondda Valley, and the Vale of Glamorgan districts. For the present year the boats will be those of Messrs Campbell Ltd of Cardiff and Bristol, but the Barry Company have not abandoned their intention to seek Parliamentary Powers to provide their own fleet of passenger steamers for the purpose.

A week later, on 23rd June, 1899, Mrs Grundy passed comment on the prospects for a pier at Minehead which, lying opposite Barry on the other side of the Bristol Channel, was naturally of interest to Barry folk, and her report read thus:

It is a gratifying fact, as showing the important future connection between Barry and the different watering places on the opposite coast of the channel, that one of the firms of solicitors of the Minehead Pier Company, which is now being promoted, is Messrs Downing & Handcock, the solicitors to the Barry Railway Company, and in their prospectus the Minehead Pier Company dwell at considerable length upon the unrivalled advantages of Barry and its new passenger pontoon.

It would be be another couple of years before what was to be the penultimate Bristol Channel pleasure pier did open for traffic although, when it did, the link with Barry which Mrs Grundy foresaw was significant.

Col Yorke inspected the Barry Pier extension railway and landing-stage pontoon on 17th July, 1899, and made a number of stipulations with which the Barry Railway were obliged to comply before permission to commence operations was granted. These were largely to do with signalling alterations, as well as the rather steep gradient in the newly-bored tunnel through which boat-trains were to descend with the utmost caution to the Pier, and which involved - *inter alia* - alterations to the buffer-stops at the platforms at Barry Pier. All his stipulations were to be complied with by 25th July, 1899.

On 21st July, 1899, the *Barry Dock News* was able to make the following announcement:

BARRY PASSENGER PIER
TO BE OPENED FOR TRAFFIC NEXT THURSDAY
ARRANGEMENTS FOR AN EXCELLENT BOAT SERVICE DAILY

We have been asked officially to announce that the Barry Passenger Pier and Pier Railway Station, having been inspected by Col. Yorke, R.E., the Board of Trade Inspector, will be opened for traffic on Thursday next, the 27th instant, and the Barry Railway Company and P. & A. Campbell Ltd have made arrangements for an excellent service of passenger boats to ply between Barry Pier and Weston, Minehead, Lynmouth, Wooda Bay and Ilfracombe daily. A feature of the arrangement is that through tickets will be issued at all stations of the Barry and Vale of Glamorgan railways. The combined rail and steamboat fares from Cardiff (Riverside Station) will be the same as from Cardiff by boat alone.

The new pier has been fitted with all conveniences for passengers, and hydraulic lifts have been provided for transferring luggage from the pontoon to the station platform and vice-versa. A bridge has also been erected for foot passengers to communicate with the roadway leading to the island. The contract for the pier and extension of the line of railway from the island railway station has been efficiently carried out by Messrs Price and Wills under the local management of Mr R. Hollowday. Sir John Wolfe-Barry KCB was the consulting engineer; and Mr R.C.H. Davison was the resident engineer.

The atmosphere in Barry was now justifiably positive, but from the perspective of P. & A. Campbell Ltd things may have seemed less than ideal: rather than having opened in 1898 as initially intended, the date now achieved in 1899 was well over a month into the season, and two vessels of their fleet had been more or less idle in anticipation of the pier being ready for traffic. One cannot say with certainty which these two were, but P. & A. Campbell Ltd records allow one to infer that *Albion* - built as *Slieve Donard* at Clydebank in 1893 for service with the Belfast and County Down Railway in Northern Ireland - had been acquired in 1899 by Alec Campbell with Barry Pier in mind. The older vessel *Glen Rosa* was also to become a frequent visitor to Barry Pier, and had been transferred to the Limited Company in 1898 from the personal ownership of Alec Campbell: he had purchased her in 1897 as expansion on the South Coast was initiated by *Cambria. Glen Rosa* supported *Cambria* at Southampton in 1898, but her retention in the Bristol Channel for local duties in 1899 was clearly with the Barry venture in mind.

In 1899, then, the White Funnel Fleet had become big and impressive. Half of the 10-strong White Funnel Fleet had been built to the order of Peter and Alec Campbell, but *Lady Margaret* had been purchased in 1896 after only one year in the service of Edwards, Robertson and the rather older vessels *Bonnie Doon* and *Scotia* were of a secondary nature to the Campbell 'flyers' *Westward Ho, Cambria* and *Britannia,* built in rapid succession in 1894, 1895 and 1896. It was to *Lady Margaret* that fell the honour of being the first steamer to call at the new Barry Pier - for invited guests only - on Friday 21st July, 1899, and Mrs Grundy commented succintly on the natural advantages of Barry Pier over the Pier Head at Cardiff:

> Another unique achievement for Barry. The first passenger boat, the *Lady Margaret,* which had the privilege of opening the Barry New Pier for traffic last Friday morning, left for Ilfracombe at dead low water, a feat never before accomplished by any boat in the Bristol Channel.

The first sailing by Lady Margaret

The account in the *Barry Dock News* of the first sailing from Barry Pier by the P. & A. Campbell Ltd steamer *Lady Margaret* is an intriguing one, as much as anything for the apology that Mr Archibald Hood J.P, the Deputy Chairman of the Barry Railway Company, had to give to guests that day regarding the absence of the Chairman and a number of his fellow Directors, whom one would have thought would have undoubtedly made every effort to be present for this significant occasion. Much money and effort had been expended on getting the Pier open for steamboat traffic, yet seemingly all was not well as Mr Thompson - a Barry Railway Company Director with extensive shipowning interests, and whose role would become of crucial importance - declined to be present. Relationships with P. & A. Campbell Ltd would still have been somewhat frosty at this stage, but Peter Campbell joined the party, together with his fellow White Funnel Fleet Directors Messrs Brown and Waite, making up around 60 guests altogether. A special train ran from Cardiff to Barry Pier and, after inspecting the new facilities there, the party boarded *Lady Margaret* which left at about 11.00 am for the voyage down Channel to Ilfracombe, in weather described as delightful, with dinner served off Foreland Point. Some of the party disembarked at Ilfracombe whilst the paddler proceeded down the coast towards Clovelly, before returning to Ilfracombe at about 3 o'clock. Tea was served on the passage back up Channel, and Barry was reached at about 5.30 pm.

Speeches were made, and Mr Hood reiterated the aim of the Barry Railway Company, which was that a facility would soon be provided on the English coast of the Channel which would enable the boats to run at fixed times daily, in connection with their railway services. There was no mention that day of the boats being operated by other than their colleagues, P. & A. Campbell Ltd, and for the moment all was well. A glowing reference to 'the teeming population of the hills and the Vale' was made, it being implied that this section of the South Wales populace had not hitherto been adequately catered for, and would wish to take advantage of the new steamboat services via Barry Pier and - of course - Barry Railway Company local passenger train services. The party dispersed on the special train back from Barry Pier to Cardiff, and a short public preview

As the Barry network expanded more passenger locomotives were acquired. The later class 'J' types also had an attractive appearance and No. 94, built by Sharp, Stewart in 1899, is seen here calling at Cadoxton station, looking towards Barry, with a smartly-turned out passenger working to Cardiff. The Barry Railway Company ran a number of dedicated boat-trains over the years between Cardiff and Barry Pier, and the principal connecting services were into and out of the main Ilfracombe boat, at around 9.30 am from Riverside station 'down' in the morning, and back from Barry Pier at about 6.30 pm or later depending on the time of year, on a limited-stop basis, after the arrival of the 'up' boat working. It is clear from contemporary newspaper reports that confusion was occasionally caused by some trains which omitted local stations, and at most times throughout the day it was the practice to extend ordinary Barry Island services to the Pier station, in accordance with steamer times as influenced by tidal variations at Weston-super-Mare and elsewhere. Trains were formed of four- and six-wheeled non-gangwayed carriages at the time the Barry Railway Company was involved in passenger shipping activities.

National Museums & Galleries of Wales

cruise from Barry Pier that evening was evidently offered by *Lady Margaret* between 7.15 and 9.00 pm, for which a special train was laid on, at a fare of one shilling from Cogan and stations to Barry. The new Barry Pier had now become part of the Bristol Channel excursion steamer scene, and duly opened fully to the public the following Thursday 27th July, 1899.

At this juncture it is worth taking stock of what had been created by the Barry Railway Company in a comparatively short space of time. The railway had been brought to the large new docks complex at Barry, an extension to Barry Island had been opened to develop passenger traffic, and now the further extension through tunnel to Barry Pier was in place. Although it may not have been publicly apparent, all was not well with the relationship between the railway and the Bristol-based company who had developed the White Funnel Fleet of steamers, but calls at the new pier had eventually commenced and initial passenger traffic levels seemed promising enough, at least to the railway company. Looking on the bright side, more new pier destinations in the Bristol Channel were in prospect: Mumbles Pier had opened in 1898 and it was confidently expected that rapidly-developing Weston would soon have a new, centrally-located pier, to which regular services could be offered free of tidal constraints. But from the P. & A. Campbell Ltd perspective, it had been building up its own fleet, and had branched out into operating on the South Coast, at Southampton, in 1897. It was only natural that it would look to earn the best returns possible from its vessels, and there had already been delays to the start-up of the Barry venture, which would have been seen very much as a commercial compromise. It was to be five years before matters finally came to a head, and the two companies waged war on one another, but in the meantime steamers were available from the English company to service the new pier in South Wales, even if the commercial relationship was to take on a rather challenging character.

The first season: traffic arrangements at Barry Pier in 1899

Whilst the new services at Barry Pier required the deployment of two vessels by P. & A. Campbell Ltd, the manner in which operations were actually carried out was not wholly separate from the already established activities at the Pier Head at Cardiff. Additional advertisements appeared in the *Western Mail* newspaper, on quite a grand scale, to promote the new joint arrangements of the Barry Railway Company and P. & A. Campbell Ltd, and sought to stress the regularity of the daily (except Sundays) Ilfracombe service via Barry Pier, which amounted to a 10.00 am departure to Lynmouth, Wooda Bay and Ilfracombe, after arrival of the connecting 9.20 am train from Cardiff Riverside station. No precise arrival time at Ilfracombe was stated, it being left to passengers to deduce that this would depend to some extent on the tides, and the numbers of passengers handled at Lynmouth by launch. Unlike at Weston's Birnbeck Pier the harbour at Ilfracombe was approachable throughout most of the day except at times of exceptional spring tides, where an arrival which happened to coincide with very low water might occasion a wait off the harbour. In the return direction departure was normally advertised during that first 1899

When Barry Pier opened for traffic in 1899 the P. & A. Campbell Ltd vessel *Lady Margaret* ran the first trip for invited guests to Ilfracombe. She is seen here departing from Ilfracombe at some point before 1903, when she was sold to the Furness Railway. *H.A. Allen Collection*

This map illustrates the 'Commercial Compromise' whereby fares between Cardiff & Weston were the same whether by White Funnel Fleet or Red Funnel Line steamer, direct from Cardiff or via train to Barry Pier. For many Cardiff folk it would always be more convenient to embark at Cardiff than travel via the Barry Railway Company system in order to cross the Bristol Channel. (NB Map contains error north of Caerphilly!) *Author's Collection*

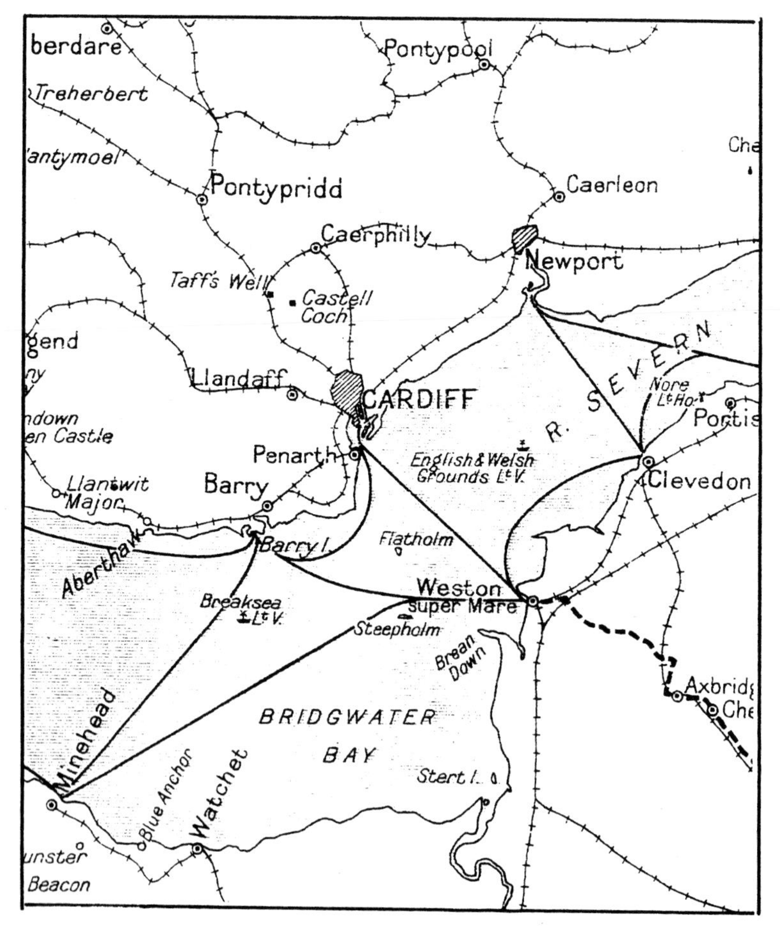

season at 4.30 pm, so that the steamer would be back at Barry Pier for passengers to catch the 6.50 pm boat-train to Cardiff Riverside. When tides were adverse this departure time would be advanced to 4.15 pm, so that sufficient margin existed for connections to be made into the same fixed-time train. The P. & A. Campbell Ltd advertisements stated that this service would normally be provided by either *Westward Ho* or *Britannia,* but with the usual rider of weather and circumstances permitting.

The pattern for sailings between Barry Pier and Weston-super-Mare was not so simple, as Birnbeck Pier at this time had no low-water landing-stage. Thus departure times varied considerably from Barry Pier, as did the number of round trips that could be programmed, but during August and September 1899 there were between two and four crossings each way offered daily (except Sundays), all with connecting trains from and to Cardiff Riverside station. The earliest departure from Cardiff (i.e. by train) was 8.20 am, which gave an arrival in Weston at 10.05, with a last departure from Weston back to Barry Pier usually no later than six or seven pm, depending on tides. On days when four round trips were performed, each allowed 45 minutes to cross the channel in either direction, the ferry steamer would be kept quite busy, and Barry Railway Company train services could be operated economically by extending ordinary Cardiff to Barry Island services through to the Pier station and vice versa if passenger numbers did not warrant special boat trains. This service was advertised quite separately to the established P. & A. Campbell Ltd service between Cardiff and Weston-super-Mare, calling at Penarth, which itself was stated normally to be provided by *Ravenswood* and *Lady Margaret.*

But herein lay the paradox: if the goal of the Barry Railway Company was indeed to move people from the Cardiff area to Weston, through Barry Pier, then it was often going to take longer for many passengers than if they continued to use the established White Funnel Fleet steamer services directly from Cardiff's Pier Head to Weston, with a comparable three-quarters of an hour crossing time. Although for many Cardiff residents a tram trip or a walk down Bute Road was needed to reach the Pier Head in order then to catch a steamer, the time taken to connect at Barry Pier after the train journey down through Cogan and past Barry Docks into a steamer often meant there was simply no time advantage. The absence of a tidally-unrestricted berth at Weston made it literally impossible to offer regularity and the fixed times every day which could have offset the tidal disadvantage of Cardiff's Pier Head, and complemented the smart new Barry facility in the way in which the Barry Railway Company Directors had envisaged. Thus, a Cardiff to Weston journey might typically take 1¾ hours via Barry Pier by train and steamer, but would often be accomplished in under the hour if one made a swift interchange between tram and a direct steamer at Cardiff's Pier Head, depending on one's place of residence.

A few variations on the basic Ilfracombe and Weston sailings from Barry Pier were on offer during the first season, and to illustrate the point about integration with Campbell's 'own' Cardiff services, it is clear that on days when the tide suited then the 10.00 am boat from Barry to Ilfracombe actually started back at Cardiff at 9.15 am. This feature gave substance to the later claim of the

Barry Directors that they had often received a poor service from P. & A. Campbell Ltd when the boat arriving at Barry for Ilfracombe was already full with Cardiff passengers, leaving Barry passengers either to stand or be left behind! It would be a finely judged affair as to whether two separate steamers would be justified from Cardiff to Ilfracombe if there was a convenient morning tide which enabled one to do the job instead of two. Another variant was offered on Thursday 8th August, 1899, when a half-holiday trip from Barry to Clevedon was advertised: this appears to have been a good use of spare time in the ferry steamer schedule when there was no water in the late afternoon at Birnbeck, and was in practice an extension of the 3.15 pm Barry-Weston ferry crossing up the coast to Clevedon for an hour or two ashore there (where the pier did permit a low-tide landing) before an 6.00 pm return departure from Clevedon to Weston, thence back at 6.45 on the ferry service to Barry Pier. Another interesting variant, on Saturday 12th August, 1899, was the use of the new facility instead of Cardiff for an afternoon excursion (with connecting train from Cardiff) to Ilfracombe leaving Barry Pier at 3.15 pm, and returning from Ilfracombe at 7.30 pm to Barry Pier. On this occasion the tides made Cardiff inaccessible for such a trip, which was a popular half-holiday one especially as Sunday sailings were still not then on offer, and many folk worked on Saturday mornings.

One might observe that the range of excursions on offer from P. & A. Campbell Ltd at this time from Cardiff was quite extensive, and as well as the usual fare to Bristol, Up the Severn, Chepstow, Clevedon, Weston, Minehead, Lynmouth and Ilfracombe, and occasionally Clovelly and Mumbles & Tenby, odd trips to Watchet and even Porlock featured, as well as to Burnham, plus optional train - via the Somerset & Dorset Railway - to Bournemouth. From a Cardiff perspective the new steamer operation via Barry Pier may well have seemed superfluous, bearing in mind that Penarth Pier had opened in 1895 and was well-served and catered to some extent for folk to the south and south-west of the city. The 1899 season rapidly drew to a close for Barry Pier, and the Ilfracombe steamer service was suspended after Saturday 23rd September, 1899, Barry Pier to Weston ferry services ceasing one week later on Saturday 30th September, 1899. A Barry Railway Company notice also stated that on this day their brake service connecting the seaside resort of Southerndown with the railway station at Southerndown Road (on the Vale of Glamorgan Railway) would also cease. As the 1899 season ended, the two companies could now review the results of that first period of use of Barry Pier, which had been something of a commercial compromise.

It is not difficult to see straightaway why P. &. A. Campbell Ltd felt so compromised by the new arrangements which it had entered into with the Barry Railway Company, and a glance at a map quickly illustrates the 'false premise' which was to bedevil the Barry steamers' operation. As fares from Cardiff to Weston were set at the same level whether direct by steamer from Cardiff's Pier Head, or by train from Cardiff Riverside station to Barry Pier, and thence by steamer, it was inevitable that the return to the Campbells was less after the Barry Railway had taken their 'cut' for the railway element. As the Barry Railway Company were arguably seeking to carry traffic from Cardiff over their own railway system, charging higher fares from Cardiff to Weston via Barry Pier than via direct steamers was clearly a non-starter. From the Campbells point of view, it might have been satisfactory if the Barry steamers were generating lots of new traffic, which would not otherwise have used their own direct Cardiff-Weston sailings. But, given the 'abstractive' nature of the new set-up, a commercial dispute was almost an inevitability and, as two steamers were being committed to the new Barry Pier enterprise in the 1899 season, the exposure to higher operating costs was considerable. And, whilst two steamers had been taken on, there were some days when maybe only one was needed, which exacerbated this financial difficulty.

The verdicts of the two companies on the results of the 1899 season were, not surprisingly, rather different. When the half-yearly Barry Railway Company meeting of shareholders had been held in mid-August, the Chairman had then been able to report that

> . . . the new Landing Stage was opened on the 27th last month, and from that date to the 8th inst. 13,206 passengers had passed outwards and inwards, a fact which showed clearly that the public were taking immediate advantage of this extra facility (hear, hear) . . .

The complete figure declared in later Accounts (for the two-month season) was 45,936 'carried via Barry Pier' which can be taken as meaning probably only around half of that number as return tickets were sold. On the other hand, it was minuted at the P. & A. Campbell Ltd Meeting of Directors on 20th November, 1899 that the results of the venture for the Barry Railway Company had clearly been unsatisfactory, and that

> . . . the Board could only consent to provide a service next year if the Barry Railway Company would undertake that the boat proportions of the bookings should not be less than £6,500 for the two steamers . . .

After the first season of Barry Pier operations, then, it was certainly clear that there was a problem. Whilst the White Funnel Fleet lay at Bristol for the winter, the Barry Railway Company felt that there was now no choice but to make a second attempt to gain its own powers for operating steamships, and again deposited a Bill in Parliament, and which again drew the predictable and spirited opposition of P. & A. Campbell Ltd.

The season of 1900: no service

If we briefly jump ahead to the period when the two companies were at war over the Bristol Channel excursion steamboat traffic, the official records of Shareholders' Meetings of the Barry Railway Company from around 1907/08 make it plain that the Bristol company had been regarded in these early years by the railway company Directors as being wholly unreasonable towards the large investment that they had made at Barry Pier. They saw their facilities there as something which any excursion steamer company should surely have wanted to take advantage of, and they believed the new pier offered a new source of traffic income for both parties. Conversely, Peter and Alec Campbell's position was simply one of seeking to protect their company from predictable losses, based on the 1899 results of operating their white-funnelled steamers at Barry Pier. But as the 1900 season approached, the expectation in South Wales was that the P. & A. Campbell Ltd vessels would again serve Barry Pier, broadly in the manner of the arrangements that had applied in 1899.

Parliamentary proceedings were underway in March 1900, as the Barry Railway Company pressed forward with its renewed attempt to become a steamboat operator in its own right, and at the end of that month it appeared that success was in sight as the *Barry Dock News* reported that the case was virtually made for: '. . . improved means of communication from Barry to the south side of the Bristol Channel . . .', and the Bill was thus allowed to proceed. Whilst considerable legal bills were being amassed, on both sides, it is reasonable to assume that P. & A. Campbell Ltd must have been mindful of the fact that only they actually had the vessels and the wherewithal available to provide a service at Barry Pier at comparatively short notice, and so it was not too surprising that this report was printed, in the *Barry Dock News*, on Friday 29th June, 1900:

BARRY STEAMBOAT TRAFFIC
TO BE RESUMED THIS SUMMER

It is reported that Messrs P. & A. Campbell Ltd, the owners of the fleet of steamers which at present monopolise the passenger traffic of the Bristol Channel, and which monopoly has been successfully threatened in Parliament by the Barry Railway Company, have now concluded a contract with their possible competitors to run regular services to Weston, Minehead and Ilfracombe from Barry. The services have not yet been started, but from enquiries we have made this week we have no reason to doubt the report.

The somewhat provocative tone of this statement would doubtless have irritated the Campbell brothers. A few days later, the same newspaper published a substantial report - very much biased towards the Barry perspective, as one would of course expect - to the effect that the Barry Railway Company could not agree to the terms sought by P. & A. Campbell Ltd, that the Bristol company had somehow enlisted the support of the Great Western Railway to oppose the Barry Railway Company's Bill, and so the preamble to the Bill was not proved, and the Bill was duly lost. One can only speculate as to what was actually said behind closed doors, in both boardrooms, in Barry and in Bristol!

The essence of the failure to agree terms on how Barry Pier could be served in 1900 by White Funnel Fleet vessels was that Alec Campbell had told Messrs Evans and Thompson of the Barry Railway Company in June that year that he would require them to commit to a charter agreement, for a period of five years. This was unacceptable to the Barry Railway Company, and so negotiations effectively ended there. The opposition of P. & A. Campbell Ltd to a Bill enabling the Barry Railway Company to run its own steamers, as it saw fit and without restriction, remained, but it had been made plain to the Welsh railway company that the view of the Bristol steamer company would be relaxed if the proposed Bill contained a clause to confine any new Barry Railway-owned steamers activity to trading out of Barry only. This would, as the Campbell brothers saw it, ensure that they had the field to themselves at Cardiff where, they reasoned, they had invested in a substantial fleet which was giving a good service to the public. They did not see that a railway company should encroach on 'their' territory, and statements were made which implied that they believed that they would be the victims of unfair competition if the operation of railway-owned steamers was cross-subsidised. The financial situation of P. & A. Campbell Ltd at that time was evidently not entirely healthy, as continued attemps to sell some of the older vessels were being made, in addition to which soft loans were being sought to ease cashflow problems. The Bristol company concluded that it could do without the risk of losses that might accompany an additional Barry commitment and, in July, the matter was finally dropped as far as it was concerned.

At the end of July 1900, well into the season, the public admission now had to be made that there would be no steamboat operations that year at Barry Pier. In one sense, both parties were losing out: P. & A. Campbell Ltd had idle vessels, and the Barry Railway had a disused new pier facility, just one year old. But equally neither party was incurring a loss on direct operations, although both had amassed considerable legal expenses. A sort of impasse had been reached, although it is doubtful if either party saw it quite like that. The Welsh company wanted to develop traffic on its railway system, to feed a steamer service, whereas the English company - which had operated Bristol Channel excursion steamers at Cardiff with some success since 1887 - simply did not see that a Barry operation was worth its involvement. There was still no substantive progress towards any new low-water pier facility at Weston, which would complement that at Barry Pier and unlock its full potential for regularity of services, and the commercial compromise apparent in 1899 was still of relevance. What would happen to unblock this unsatisfactory state of affairs?

As it happened, a glimmer of hope was flickering for 1901, not at Weston-super-Mare, but further down the Somerset coast, at Minehead; the prospect of completion of the new pier there appears to have been the defining event of the period which was to bring the parties back together. Talks between the parties continued during the winter of 1900/01, and the ice had clearly thawed a little as Mrs Grundy was able to report in the *Barry Dock News*, on 12th April, 1901, that '. . . passenger boats ran channel excursions between Barry and Weston on Easter Monday when, notwithstanding the unfavourable weather, a large number took advantage of the trips . . .' These trips were probably simply calls at Barry Pier in between the Cardiff to Weston-super-Mare ferry duties of the early-season White Funnel Fleet vessel, at low water, when the 'ferry' steamer would otherwise be idle but nonetheless, it was not long now before a proper resumption of activity at Barry Pier could be considered for the 1901 season.

PLEASURE SAILINGS

FROM ILFRACOMBE, BY

P. & A. Campbell, Ltd.

MAGNIFICENT SALOON STEAMERS

Britannia, Westward Ho!
Lady Margaret,
Ravenswood,
Glen Rosa,
Waverley, etc.

Largest, Fastest, and most Palatial Steamers in the Bristol Channel.

☞ For Times of Sailing see Bills.

Further information from the Agent—

F. W. BIRMINGHAM,
Quay, Ilfracombe ;

Or P. & A. CAMPBELL, Ltd.,
Cumberland Basin, Bristol.

1474

BARRY RAILWAY

AND

P. & A. CAMPBELL, Limited.

MONDAY, 20th May, 1901.

RE-OPENING OF DAILY SERVICE

Without Break of Journey, between

Porth, Cardiff, Barry, Pontypridd, &c.,

AND

Minehead, Lynmouth, Ilfracombe, &c.,

Via BARRY PIER.

The FARES (combined Rail and Steamer) from Cardiff (Riverside Station) to all places visited by the Steamers going from Barry Pier, are the same as from Cardiff by Boat alone.

For further particulars as to Fares, Times, &c., apply to Mr. WM. GUY, 70A, Bute Street, Cardiff; Mr. R. H. WARD, The Pier Gates, Weston-super-Mare; Mr. H. J. PULSFORD, The Quay, Minehead ; Mr. F. W. BIRMINGHAM, The Quay, Ilfracombe ; or to the GENERAL MANAGER, Barry Railway, Barry Dock.

(By Order.)

Barry Dock, May 8th, 1901.

1190

The steamer services provided at Barry Pier by P. & Campbell Ltd for the Barry Railway Company had not operated in 1900 but were resumed for the 1901 season. This advertisement appeared alongside the regular P. & A. Campbell Ltd entry in the *Ilfracombe Gazette and Observer* on 18th May, 1901, just prior to the start up before the important Whitsuntide period. When the service re-commenced, Ilfracombe enjoyed an additional daily boat at set times down from Barry in the morning, and returning up-Channel in the afternoon, giving easy links with much of South Wales.

Ilfracombe Museum

1901/02: P. & A. Campbell Ltd services restored

Ideas for a pier at Minehead dated back to 1895, but only really got seriously underway in 1899 when a company created for the purpose finally raised the necessary capital to begin work. Judging by the fulsome speeches recorded in the *West Somerset Free Press* newspaper which described the formal opening of Minehead Pier on Saturday 25th May, 1901, not everyone in Minehead had welcomed this new development. Whereas a faction wanted Minehead to retain an air of peace and quiet, and not develop into a seaside resort, others thought differently and actively welcomed the development prospects the new pier was expected to stimulate, both in terms of increased property values and extra custom for tradespeople from an influx of visitors from rapidly developing South Wales, just a few miles away across the Bristol Channel, and clearly seen by the Minehead interests as an important generator of economic wellbeing.

The prospect of this additional source of traffic clearly appealed to P. & A. Campbell Ltd, who naturally appreciated the benefits of a pier which would be available virtually without any tidal constraints. The new Minehead promenade pier was built out far enough from the shore, for some 700 ft, to overcome the problems of the wide tidal range experienced further up-Channel, notably at Bristol, Newport, Cardiff and Weston's Birnbeck Pier where the tides dictated varying departure times every day and prevented regularity of timetabling from being achieved. Whilst offers for some of their older steamers had been solicited during the previous couple of years, the fleet strength in numbers was still there, and so a pattern was developed again to deploy two steamers in 1901 on rail-connected services from Barry Pier, but somewhat differently to the 1899 arrangements. The announcement made in the *Barry Dock News* on 12th April, 1901 entitled SUMMER SAILINGS FROM BARRY: DAILY SERVICE OF PASSENGER BOATS was slightly misleading, but certainly positive:

> We are pleased to learn that the Barry Railway Company have now definitely arranged terms with Messrs P. & A. Campbell, whereby their daily service of passenger boats will regularly work to and from Barry Pier in connection with the Barry Company's trains during the approaching summer season. The service will commence on 20th May, a week before Whitsuntide, and the boats will run to and from Ilfracombe, Lynmouth, Minehead and Weston, and probably Clevedon. Details of the services will shortly be published.

As Whitsun approached, a large announcement regarding the re-opening of the joint Barry Railway Company and P. & A. Campbell Ltd service via Barry Pier, 'without break of journey', was duly placed in the *Western Mail* newspaper. But this time, at least at the opening of the 1901 season, there was no daily Barry to Weston service as had been offered in 1899, and instead two round trips daily between Barry and Minehead were initially advertised, at nominally fixed times during the first week, but with a few daily variations in the small print. The daily boat to Ilfracombe was in similar timings to those that had applied in 1899, and departed from Barry Pier at 10.10 am after the arrival of the 9.20 train from Cardiff Riverside station, calling *en route* at Lynmouth. As the short-lived pier at Wooda Bay had been destroyed during the winter of 1900/01, calls there were no longer possible. The same boat train from Cardiff Riverside also provided the connection into the second boat, for Minehead, which also departed from Barry Pier at 10.10 am and returned straightaway from Minehead at 11.10 am to Barry.

The afternoon round trip to Minehead involved departure from Barry Pier after the arrival of a train leaving Cardiff Riverside at various times between 1.13 and 3.42 pm during that first week before Whitsuntide. The last run of the day was at the set time of 6.40 pm from Minehead to Barry Pier, and the boat operating this run arrived back at Barry Pier somewhat later than the Ilfracombe boat, which (as in 1899) did not leave Ilfracombe at a set time, but at times which ranged between 4.00-4.45 pm. Two separate boat-trains were thus necessitated in the evening to return steamer passengers arriving at Barry Pier to Cardiff Riverside. Connections to other stations on the Barry Railway Company network, notably westwards on the Vale of Glamorgan line, were possible by means of a change of trains at Barry. Perhaps coincidentally, the evening train at 7.48 pm from Barry Island to Porth, up the Barry 'main line' via Wenvoe, was advertised to run from Barry Pier at 7.45 pm, immediately after the Minehead boat arrived, and this would have been a very marginal adjustment for the Barry Railway Company to make to its normal timetables, with little additional operating cost.

In a nice touch of symmetry with the end of the season of Barry Pier steamer services after September 1899, the re-opening in 1901 coincided with the re-introduction on Saturday 25th May of the seasonally-operated Barry Railway Company brake service between Southerndown Road and Southerndown, where passengers could look over to the high cliffs of the magnificent North Devon coast. Here, a comparable coaching operation still linked Lynton with Ilfracombe. South Walian travellers could also contemplate the scenic transport delights across the Channel such as the Lynton & Lynmouth funicular and the Lynton & Barnstaple narrow-gauge railway. Those already in North Devon on its somewhat higher cliffs might be just as impressed as they gazed across at Nash Point, its prominent lighthouses and the rocky Vale of Glamorgan coast from Porthkerry to the mouth of the River Ogmore.

Opening of Minehead Pier

Minehead Pier had opened to the public a few days before the formalities of the official ceremony on that Whit Saturday in 1901, and everything must have seemed delightful on that sunny day when the honour fell to *Glen Rosa* of being the first steamer officially to inaugurate the landing-stage at the new pier on her arrival from Barry. No mention was made locally of any of the past difficulties between the popular Campbell steamers and the railway company owners of Barry Pier, and Minehead's new link with South Wales was duly greeted with all the usual speeches and sentiments over a recherché repast at the Hotel Metropole. The number of steamer calls at Minehead that day was exceptional: it was recorded that *Glen Rosa* called twice from Barry, *Westward Ho* called in

When the new Minehead Pier opened in 1901 the first vessel to call, from Barry, was the P. & A. Campbell Ltd-owned *Glen Rosa*. Much of her later career was spent away from the Bristol Channel on the South Coast of England. *H.A. Allen Collection*

whilst on her down-Channel run from Bristol and Weston to Ilfracombe, and again on her up-Channel return voyage, and in addition both *Waverley* and *Ravenswood* made calls from Cardiff and Weston. It was noted that, at one point, three steamers lay abreast at the new landing stage: this certainly seemed like a splendid start for Minehead Pier, and its Directors might well have now thought that their problems in securing an adequate steamer service with South Wales were behind them.

One cannot now glean precisely from the Minute Book how Alec Campbell and his fellow Directors had decided to re-enter the fray at Barry Pier, or whether they had secured some kind of guarantee from the Barry Railway Company against possible losses, but it is reasonable to assume that the opening of Minehead Pier gave them optimism, albeit in a somewhat indirect manner. After a meeting in March 1901 with a Mr Vincent, the confidential clerk to Mr Evans, the Barry Railway Company General Manager, Alec Campbell explained to his own Board that there might be overall advantage to them if Minehead was connected to Cardiff, so that the Bristol-Ilfracombe boat could serve Weston more frequently (i.e. rather than call in at Cardiff) and thus give an improved service between Bristol, Weston and Ilfracombe, which could also occasionally embrace a Minehead call too. At first glance this seems a slightly convoluted reasoning, but is quite rational if one was assuming that Minehead would act as an attractive new destination for people from Bristol and Weston - and of course from Cardiff and Barry - as well as opening up a new market for holidaymakers in Minehead who might wish to sail to Lynmouth and Ilfracombe. Perhaps a weak link was that the two sailings a day between Barry and Minehead were not timed to provide the opportunity for a day out in Cardiff for Minehead folk - but with hindsight the sailing arrangements in 1901 for Barry Pier can perhaps be seen as having been partly experimental in their nature. The option still existed for P. & A. Campbell Ltd to sell some of its potentially surplus steamers - *Scotia*, *Bonnie Doone* and *Lady Margaret* were the ones for which offers evidently had been considered - if Barry Pier traffic results still did not meet its expectations.

After the exciting first few days of the 1901 season, Mrs Grundy was thus able to briefly mention in her jottings that things were now more as one would have wished. On 31st May, 1901 she recorded these words, a little abruptly as if to imply that valuable time had been wasted by the non-provision of a service in 1900: '. . . Good news for Barry excursionists. The new pier at Minehead was opened with due ceremony last Saturday. It is now used by the Barry passenger boats every day'.

During the research for this book, a charming piece of memorabilia came to light which gave a fascinating insight into how the steamer services at Barry Pier in that early stage of its existence were actually used. A beautifully printed programme, on embossed quality paper, had survived as a memento of a picnic outing for staff of the Barry Railway and invited friends which involved a day out - via the still novel, new Barry Pier - by steamer to Weston, with horse-drawn conveyances provided to Cheddar via Banwell and Axbridge, arriving in time for luncheon, and sports in the afternoon before tea and the return to Birnbeck Pier. Here, a couple of hours were available before the boat returned - doubtless a special charter, for the exclusive use of this important party - back to Barry Pier where a special train was waiting to take everybody home to Barry, Cadoxton and on to Cardiff Riverside, calling at all stations. The programme belonged to Miss Gwyneth White of Penarth, who had acquired it from her father who, she explained to the author, had a been an officer of the Taff Vale Railway before the Great War, and who had a close friend who had similarly been in the service of the Barry Railway Company. On 21st June, 1901 the *Barry Dock News* duly recorded the Midsummer excursion, in a brief account entitled:

BARRY COMPANY'S CLERICAL STAFF OUTING:

The annual outing of the clerical staff of the Barry Railway Company was held on Wednesday last. The company, numbering about 200, proceeded by boat to Weston, thence by brakes to Cheddar, where dinner was partaken of at the Cliff Hotel, and the afternoon was very enjoyably spent in visiting the historic caves and other places of interest and attraction in the charming neighbourhood.

Regrettably the steamer on this duty was not identified, but one imagines it might well have been one of the 'secondary' White Funnel Fleet vessels such as *Glen Rosa* or *Bonnie Doon* rather than one with a higher passenger capacity or more regularly advertised in connection with Cardiff-Weston ferry duties: these were stated to be *Ravenswood* and *Lady Margaret* in 1901. The souvenir programme printed for the participants recorded that picnic outings in previous years had been operated to Tintern (1897), Symonds Yat (1899) and Caswell Bay (1900) and this seems to have been the first to take place by steamer rather than by train. Cheddar was clearly an attractive venue, and some of the party would have taken the opportunity to go on by train from there to Wells after luncheon.

A little later in the season *Mrs Grundy's Jottings* listed the outings made by other groups from Barry, such as the Barry Master Bakers Association who went to Minehead on 17th July, for a special inclusive fare of two shillings and sixpence. Other groups mentioned with this party booking were the Shopkeepers Union, the Cadoxton Conservatives and the Barry Chamber of Trade. She elaborated further on 5th July:

> . . . further reference to 10.00 sailing on 17th July to Minehead, arr. 11.00. One hour at Minehead, then dinner at Pier Hotel, brake trip at 2 pm to Cleeve Abbey & Watchet where Messrs Stoate and Sons, the Watchet firm of millers, will entertain them to a cream tea at the Recreation Grounds. The brakes will start on the return journey from Watchet at 6 pm, boat will leave Minehead for home at 8 pm. All for the moderate sum of eight shillings and sixpence.

Around 150 folk apparently participated in this grand day-out but, again, regrettably, no steamer was named.

A third snapshot of this era, albeit not specifically related to the Barry Railway Company or its pier and steamer services is included here because of its delightfully euphemistic observation on the attitudes and behaviours of the time, taken from the *Barry Dock News* of 9th August, 1901:

> A WORTHY AMBITION
> WANTED TO SWIM TO BARRY
>
> Some consternation was caused on board Messrs Campbell's excursion boat *Scotia* which ran on Thursday evening last a trip from Newport to Clevedon and back. A man took off all his clothes except his shirt and trousers and said he was going to jump overboard and swim to Barry. It is thought that perhaps the sun had affected his head. He was secured by the crew and kept under observation till he reached Clevedon, when he was taken care of by some friends.

Traffic arrangements in 1901

The pre-season announcement for 1901 services had alluded to possible services from Barry Pier to Weston and Clevedon in addition to those to Minehead and to Lynmouth and Ilfracombe already described. Perusal of the *Western Mail* newspaper for the three months period between July and September revealed that whilst the norm was for the two Minehead round trips to be offered, the times of these were by no means fixed, and regularity on this route was sacrificed in order that Barry-Weston trips - all with their own advertised train connections from Cardiff Riverside - could run on some days. For those that liked timetabling variety, the Bristol Channel tides and some ingenuity on the part of the Barry Railway traffic staff gave rise to services that seemed to vary on an almost daily basis. Often, the morning boat to Minehead would leave Barry Pier earlier than the standard 10.10 am in order to be back earlier, and offer an early afternoon Barry-Weston round trip. A second round trip from Barry to Weston would then run after the evening crossing from Minehead to Barry Pier had disgorged its passengers. This gave the opportunity for a full day out from Cardiff at either of the Somerset resorts.

On different tides, another pattern was for an early Barry-Weston round trip to be performed before the 'normal' morning Minehead trip. As high summer

This very rare view of Birnbeck Island and Pier, included in the 1902 edition of the P. & A. Campbell Ltd Bristol Channel District Guide, illustrates (*on the left*) the intended low-water extension as it should have appeared had it not been largely destroyed by extreme weather conditions in September 1903, before it had even been opened. It took many years before the replacement was finished. *Author's Collection*

The delightful tramway system at Weston-super-Mare opened in 1902 and provided a very useful service for steamer passengers at Birnbeck Pier. This postcard possibly dates from around 1907/8, before the completion of the (replacement) low-water extension. After the Grand Pier opened in 1904, Birnbeck was often referred to as 'The Old Pier' to distinguish it from its much newer rival in the centre of town. A P. & A. Campbell Ltd paddler is berthed at what was known as the North Jetty, and the tide is fully in. Horse-drawn transport is in plentiful supply for arriving steamer passengers. The tramway closed in 1937. *Author's Collection*

approached, there were some days when three round trips between Barry and Minehead were offered - at different times every day, in the week before the Bank Holiday on Monday 5th August, 1901. The weather that day was evidently favourable as according to the *Western Mail* newspaper, describing the crowds that flocked to Cardiff.

> . . . the vast majority of visitors either proceeded across the water in Messrs Campbell & Co's steamers or to Penarth or other places of interest along the coast. In recent years Barry has become a favourite resort on Bank Holidays for the teeming population of the valleys north of Cardiff, and on Monday there was an immense number of visitors on the island . . . the weather was fine without being too warm . . .

It is worth mentioning that whilst the Ilfracombe boat from Barry Pier, known as the 'railway run', was perhaps the only fixed element of the offering throughout the 1901 season, up at Cardiff there was generally a boat at 9.30 am direct to Lynmouth and Ilfracombe whenever tides permitted. Furthermore, Minehead was by no means exclusively linked by White Funnel steamer to Barry Pier, as frequent excursions ran from Cardiff to Minehead. Finally, on some (high season) days it was now possible with these more frequent crossings for Minehead folk to take the opportunity for a reasonably full day out across the water in Cardiff, courtesy of the Barry Railway Company boat-train connections to Cardiff Riverside which met every steamer arrival at Barry Pier. All in all, Minehead Pier was generously served by steamer in that opening year of 1901.

Services at Barry Pier ceased after 21st September, 1901 for the duration. The view taken by the Barry Railway Company Directors in August 1901 of the season had been expressed at the half-yearly Shareholders' Meeting in just a few words, worth quoting verbatim ' . . . the . . . arrangement for passenger steamers from 20th May . . . was working satisfactorily, and the advantages afforded appeared to be increasingly appreciated'. By late-Autumn, the arrangements made between P. & A. Campbell Ltd and the Barry Railway Company had been reviewed and appeared to have been acceptable to both parties, and Captain Alec Campbell met with Richard Evans, the General Manager, in November 1901 as a result of which he recommended to his fellow Directors that similar services should again operate in 1902.

1902: more of the same

The development of a low-water pier at Birnbeck Island had not yet been completed, but was regarded as imminent, and the prospect of such a facility was clearly of interest to both the Bristol steamer company and to the Barry Railway Company, which saw it as the means by which the superiority of its own facility on the Welsh side of the Bristol Channel would be secured. There is evidence that the Weston-super-Mare Pier Company was keen to persuade P. & A. Campbell Ltd to take a lease on its pier, probably in order that some guaranteed income might make the business of funding the new works a little less onerous. But this appears not to have happened, and the continued development of Weston was such that plans for the new Grand Pier started to firm up in 1902 and which, its promoters said, would also have a low-water facility.

The 1902 Bristol Channel District Guide published by P. & A. Campbell Ltd had this to say, slightly ambivalently, about developments at Birnbeck where their steamers already called:

> . . . a new low-water pier is being constructed at the western end of the island, and when completed this will give increased facilities to the steamboats for the embarkation and the landing of passengers. There is already a low-water pier at Barry, and when similar provision is made at Cardiff, the cross-channel traffic will doubtless be greatly augmented, to the advantage of the public as well as of the steamboat company.

A sort of race was on now in Weston-super-Mare, to be the first pier that could accommodate the steamers from South Wales at all times of the day. The winner of this race would, it seemed, reap the benefits through pier tolls, but as things turned out Weston had to make do without this luxury for quite a few more seasons. The significance of all this was the effect it had on the subsequent actions of the Barry Railway Company after the 1902 season.

Less was recorded in the *Barry Dock News* of the comings and goings of the Barry Pier traffic in 1902 than in the previous year, as the novelty would doubtless have worn off a little. Mrs Grundy did record that in mid-August the members of the Barry Dock Conservative Club were again to cross the Channel for their annual outing. This time they were to proceed by boat leaving from Barry Pier for Clevedon at the early hour of 7.30 am, with dinner at the Bristol Hotel, and an expectation that the Grand Athletic Sports planned for the afternoon would prove to be 'an irrestisible draw'. After tea at six o'clock the homewards departure was planned for 9.00 pm, making a very full day out. After the event she solemnly recorded that *Glen Rosa* had conveyed 200 or so worthies at an early hour to Clevedon, of whom some had proceeded by motor-car to Portishead and others to Wells Cathedral. The return vessel was not named but departure from Clevedon was evidently at 9.30 pm with arrival back at Barry at about 11.00 pm. Such a working would almost certainly have been an add-on to the duties of either of the Campbell steamers allocated to the Barry station that day, before and after the regular Minehead and Ilfracombe workings.

In comparison with the 1901 traffic arrangements of P. & A. Campbell Ltd for serving Barry Pier jointly with the Barry Railway Company, matters in 1902 were more straightforward. The Ilfracombe boat operated as it had in the preceding season, and there appear to have been no Barry-Weston services. The basic, twice-daily Minehead calls thus followed a more regular pattern, and the usual weekday service featured trains from Cardiff Riverside at 9.20 am and 2.32 pm for Barry Pier, and steamer to Minehead, returning from Minehead for Cardiff via Barry Pier at 11.10 am and 6.30 pm. On some Saturdays this was increased to three round trips, which involved altered train times, namely Cardiff Riverside departures at 8.35 am, 2.32 and 5.10 pm, returning from Minehead for Cardiff via Barry Pier at 10.15 am, 4.45 and 8.00 pm. As a further variation, on the Bank Holiday Monday on 4th August, 1902 there were four round trips between Barry and Minehead, again at mostly altered times (rather than extra journeys added to the core times of the base two trips), and additional advertising drew attention to these as 'Special Excursions via Barry Pier' at this peak traffic time. Cardiff Riverside connecting train departures, on this one-off occasion, were at 8.35 am, 1.13, 4.23 and 7.15 pm, returning from Minehead for Cardiff via Barry Pier at 10.15 am, 3.00, 6.30 and 8.45 pm. One does wonder how many intending passengers turned up for what they might have thought of as a regular timetable of rail & steamer services, only to find on the day that they would actually travel at different times to those which they had expected - or missed the boat entirely.

It would be misleading to think that everything went smoothly in those days, and at the end of August Mrs Grundy sniffily recorded her views on what presumably had been an error of judgement up at the rival port of Cardiff:

> Several Barry excursionists were amongst those who participated in the all-night vigil on board the stranded *Bonnie Doon* on the mud off Cardiff Pier Head last week. Such a ridiculous contretemps, it is impossible by the Barry boats. Moral, patronise home boats. Query, why go to Cardiff and fare worse?

Her closing remarks for 1902 in respect of the local steamers were to the effect that services would cease on Saturday 13th September. At this point all seemed to be going well at Barry Pier, and few would have anticipated that an era had in fact already ended.

1903/04: No steamers at Barry Pier

The autumn of 1902 can be seen, in retrospect, as something of a turning point for P. & A. Campbell Ltd and at the Directors' Meeting that took place on 3rd November, 1902 two major decisions were made which reflected the overall trading results of the season that had just ended, and directly led to significant fleet deployment changes. Though not directly related to the Barry activities, it was agreed that trading at Southampton had been unsatisfactory and Alec Campbell recommended that in future his *Brighton Queen* should concentrate on excursions from Brighton, and that *Cambria* - which had largely performed Solent excursions - should return to the Bristol Channel. Secondly, he stated that '. . . the results of the season's trading from Barry . . . were unsatisfactory . . .' and recommended to the Board that the Minehead service could not continue on the same terms. The Secretary was therefore instructed to write to both the Barry Railway Company and to Mr Holman of the Minehead Pier Company accordingly.

It will be recalled that a similar situation had happened after the 1899 season, when P. & A. Campbell Ltd had sought a guarantee from the Barry Railway Company against losses it might incur in running steamer services from Barry Pier. This time, as the Bristol company saw it, it had tried to run for two seasons, and yet the results were still insufficient to warrant its continued involvement at its own risk. Whilst Alec Campbell did not quote figures to his Board colleagues, later Barry Railway Company records do state that the numbers of passengers through Barry Pier were down in 1902 to 45,791 compared to 50,489 in 1901, a reduction of around 10 per cent. There was clearly a very different interpretation of the value of the Barry Pier traffic by the two companies: one had invested a large amount of capital in the pier and railway works, and sought increased passenger flows over its local railway network as a return, whilst the other had retained additional steamers in its fleet only to find that the return to it was inadequate. The collective view of the Barry Railway Company seems to have been that, having invested heavily in the infrastructure at Barry Pier itself, it should not have had to own and operate steamships in its own right, and the railway company believed ideally that others would gladly do this.

It is clear that opinion was divided on this point, though, as the reluctant attitude of P. & A. Campbell Ltd had been such that the Barry Railway Company had felt obliged to seek the necessary Parliamentary Powers (that is, for a ralway company to operate steamships) on two occasions already. On both occasions a compromise had subsequently been reached. It now seemed that the worst fears of the Barry Railway Company were realised by the failure to agree terms with P. & A. Campbell Ltd for the 1903 season, and the inevitable outcome was a third engagement with Parliamentary proceedings in order to seek the requisite Powers. The Welsh railway company clearly hoped it would be a case of third time lucky, as opposition from the Bristol excursion steamer operator would again be inevitable.

It will also be recalled that certain Barry Railway Company Directors had declined to be present at the inauguration of Barry Pier by the white-funnelled *Lady Margaret* in 1899, and this is perhaps the point at which Mr T.R. Thompson should be introduced as the key dissenter. I have taken these remarks from a speech he made to Barry Railway Company shareholders at the 47th Half-Yearly meeting on Friday 7th February, 1908. The Right Hon. Earl of Plymouth was in the chair, and it should be explained that at this time there had been lengthy litigation between the companies, which had caused shareholders to demand full and frank explanations from their Board. T.R. Thompson was eloquent in his address to the shareholders, and I have quoted him here at some length as his statement set out precisely the unsatisfactory state of affairs from the Barry perspective:

> . . . the Barry Company were not, at the outset, desirous of running Passenger Steamers . . . the Company communicated with Messrs Campbells, and invited them to perform that service by their steamers . . . I must tell you that I always stood in dread of this alliance, and, as a matter of fact I dissented, and I warned my brother Directors that so soon as the service was started, and was established, the Company's Railway Service and Pontoon would be entirely at the mercy of private shipowners, owing to the fact that they held the monopoly of the Steamship Service of the Bristol Channel; and I also warned my brother Directors that a pistol would be held at their heads, and extortionate sums demanded for performing the service, under threats of closing that service, and dislocating an important part of the Barry Company's Railway Service. My colleagues were anxious to avoid providing the capital for steamers, before trying to work the service jointly with Messrs Campbell. They offered to Messrs Campbell such advantageous terms that these terms were at once accepted . . .

This, then, in late-1902 was the parting of the ways. The Minute Book of P. & A. Campbell Ltd made no further reference to the Barry Railway Company or Barry Pier during the following year. What the book does reveal is that Alec Campbell acted swiftly and decisively to reduce his company's operating costs by trimming the fleet, which suggests that he and his fellow Directors had in effect discounted the possibility of any resumption of activity (i.e. that requiring vessels to be allocated for 'dedicated' services) at Barry Pier in 1903 or thereafter on their account. By January 1903 offers had been received and accepted for *Scotia* and *Lady Margaret*, the former vessel going to Italian owners and the latter to the Furness Railway. The net proceeds of these sales were recorded as £17,500 and, at the same Board meeting on 24th February, 1903 Alec offered to sell *Brighton Queen* to the Limited Company for £23,000. In the ensuing weeks the arrangements for P. & A. Campbell Ltd to begin operations at Brighton were put in place. Although the smaller-sized fleet which remained for Bristol Channel duties in 1903 could have been timetabled to make calls on services passing by Barry Pier - rather than provide dedicated rail-connected daily services to Minehead and Lynmouth & Ilfracombe - no such calls were made, and this was also to become a sore point with the Barry Railway Company. Exactly what the Campbell brothers thought the Barry Railway Company were now going to do with its new railway and pier is unclear, and they may have hoped that their one-time Welsh partners would eventually feel obliged to meet their terms or settle for some other compromise. It seems reasonable to infer that P. & A. Campbell Ltd had had its own trading difficulties and, quite simply, put its own primary business needs for Bristol, Newport, Cardiff and now the South Coast station at Brighton first.

During 1903 Mrs Grundy seems to have been silent in the *Barry Dock News* on the absence of boat services from Barry's own local pier, and although the public may have assumed negotiations were still going on behind the scenes to provide such services, there seems not to have been a formal admission that there would be no 1903 excursion season. The normal Whitsuntide start-up time for the excursion season came and went and no services commenced. The Barry Railway Company must have taken a while to decide on its own next steps, but did not dally long as it became publicly apparent by November that year that a new Bill had been lodged, and the legal processes - which would have necessitated the instruction of a Solicitor to instigate the necessary Parliamentary proceedings to advance this - must therefore have commenced a few months earlier. Local pride was at stake as well, and when news did eventually break that a fresh Parliamentary attempt by the Barry Railway Company to gain the rights to run its own steamships was underway, the statement was interesting inasmuch as it played down any notion of generating future traffic from Cardiff, relative to the potential for capturing new sources of passengers from the valleys which could be channelled down to Barry Pier via their 'main-line' route from Porth via Criegau and Wenvoe.

A splendidly subtle reference to the 'opposition' was made in the *Ilfracombe Gazette* on Friday 14th August, 1903:

> . . . the public should do all in their power to support Messrs Campbell's boats - the *Britannia*, *Cambria*, *Westward Ho* etc.; also Messrs Pockett's *Brighton* - at the same time we

> are pleased to learn that these boats have not in any way suffered from the attempted opposition, marine excursionists no doubt preferring these popular steamers which have run for so long a period without a single accident, in preference to those of a temporary character.

The Local & General Notes section of the *Barry Dock News* on 27th November, 1903 published this paragraph saying that a new Barry Railway Company Bill had been lodged which, if passed, would

> . . . enable the Company to provide adequate and convenient passenger boat service for the thousands of holiday-seekers from the Rhondda and neighbouring valleys who make excursions across the Channel during the summer . . . by the establishment of a regular service of boats daily from their pier head landing stage at Barry.

The corresponding formal notification that Powers were to be sought had been placed in the Parliamentary section of the *South Wales Daily News* on 20th November, 1903, and stated that the Bill would be deposited in the House of Commons by 17th December, 1903.

A process had now been set in motion, the outcome of which would be dictated by Parliamentary timescales as the Bill went through its hearings in early 1904. One can infer from P. & A. Campbell Ltd records that the Bristol company was very much aware of what the Barry Railway Company was seeking to do in the general sense, and the difference of opinion between the two parties centred on whether a railway company could or should be permitted to compete head-on with a private company for the lucrative traffic at Cardiff. Later testimonies from the ensuing legal battle that raged between 1905-1907 make it clear that the Welsh faction saw an abuse of monopoly by the Bristol company, which for its part saw no reason why an admittedly successful railway company should use its resources to subsidise a steamer operation when Campbell's were catering for the traffic adequately.* Whilst the argument for the Barry Railway Company was presented as being about catering for steamer passengers at Barry, in reality it was about the far more important Cardiff traffic, and we have already seen that the inherent nature of attempting to persuade the public to be routed from Cardiff to Weston via Barry Pier was questionable in terms of journey time, fares and general convenience.

Before concentrating on how matters developed in Barry, and how Mrs Grundy saw them, the business of the provision of pier facilities across the other side of the Bristol Channel at Weston-super-Mare was now of relevance to the actions of the two companies. During the summer of 1903 construction of the new Grand Pier was well underway, and P. & A. Campbell Ltd subscribed to a £500 equity stake in its funding. It was still expected that a low-water landing stage would be built on to the new pier, and that this would transform the

* In this context, the term 'subsidy' can be taken to mean that the Campbell brothers feared that the Barry boats might be run in a way where low steamer fares would be offered to attract travellers in order to increase their own railway booking office takings, for through rail/boat journeys by means of Barry Railway services, even if direct steamer operating costs were not being covered. The Campbell steamers basically had only their steamer takings as revenue.

ability of a steamer company to ferry across many more excursionists from South Wales at less anti-social times of day than the tides dictated at the Birnbeck Island pier. Obviously the tidal range at the Cardiff Pier Head would still impose a constraint as far as P. & A. Campbell Ltd was concerned, but for the Barry Railway Company in 1903 it would have seemed that for them, the moment a low-water facility was completed at Weston-super-Mare, commercial success would be assured, and steamers could operate to fixed schedules to a more central part of the fast growing Somerset resort. But construction of a new low-water facility at Birnbeck Island was also underway in the summer of 1903, and disaster struck there in September that year when gales not only destroyed much of the new works there but also wrecked the larger part of the original (i.e. north) jetty.

Thus, there was briefly a point in the Autumn of 1903 at which both P. & A. Campbell Ltd and the Barry Railway Company would have seen a principal source of income, real or intended, in jeopardy. And at the same time the promoters of the Grand Pier would have seen a heightened opportunity for their venture if they could press on with construction works in readiness for the 1904 season, and snatch traffic away from Birnbeck, or the 'Old Pier' as it was to be known. However, construction of the Grand Pier low-water extension was to prove a long drawn-out and ultimately ignominious affair, and a massive effort on the part of the Weston-super-Mare Pier Company who owned Birnbeck ensured that their ruined north jetty was rebuilt in time for May 1904, and so the Campbell steamers could resume calls as normal. Shortly afterwards, the Grand Pier opened to the public, initially without any facility for steamers

The Grand Pier at Weston-super-Mare in its early days before the addition of its landing-stage extension. (A fire later led to major reconstruction and today's pier has a very different appearance.) *Author's Collection*

to berth at a low-water extension, but with every intention of pressing on to add this as soon as possible. The setback at Birnbeck was serious, especially financially, and it was still to be some years before the low-water pier there was completed. To sum up, at the time the Barry Railway Company's Bill was proceeding on its Parliamentary course, the stated objective of the Welsh railway company was to create a link between South Wales and Somerset via tidally-unconstrained piers on either side of the Bristol Channel at Barry and at Weston-super-Mare, to offer regular services. It had built the facility on the Welsh side itself, and was wholly aware of the opposition from P. & A. Campbell Ltd which had been registered on earlier occasions, but had now fallen out irretrievably with the Bristol company.

The Barry Railway (Steam Vessels) Act, 1904

Moving on to 1904, Mrs Grundy reported in the *Barry Dock News* on 22nd April that year that 'The Tenby Harbour Commissioners have passed a resolution in favour of the Barry Company's steamboats Bill, and have authorised the town clerk to give evidence of the same in Parliament'. This might have sounded a little like clutching at straws, but in the same edition a report of a Barry Chamber of Trade Dinner on Wednesday 13th April noted that there had been various expressions of support for the steamboats Bill, and that E.F. Blackmore, the Secretary of the Chamber of Trade, had stated '. . . Barry Railway Company should be strongly supported in their endeavour to carry their steamboats Bill through Parliament. Barry possessed excellent facilities, for embarkation and landing, and he hoped the Bill would be passed this Session'. Matters were moving positively now and, on 6th May, 1904, Mrs Grundy could note that 'The preamble of the Barry Railway Coy's Steam Boats Bill was proved last Friday, and was ordered for report and third reading, and a report of the evidence given before the Committee will appear in our next issue'. An impressive array of supporters had been lined up by the Barry Railway Company to present this evidence, and statements were given by representatives of Ilfracombe Urban District Council, the Ilfracombe Harbour Committee, Lynton Urban District Council, Minehead Council and Mr Walton King of the Weston-super-Mare Pier Company, who reiterated the intention of his colleagues to complete the proposed deep-water berth at Birnbeck Island.

Notwithstanding the failure to agree terms for Campbell steamers to service Barry Pier in 1903 there had been dialogue between the companies over the six-month period or so before this stage was reached, and whilst P. & A. Campbell Ltd remained formally opposed to the Bill, there had been progress with the insertion of a clause which - at the request of P. & A. Campbell Ltd - restricted the proposed Barry Railway Company steamer services *inter alia* from carrying passengers from or to Cardiff. The Bill contained another clause which prescribed the amount of additional funds by which the railway company could increase its capital in respect of the extended Powers, the figure being put at £60,000. By late July the Bill finally received the approval needed from the House of Commons Select Committee and the preamble was proved, subject to a limitation that there would be no general goods traffic, and the imposition of a condition that the powers granted would need to be exercised within three years. A jubilant Mrs Grundy could therefore announce, in the *Barry Dock News* on 5th August. 1904, that 'The greatest satisfaction is felt in the Barry district at the passing of the Barry Company's Steam Vessel Bill through Parliament'. She went on to add: 'It is rumoured that in the event of . . . the Bill receiving Royal Assent this month, a passenger boat will be run from Barry this September'.

This news would have been enthusiastically received in Barry, and doubtless interpreted as an imminent victory for local interests after the humiliating period when Barry's new pier had lain idle. One can imagine the conversations that took place between the more erudite members of the Barry Conservative Club on their annual outing a few days beforehand, which had involved a special train from Barry to Cardiff Clarence Road station in order to catch a sailing by *Ravenswood* from the Pier Head to Weston, prior to numerous groups travelling by 'four in hands' to Clevedon and by train to Wells, Cheddar and Glastonbury, after dinner at the Bristol Hotel. Now, it appeared, the good citizens of Barry would shortly be able to enjoy the delights of travelling from their own pier, on their own, local steamers, without any need to patronise the 'foreign' White Funnel Fleet up at the rival port of Cardiff. Mrs Grundy could well feel satisfied that justice was now about to be done, and that six years after Barry Pier had opened - during which period there had been three seasons during which the pier had not been used - a bright new era was in prospect.

The Bank Holiday period came and went, and on 12th August, 1904 the *Barry Dock News* was able to report enthusiastically that a party of four senior Barry Railway Company Directors and officials, namely Messrs Thompson, Evans (the General Manager), Davies (Dockmaster) and Hosgood 'proceeded to Glasgow Saturday last . . . visit believed in connection with just-sanctioned passenger steamer service from Barry'. Such was their confidence that the Royal Assent would be forthcoming that no time was wasted in making arrangements to purchase new steamers and, on 26th August, 1904 a report by Mrs Grundy in her Jottings duly but tersely confirmed the good news: 'Barry Railway Company's Steam Vessels Bill has received Royal Assent, Bill is now law'. Mr Thompson must now have felt thoroughly vindicated; not only had he been proved right in his distrust of P. & A. Campbell Ltd, but the highly successful railway company in which he took such pride as a key Director was now about to branch out into steamship operation. For good measure, they were going to procure the best-quality steamships available - and for the time being nobody in Barry paid too much concern to that little clause in the Bill which had been added to overcome the objections of the Bristol company. Thus, this part of the story really ends with the simple announcement, in the *Barry Dock News* on 21st October, 1904, that two steamers were being built, which were due next April, for the cross-channel passenger traffic. It was significant that the exact plans of the Barry Railway Company were not at this stage being revealed, but one might have reasonably inferred that the two vessels were to handle anticipated traffic flows by rail through Barry Pier - from all points on the Barry Railway network - to Weston-super-Mare and to Ilfracombe.

Chapter Two

The Barry Railway Company Move into Steamship Operations

Phase One: The New Order, 1905/1906

. . . a pontoon was constructed within the breakwaters, at which passenger steamers land or take in passengers. The pontoon is served by railway lines made from Barry through Barry Island, and it is now possible for passengers from Cardiff, and the districts containing the teeming population of South Wales, to travel by train to the pontoon, and embark for the various watering-places and towns in the Bristol Channel. To further assist in the development of business, the Barry Railway . . . has obtained Parliamentary powers to work, or arrange for, steamers to ply in the Bristol Channel to and from this pontoon . . .

E. Lake, General Manager Barry Railway Company
Interview in *The Railway Magazine*, October 1906

1905: The new venture

We need now to recap a little, and consider what exactly was intended by the Barry Railway Company once it secured the hard-won Parliamentary Powers in 1904 which enabled it to become an operator of steamships. The major investment to construct Barry Pier and the extension railway from Barry Island had been completed back in 1899, but in the six intervening years the pleasure steamers had only plied there for three brief seasons and a fraught commercial relationship with P. & A. Campbell Ltd had to all intents and purposes now ended. The Bristol company had concluded that the traffic returns from its on-off involvement in serving Barry Pier were inadequate to warrant continuing, despite the completion in 1901 of Minehead Pier as a new source of Bristol Channel traffic. There was still no definite sign of a tide-free berth at the key Somerset resort of Weston-super-Mare, to which regular services from South Wales without daily tidal variations could then operate, as on the Firth of Clyde where Scottish railway companies happily provided connecting rail and steamer journeys from Glasgow on largely fixed schedules to take the crowds to resorts across the Firth. But the Barry Railway Company was confident - with some justification - that such a facility was now imminent at Weston-super-Mare, and in the Barry Railway Steam Vessels Bill there existed a clause which provided for the railway company to increase its capital in order to construct, own and operate the new steamships.

Scrutiny of the Minute Books of the Barry Railway Company from this period is frustrating inasmuch as those few references that are made to the steamships venture tantalise rather than fully inform one of exactly what was intended. However, it is possible to piece together what the Directors of the company must now have thought of the bigger picture - namely, that their Pier extension railway beyond Barry Island had lain disused in 1900, 1903 and 1904, and it had become a matter of pride and urgency to take control of the situation at Barry Pier and generate income that represented a worthwhile return on the very considerable expenditure that had been incurred. When the steamers of the

White Funnel Fleet had been serving Barry Pier, in 1899 and in 1901/02, the basic pattern of traffic had deployed two vessels, and at the prevailing prices for new paddle-steamers at that time, a capital amount of £60,000 should have been ample if two vessels were to be operated by the Barry company. One would serve down-Channel demand, to Lynmouth and Ilfracombe and the other could serve the up-Channel requirements for the lucrative Weston traffic. Just where the port of Cardiff fitted into this vision was not mentioned. Nonetheless, two identical vessels could interchange between these duties and when the Board of Directors met on 1st July, 1904, some basic decisions were made, and the full text of the relevant Minute was straightforward and to the point:

> *Steam Vessels Act:* The discussion of how the Company's powers under this Act are to be brought into operation was continued. It was decided to appoint Messrs Thompson and Forrest (as) a Committee to proceed to the North with the Company's officials to enquire what can be done in the way of getting tenders for two boats suitable for this service and that a special meeting should, if necessary, be thereafter called at the Solicitor's office to further consider the matter.

A statement made in the *South Wales Daily News* on 28th July, 1904 was prompted by the passage of the Bill through Parliament that day, and it was noted that the Barry Railway Company was to be one of a select few railway companies, along with the Lancashire and Yorkshire Railway, to be granted the requisite Powers to own and operate steamships: '. . . the object of the Barry is to develop a passenger and excursion business. The boats . . . are to work between Barry Dock and the various English ports on the Bristol Channel'. It was also noted that, on account of an objection by the Great Western Railway, a clause had been added to the Bill which prevented the Barry Railway Company from carrying goods, as it was feared that a possible alliance between that company and the London & South Western Railway with a 'combined sea and land route' might be detrimental to GWR interests.

At the special meeting which was duly held on Friday 19th August, 1904 at Vienna Chambers, Cardiff, chaired by Lord Windsor, Mr Thompson reported that the Committee (which had been constituted on 5th August) had been to Glasgow, and that tenders had been received from 'certain builders', and these were all carefully considered, although the tenderers were not named. The Secretary reported that Royal Assent to the Bill had been granted on the 15th inst. and Lord Windsor moved that the tender from the John Brown shipyard in Glasgow be accepted for one steamer, at the price quoted, and that a reduction in price should be sought for a second such steamer. Mr Thompson apparently suggested how two steamers might be worked, but this aspect was deferred without any details of the discussion being minuted. Finally, it was resolved that help should be sought from Captain Williamson, the Marine Superintendent of the Glasgow & South Western Railway (G&SWR).

The weeks that followed this would have been a demanding but fulfilling time for Mr Thompson, a shipowner of some repute but whose professional experience and involvement had mainly been in the owning and operation of cargo vessels. The reference to seeking assistance from the Glasgow & South Western Railway was notable, and it is worth briefly stating how this company had become involved in passenger shipping on the Firth of Clyde in order to set the context for how the Barry Railway Company now decided to proceed themselves. One thing which is clear from press reports of the time is that no direct statements were made in which the precise traffic at which the new steamers would be targetted was defined. Although it was implied that the steamers would just serve Barry Pier, the Barry Railway Company chose not to reveal their hand regarding the more obvious goal of the far greater traffic potential at Cardiff. Communications with P. & A. Campbell Ltd had been more or less severed, and so Mr Thompson and his fellow railway Directors were hardly likely to do anything to arouse the suspicions of Peter and Alec Campbell by way of inadvertent reporting in the newspapers. A straight reading of the recorded Barry Railway Company Minute Book suggests law-abiding intentions, but whether these were wholly sincere is questionable. In ordering steamers that were going to be bigger and - at least in the minds of the Barry Railway Company Directors and officials - better than those of the White Funnel Fleet, a skirmish was clearly inevitable. Had there truly been plenty of new traffic on offer at Barry itself, then less lavish steamers might have been procured, with more of an eye on operating economy than challenging and competing head on with an established organisation whose vessels had already clearly won the loyalty of much of the travelling public.

There were a number of parallels between the maritime activities of the Glasgow & South Western Railway and the newcomer to shipping in South Wales. In taking on the private steamboat owners on the Clyde the Caledonian Railway had, through its subsidiary the Caledonian Steam Packet Company, acquired a considerable fleet of steamers with which it was able to substantially influence traffic patterns to its own advantage. It had been necessary for the Caledonian Railway to distance itself somewhat from the steamship activity because of concerns that it might gain undue control of Firth of Clyde traffic, and that the public would be disadvantaged through a reduction of competition. Channelling people from the centre of Glasgow by train to Gourock was held to threaten the survival of the established pattern of sailings from the Broomielaw, and be disadvantageous to the public. A legal loophole had been exploited by the Caley, in setting up the Caledonian Steam Packet Company expressly to circumvent the need to acquire steamship Powers, which had not gone unnoticed. Thus, for the Glasgow & South Western Railway to regain ground lost to the Caley in the 1880s and 1890s it had to fight hard for the Parliamentary Powers then necessary to enable it to run ships itself, and claw back traffic to its Greenock railhead. Opposition to the granting of these Powers was fierce, and in much the same way as the Barry Railway Company had been obliged to compromise in the face of spirited opposition from P. & A. Campbell Ltd, the compromises which the Glasgow and South Western Railway was obliged to accept reduced the earning potential of its fleet. In seeking help from the G&SWR before placing its order for new vessels, the Barry Railway Company may very well have had empathy with the feeling of oppression that had been experienced in Scotland.

The help they sought was evidenced in the decision to order what amounted to copies of a proven design from the Clydebank yard of John Brown and

Company Limited (previously J. & G. Thomson), who had built the paddle steamer *Juno,* and which had entered service with the Glasgow and South Western Railway in 1898. The two new Barry vessels were to be built to the same general arrangements, albeit with certain exceptions, the most visually obvious of which was to have two funnels rather than *Juno's* single funnel. The other important difference was that the Barry Railway Company chose to have the navigating bridge of its paddlers placed forward of the leading funnel, comparable with what had become standard P. & A. Campbell Ltd practice in the Bristol Channel. There were to be further differences in detail, but essentially the starting point for the Barry pair was the sturdy and speedy *Juno.*

In choosing a proven design, the Barry Railway Company was not taking any of the risks associated with innovative features. At 245 ft long, the new paddlers were to be the longest that could turn in the River Avon off the entrance to the Cumberland Basin, and by going for quality and size as well as speed comparable to the three Campbell 'flyers' - *Westward Ho, Cambria* and especially *Britannia* - the statement was being made that here was direct competition to the enemy in Bristol. Another advantage of copying an earlier design was the obvious one of speed of construction, and the shipbuilder's tender documentation quoted for delivery on the River Clyde within seven and a half months. Thus, it was expected that the two new ships would both be ready in time for the start of services in April 1905.

At a Special Board Meeting of the Barry Railway Company on Friday 28th October, 1904 it was proposed by Mr Forrest and seconded by Mr Insole that there be a special vote of thanks to Mr Thompson 'for the valuable services rendered to the Company in connection with the letting of the contract for the two passenger steamships and the detailed work relative thereto'. The Secretary reported the sealing of the Agreement with John Brown 'for construction of two passenger steamships, the first ship to cost £29,790 and the second ship to cost £29,000'. Messrs Forrest & Thompson were to form a Committee '. . . to consider the best scheme for the provision and working of a steam vessels' service under the Act of 1904, and to report to the Board thereon'. Finally, at this momentuous occasion, the Manager of the Barry Railway Company (an official as distinct from a Director) was 'instructed to obtain prices for table linen, cutlery and other equipment of a like nature'. At this point, the two new vessels were still unnamed, and during the next four Board meetings (in December 1904, January, February and March 1905) there was no further reference to how the shipping operation would be set up, or who exactly would take charge.

Thus was the scene set in Barry for the entry into service of the two new ships, in the Spring of 1905. It is worth noting from the P. & A. Campbell Ltd records of this time that although a new vessel was being advocated by Alec Campbell, no decision to proceed was made. That another body over the Channel in South Wales could so easily find the finances for not one but two front-line excursion steamers did not go unnoticed, and this became a fundamental feature of the dispute that was to flare up in the early summer of 1905.

Portrait of T.R. Thompson, Director of the Barry Railway Company. At the opening ceremony of Barry Dock on Thursday 18th July, 1889, the report published in the *South Wales Daily News* noted that the first ship to enter the dock was SS *Arno*, steered by T.R. Thompson. The paper gave a detailed profile of this key figure in Barry's development:

If only as a parliamentary witness, Mr Thomas Roe Thompson deserves special notice. He appears to have been created as a set-off to the acuteness of the legal profession, for the smartest man at the bar cannot double up Mr Thompson. He was born at Sunderland about 43 years ago, and came to Cardiff with his father, Mr Matthew Thompson, in 1858 . . . in conjunction with Captain John Cory, Mr T.R. Thompson embarked into the perilous enterprise of ship-owning. But he chose the right time, and before long he became noted for his smartness as a business man. From his earliest acquaintance with Cardiff, Mr Thompson made himself thoroughly *au fait* with the requirements of the port. He was a careful reader of every document, parliamentary blue book, Board of Trade returns, statistical compilations, and the rest, bearing upon the development of the trade of the town and perused the evidence of all who had appeared before Parliamentary Committees dealing with South Wales bills. Consequently, when Mr T.R. Thompson went into the box himself, he was armed at all points, and was a match for any Counsel.

In former years he has given much assistance to the Bute Trustees when they undertook anything tending towards the development of Cardiff. But they did not go far enough to meet his ideas of what ought to be done for the port. Consequently, when Barry loomed through the mist he eagerly espoused its cause and there has been no more determined and capable champion of its rights than he. In regard to the pilotage question he has, from his special acquaintance with maritime matters, assumed a leading position from the outset, and has given the opponents of the Barry bills some hard nuts to crack. Mr Thompson is quite an object of veneration for the Cardiff Pilotage Board.

National Museums & Galleries of Wales

Construction of Nos. 368 & 369 at the Clydebank Yard, Glasgow

As a result of the survival of comprehensive records from the final closure in the 1970s of Upper Clyde Shipbuilders, who had taken over the famous company of John Brown and Co. Ltd, a good picture can be built up of the construction of what were at first hull numbers 368 and 369, and which were to become the paddle-steamers *Gwalia* and *Devonia*. At the time that Mr Thompson (acting on behalf of the Barry Railway Company) invited tenders in the summer of 1904, timely delivery for the 1905 season would have been of crucial importance. The John Brown and Co. Ltd concern was a very substantial one, and nine building berths were in place at the Clydebank shipyard. At the point that construction of the two new paddlers got underway two Cunarders (one of them, hull No. 366, already named *Carmania,* the other still known as hull No. 367) were under construction and therefore with seven available building berths John Brown & Co. Ltd was able to commence work readily.

In all, four different tenders had been submitted by John Brown & Co. Ltd to the Barry Railway Company, all dated 16th August, 1904, the first three of which were for paddle-steamers and the fourth for a turbine steamer. The first and second tenders were basically for paddlers of a similar description, the first - priced at £29,020 - being for a vessel with a No. 3 Certificate, and the second for one with a 'limited No. 2 Certificate', at £29,790. The third was for a slightly longer vessel than the second, with five Navy-type boilers, at £32,320. The fourth was for a 240 ft-long turbine-steamer, of 20 knots capability and again with a 'limited No. 2 Certificate', at £31,440. The second tender explicitly stated that this vessel would be a copy of *Juno,* and was endorsed to the effect that the price for a second (identical) vessel would be for £29,000. In each case the tender breakdown showed that the hull would account for about half the total cost, with machinery and profits making up the balance. What is striking about these tenders a century later is the stark simplicity of a simple, single sheet of a paper with minimal specification details, as being the documentation which would underpin something as major as the purchase of an expensive and complex seagoing ship.

It was the second tender that was accepted, and one imagines that Mr Thompson must have had to do some hard bargaining with John Brown and Co. Ltd to negotiate the discount agreed contractually for the second vessel as directed by Lord Windsor, in his role as the Chairman of the Barry Railway Company. The detail differences required by the Barry Railway Company were hardly inconsequential, but there clearly cannot have been time to make other than minimal changes to the plans and rely on the skill of the craftsmen at the yard to execute the differences necessary for the extra uptake for the second funnel, a different style of windows forward compared to the G&SWR *Juno,* and the relocated bridge. A little more time was presumably available to make engine design modifications. The Minute Book of the shipbuilder's Board Meetings is silent on this matter, and merely noted at its 25th October, 1904 meeting that the contract documentation with the Barry Railway Company had had the Seal affixed.

No time was wasted in laying the keels of the two Barry paddle-steamers in September 1904, side by side in building berths Nos. 1 and 2 of the West Yard

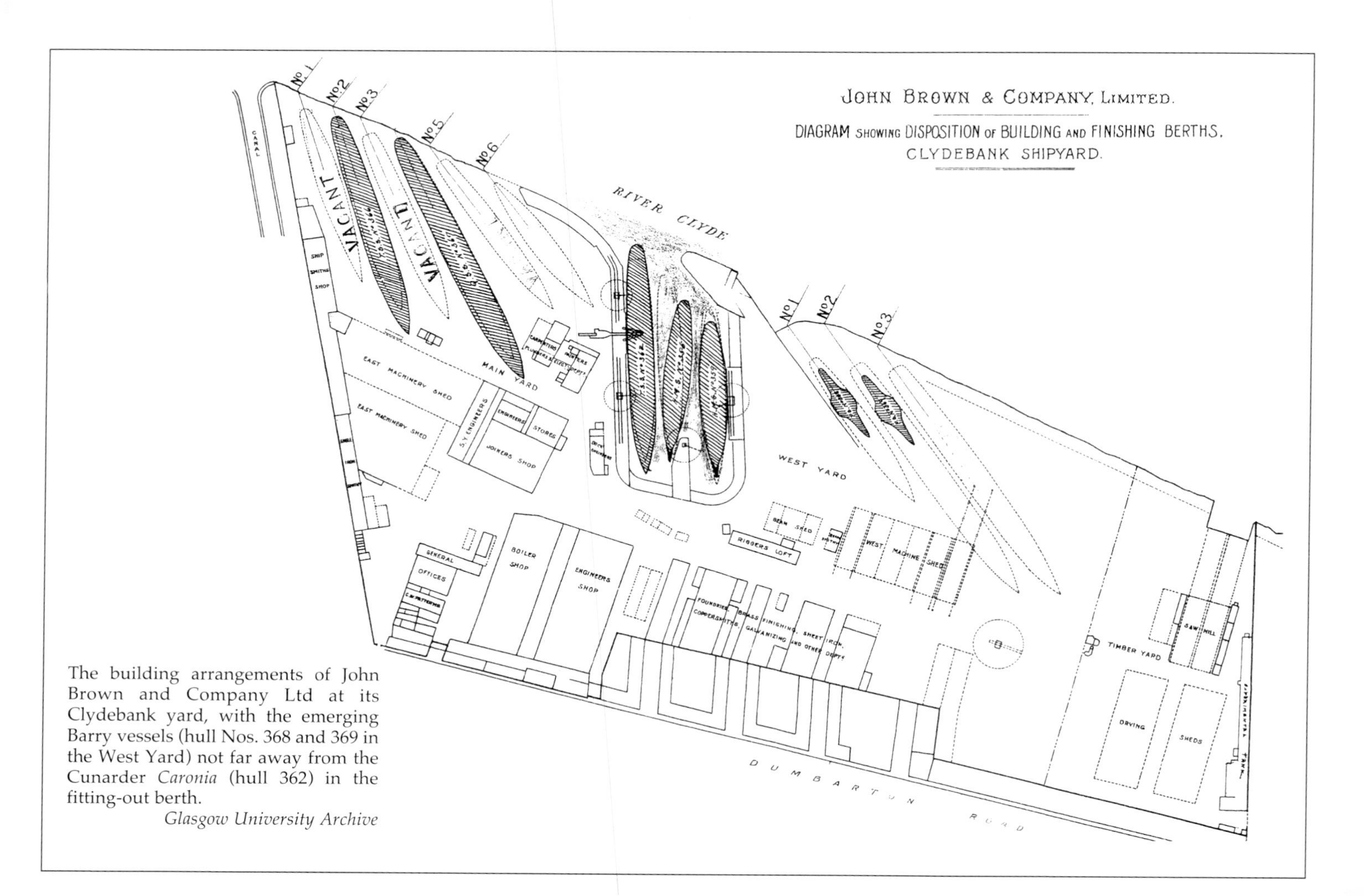

The building arrangements of John Brown and Company Ltd at its Clydebank yard, with the emerging Barry vessels (hull Nos. 368 and 369 in the West Yard) not far away from the Cunarder *Caronia* (hull 362) in the fitting-out berth.

Glasgow University Archive

at Clydebank, just downstream of the emerging Cunarders in the Main Yard and the Dock fitting-out berths, which then contained *Caronia* (hull No. 362) and two naval vessels HMS *Hindustan* and HMS *Antrim*. The monthly returns and progress reports of shipbuilding showed that there were then 4,735 workers employed at the yard, rather less than an earlier high of 5,417. Both paddlers were framed by October, and by November No. 368 was nearly half-plated with bulkheads all complete, keelsons fitted, and the sponsons and paddleboxes commenced. Progress was rapid into the winter, and by December deck-laying had commenced on No. 368 whilst on No. 369 plating was well advanced. By January 1905 both were plated and riveted, with No. 368 declared ready for launching in the February 1905 report. No. 369 had now nearly acquired all her wooden decking, caulked, and was being prepared for her launch. During the construction period of the Barry vessels, the other Cunarder gradually took shape, and was to become the mighty *Lusitania* which would be commissioned in 1907.

A diary of shipping movements of newly-built vessels was kept at the Clydebank yard, and *Gwalia* was duly recorded as having been launched on 24th February, 1905. She left for preliminary trials on 16th March, 1905, was dry-docked at Govan during the period 21st-22nd March, 1905, and left for her official trials on 23rd March, 1905. The Engine & Boiler Works report recorded her speed as being 19.8 knots. After further trials on 27th March, 1905 she moored at Greenock, and finally left there for Barry on the morning of 11th April, 1905, although John Brown & Co. Ltd had expected that she would have been away sooner, on 1st April, 1905.

In the meantime, *Devonia* was recorded as having been launched at 11.30 am on 22nd March, 1905, carrying out her preliminary trials on 21st April, 1905. Her dry-docking at Govan took place on 24th-26th April, 1905, with her official trials being run on 27th April, 1905, prior to further trials on 29th April, 1905. Finally, she left the River Clyde for South Wales on 2nd May, 1905. The initial colour scheme carried by *Gwalia* and *Devonia* was a black hull, white saloon strake, and buff funnels with an extremely narrow black top, and trials photographs show this arrangement clearly, although it turned out to be extremely short-lived. The Directors of the Barry Railway Company, it can be assumed, felt that the buff funnel would clearly distinguish the vessels of the so-called Barry and Bristol Channel Steamship Company from those of P. & A. Campbell Ltd which carried the now well-established white funnel around the ports of the Bristol Channel and along the south coast of England and as far afield as France.

The Welsh connection at the John Brown & Co. Ltd Clydebank yard was not quite over after the two Barry Railway Company paddlers had been launched, as their building berths were immediately allocated (in March 1905) to the construction of two new turbine-steamers for the Fishguard and Rosslare Railways and Harbours Company, to be named *St David* and *St Patrick*.

What, then, had the Barry Railway Company acquired for its new maritime venture with around £60,000 of investment committed to the fleet, disregarding the substantial amount already spent on the construction of Barry Pier and its attendant extension railway from Barry Island? The basic specification details at the tender stage called for a paddle-steamer design of 240 ft length, 28 ft 6 in.

Gwalia under construction, John Brown & Co. Ltd, Clydebank. *Richard Clammer Collection*

Gwalia receiving final attention, John Brown & Co. Ltd, Clydebank. *Richard Clammer Collection*

breadth and 9 ft 9 in. depth, with compound diagonal machinery with cylinders of 33 in. and 71 in. with a 5 ft 0 in. stroke. The indicated horse-power, with forced draught, was to be 2,900 with steam supplied from a double-ended boiler measuring 16 ft 6 in. by 18 ft 4 in., at 150 psi, to give a contract speed of 19½ knots. The details recorded at the time of actual tonnage measurement by a Board of Trade Surveyor prior to registry corresponded to these tender specifications, and defined the number of decks as 'One and Cabin Sole', with an elliptical stern and straight stem, fore and aft rigged, clincher-built. *Gwalia* had six bulkheads, and a displacement of 933 tons. One curious feature of the builders' certificates for a pair of supposedly identical vessels - issued a few weeks apart, on 28th March, 1905 for *Gwalia* and on 28th April, 1905 for her sister *Devonia* - is a slight variation in net register tonnage, 165.93 for the former and 167.61 for the latter. One imagines different surveyors were responsible, unless some very minor builder's deviation had intervened.

The basis of the new Barry Railway Company pair in comparison with the vessel that the Clydebank yard had built in 1898 as *Juno* for the Glasgow & South Western Railway was interesting and the words of Andrew McQueen nicely emphasise a basic feature that was to have repercussions in the later lives of *Gwalia* and *Devonia* in terms of their relative operating costs: *Juno*, he stated, had been built on

> . . . the same general lines as *Jupiter*, but considerably larger and altogether a more massive, weatherly boat. This is the only one of the Clyde boats, so far, constructed with joggled plates. Her engines are powerful and she travels fast. Most of her work has been in the form of excursion-running out of Ayr, and her qualities suit her well for these comparatively exposed waters . . .

Another oddity apart from the net register tonnage difference between the pair was that the John Brown & Co. Ltd paperwork with the Board of Trade formally noted the owners of *Gwalia* as being the Barry Railway Company, the vessel being intended for the Excursion trade. By the time *Devonia* was completed her owners were named as the Barry and Bristol Channel Steamship Company of Cardiff, and she was evidently intended for the Home trade. One detects here the first indications of an awareness by the Barry Railway Company that their moves were being watched by the Campbell brothers. Compared with *Juno*, whose gross registered tonnage was recorded as 592 grt, *Devonia* measured at a rather greater 641 grt. The most obvious difference in appearance - aside from the two funnels and forward bridge already referred to - was the smaller forward windows on the Barry vessels, compared to the large square windows fitted to *Juno*. It seems that, having taken the order from the Barry Railway Company for both vessels, and received payments from that body, then what was subsequently recorded was of rather less consequence in Scotland than it was to be in the Bristol Channel, where some subterfuge was now in prospect as the two vessels departed successively from the Clyde for their intended duties.

A trials photograph of *Gwalia*. *H.A. Allen Collection*

The site of the former John Brown and Company Ltd Clydebank shipbuilding yards, seen from PS *Waverley* on a passing excursion, 10th April, 2004. *Author*

BUILDERS' CERTIFICATE FOR STEAMERS,

MEASURED UNDER MERCHANT SHIPPING ACT, 1854.

Copy

We do Certify that we Built in our Building Yard at CLYDEBANK, in the COUNTY OF DUMBARTON, in the Year Nineteen Hundred and five the SHIP or VESSEL called the "Gwalia" of Barry Port of Cardiff for and on account of

William Thomas Symonds, Howard Edmonds Radford, William North Lewis, Herbert Rees Jones } all of Cardiff

said Vessel being of the following Description and Dimensions:—

Material,	Steel	Stem,	Straight
Number of Decks,	One and cabin sole	Stern,	Elliptical
Number of Masts,	One	Build,	[illegible]
Rig,	fore & aft	Head,	None

		Feet.	Tenths.
Length from the forepart of the Stem to the aftside of the Stern Post,		245	0
Breadth to outside of Plating,		29	0
Depth in Hold from Tonnage Deck to Ceiling at Midships,		9	7
		Tons.	
Tonnage under Tonnage Deck,		433.42	
~~Space or Spaces between Decks,~~ Forecastle		18.31	
Break,		7.24	
Houses, Round / Side	16.89 / 43.63	60.52	
Light and Air Space,		42.79	
GROSS TONNAGE,		562.28	
Deduct for Space required for Propelling Power under Merchant Shipping Act, 1854,	317.57		
Deduct for Crew Space,	61.17		
" Act, 1894	17.61	396.35	
NET REGISTER TONNAGE,		165.93	

That she is Propelled by Paddle wheels has [illegible] Engines, the estimated Horse-Power of which is 2900 Horses; and that the above named and designed Individuals were the first Purchasers thereof, in the following proportions, viz.:—

William Thomas Symonds, Howard Edmonds Radford, William North Lewis, Herbert Rees Jones } Sixty four — Sixty fourths

Given under our hands at CLYDEBANK, *this* 28th *day of* March *Nineteen Hundred and* five

JOHN BROWN & COMPANY, Limited.

[signature] Director.

[signature] Asst. Secretary.

Seal

Builder's Certificate for *Gwalia* made out in the names of Messrs Symonds, Radford, Lewis and Jones as the supposed owners. *Glasgow University Archive*

The Barry Railway Company reveals its hand

After the launch of the first Barry Railway Company ship *Gwalia* it would have been increasingly difficult to evade the issue of just what new shipping service in the Bristol Channel was about to be commenced and, indeed, the wish to start to actively promote the steamship venture would have been a natural one given that so much was now at stake. On 14th March, 1905 the *South Wales Daily News* carried the message that very quickly caused consternation in the P. & A. Campbell Ltd camp at Bristol - Captain James, formerly one of their own 'most popular skippers' had been recruited and was standing by the newly-built *Gwalia* at Glasgow as she completed fitting-out. *Devonia* was at that point apparently expected to be ready by 21st March, 1905, and was to be christened by Mrs Radford. The item stated that '. . . the syndicate will probably run occasional trips from Barry, but it is understood most of the excursions will be from Cardiff, and that they will also run trips to and from other places in the Channel'.

The name of the so-called syndicate was to be the Barry and Bristol Channel Steamship Company, and when advertisements for sailings duly appeared in newspapers such as the *Barry Dock News* at the beginning of the season they were clearly under this name, with no mention either of the Barry Railway Company, or of anything involving references to the Red Funnel Line. But P. & A. Campbell Ltd were not deceived and, at their 3rd April, 1905 Board Meeting in Bristol, resolved straightaway to seek a legal opinion with a view to instigating proceedings against the Barry Railway Company who, it seemed, were not only going to operate outside the terms of the 1904 Act by running from Cardiff but were also going to operate anywhere they pleased by means of using the alias of the syndicate. A fight was now on, and Counsel engaged as a *prima facie* case was felt to exist.

Whereas the intentions of the Barry Railway Company may very well have been broadly law-abiding back in the summer of 1904 when its hard-fought Powers were won, things had now moved on but one is tempted to infer that Mr Thompson and his fellow Directors actually believed that setting up the syndicate would be sufficient to fend off the concerns of P. & A. Campbell Ltd. At the Barry Railway Company Board meeting on 7th April, 1905 Mr Thompson proposed a resolution '. . . that the arrangements made with Messrs Symonds, Lewis, Radford and Jones for the sale to them of the steamboats now in course of construction . . . and for the provision of a service in accordance with the Company's Act of Parliament be confirmed . . .', and which was agreed unanimously. The next relevant Minute, on 5th May, 1905, went on to note that the shipbuilders John Brown were to make out the Builder's Certificates for the two new paddle-steamers *Gwalia* and *Devonia* in the names of these four gentlemen. Thus, as far as the Barry Railway Company was concerned, a separate company would own and operate the new ships, and indeed the ships registry at the port of Cardiff documented that the ownership of all 64 shares of each of the two vessels - registered on 7th April, 1905 and 2nd May, 1905 respectively - was in the joint names of William Thomas Symonds, Shipowner, Howard Edmonds Radford, Merchant, William North Lewis, Colliery Agent and Herbert Rees Jones, Shipowner.

Equally one can infer that P. & A. Campbell Ltd saw straight through this and believed it to be a ruse by which the true ownership of the ships - as they perceived it - still rested with the Barry Railway Company, who had ordered and paid for them. The only other hard evidence from this period is that recorded in the Port of Cardiff Registry transactions, namely that on 12th April, 1905 (for *Gwalia*) and 20th June, 1905 (for *Devonia*), ownership was stated to have passed by means of mortgages to the Metropolitan Bank, with Mr Symonds now being named as the Managing Owner. Peter and Alec Campbell simply did not believe that four men associated with the Barry Railway Company could really own the vessels, and this was to be the basis of the litigation that ensued - but what was probably not realised, in the early Summer of 1905, was that over two years would pass before the case was determined. The scene was therefore set for what was to become an exceptionally interesting period of intense competition for the traffic of the Bristol Channel. The fact that *Gwalia* was to run her maiden voyage from Cardiff tended to ram the point home to P. & A. Campbell Ltd - one of the biggest threats to its livelihood that it had ever had to face had now arrived. So, whilst the foundations of the legal challenge were laid, for the moment the Barry Railway Company would simply start to put their plans into action whilst the Campbell brothers and their fellow Directors could only look across the Bristol Channel with dismay - at that stage their own finances did not run to purchasing a new steamer themselves, and much would inevitably depend on a successful legal action finding in their favour.

The start of the 1905 season

The main goal of the new Barry steamers was, of course, to capture a share of the traffic from South Wales to the prime North Devon resort of Ilfracombe. The basic down-Channel run (from Bristol or from either Newport and Cardiff & Penarth) to Ilfracombe had generally featured a call by launch at the pretty little resort of Lynmouth and, from 1901, Minehead Pier had opened and a call there could easily be added to the basic Ilfracombe voyage without going unduly out of the way. A good relationship had been built up since the 1880s between the resort of Ilfracombe, its municipally-owned harbour and the White Funnel Fleet of excursion steamers which, most townsfolk appreciated, played a large part in the economy of the town. The Pockett's steamers which linked Swansea with Ilfracombe were also popular, and a faction at Ilfracombe may well have been concerned that the prospect of an additional operator of steamers was simply not necessary. The Agent of P. & A. Campbell Ltd at Ilfracombe, Fred. W. Birmingham, was a prominent local citizen and oft-times Councillor, and a key influence in the affairs of the important Harbour Committee for whom the Campbell steamers represented a major source of income. His father, Captain T. Birmingham, had at one time occupied the important position of Harbour Master at Ilfracombe.

Of the two weekly newspapers which circulated in the resort at the time, the *Gazette* was distinctly loyal to the Campbell cause. Practically no mention was made of the imminent appearance of the new Barry boats - and every opportunity was taken to remind folk of the advantages of the '. . . greyhounds of the Bristol Channel . . . the prettiest, most comfortable and luxuriant steamers between Lundy Island and Bristol . . .'

The *Chronicle*, on the other hand, conceded that a new service was to be provided which ought to benefit Ilfracombe interests, and on 1st April, 1905 published a suitable statement:

> The Barry and Bristol [*sic*] Steamship Company has just built a new steamer, the *Gwalia*, to run between South Wales and the watering-places in the Bristol Channel . . . she is acknowledged on the Clyde to be the handsomest, fastest and in every way the best boat ever launched there for passenger and excursion service. The *Gwalia* will be captained by one of the most capable of the Channel seamen, Capt. J. James, who is known and will be heartily welcomed by many 'Combeites, for his genial and courteous spirit. Mr William Jones, who is also well-known in the town, being both courteous and energetic, has been appointed the local representative, and the interests of the town will be well looked after by him. It is expected that the *Gwalia* will make a complimentary trip to Ilfracombe in about a fortnight, when the townspeople will have the opportunity of inspecting this fine craft.

In Barry there would have been mounting excitement as the day drew near for the new local steamer venture to start up and put Barry Pier back on the excursion map. This report duly appeared in the *Barry Dock News* on 14th April, 1905:

> BARRY PASSENGER STEAMER CHANNEL SERVICE
> ARRANGEMENTS TO OPEN THIS MONTH
>
> The new passenger steamer *Gwalia* reached Barry on Wednesday last. The arrangements of the Barry & Bristol Channel Steamship Company for the month are now complete, and sailings from Cardiff, Penarth & Barry to Weston, Lynmouth and Ilfracombe, will commence on Thursday 20th instant. The fares will be those usual in the Channel and half-fare coupon books and a limited number of season-tickets will be issued. The *Gwalia*, and her sister ship *Devonia*, which will shortly join her, are most luxuriously appointed. In addition to the usual saloon accommodation, there will be ladies tea-room and cloakroom, gentleman's smoking room, private cabin, and promenade deck, and a stall at which fruit, sweets & c. will be sold. An express boat-train will leave Cardiff (Riverside) daily at 9.30 am and will proceed without a stop to Barry Dock Pier to catch the steamer, the fare charged being the same as from Cardiff all the way by steamer. Coupons and season-tickets will not, however, cover the railway journey for which season-ticket and coupon-holders, on their production, will obtain specially cheap tickets at a shilling return (including Barry Pier toll). By means of train and steamer, passengers leaving Cardiff at 9.30 am will reach Ilfracombe about noon.
>
> The *Gwalia*, which is an exceedingly fine boat, arrived at Barry Docks, as we have stated, on Wednesday, and is now moored in the Basin. From noon today (Thursday) till 7.30 pm the vessel will be open for inspection by the public.
>
> The master, Captain James, is highly pleased with the speed maintained by the *Gwalia* in her maiden run from Greenock to Barry, which was accomplished in just over 24 hours, representing an average speed of about 18 knots per hour. A large number of visitors lined the quay on both sides of the Basin during the day to obtain a glimpse of the new boat, which, with her two funnels, and attractive tints of black, white, red and yellow, looks an exceedingly fine craft, and will probably prove the most popular boat that has yet plied the Bristol Channel for passenger traffic. Her first run will take place on Thursday, the 20th instant, to Ilfracombe.

The appearance of *Gwalia* was undoubtedly most impressive, and certainly on an equal with the established Campbell White Funnel Fleet of steamers, and gave substance to the wish of the Barry Railway Company to now do better with its affairs wholly under its own control, albeit through the syndicate arrangements that it had seen fit to create. It seems that the public were not deceived by the ownership ruse any more than the Campbell brothers - one early-season report at Ilfracombe jocularly referred to '. . . the big seaworthy crafts of the Barry Railway Company'. The initial colour scheme carried by *Gwalia* was not greatly different to that of the Campbell steamers, particularly when seen from a distance, and to the untutored eye it was perhaps only the buff funnels that clearly set her apart from the equally handsome newer vessels of the White Funnel Fleet. Her paddleboxes were particularly striking, and were elaborately decorated with a crest encircled by the words 'Barry Steamships 1905', adjacent to a pair of unicorns rampant.

Also reproduced in full here is the account of the maiden voyage of *Gwalia* published in the *Barry Dock News* on Friday 21st April, 1905. One would imagine that the Editor of this journal - which was of course wholly sympathetic to the local cause - could be relied upon to give the new company its correct official name!

BARRY & BRISTOL CHANNEL PASSENGER SERVICE
SUCCESSFUL TRIAL TRIP OF THE STEAMSHIP GWALIA

A most successful and pleasurable trial trip of the handsome and commodious new passenger steamer *Gwalia*, belonging to the Barry & Bristol Channel Steamship Company, took place on Wednesday last, when the boat made a very satisfactory run from Cardiff to Ilfracombe, calling at Penarth and Barry. The party on board numbered nearly 150. The boat behaved admirably, and the average speed attained was nineteen and three-quarter knots an hour, the return trip from Ilfracombe to Barry being made in less than two and a half hours. Amongst the party on board were Messrs T. R. Thompson (Director of the Barry Railway Co.), W. North Lewis, H.E. Radford & H. Rees-Jones (Directors of the Steamship Company), H.J. Vincent (deputy manager of the Barry Railway Co.), W. Waddell (Engineer), R.J. Duncan, H.H. Powell, Councillors J.A. Manaton & J.C. Meggitt, Dr Lloyd Edwards, Dr Gillon Irving, Dr Powell (Barry) etc. The *Gwalia*, which will make daily trips to Ilfracombe from Cardiff, Barry and Penarth, is one of the best adapted and most perfectly constructed steam passenger boats which has ever been built on the Clyde. She has accommodation for between 1,200 and 1,500 passengers, and her behaviour on the opening trip was in every respect satisfactory.

A very similar report was carried in the *Western Mail* newspaper but a little more detail of the comfort and high-quality interior of *Gwalia* was described:

. . . the highest praise must be given to the new boat. She behaved very well in the slight sea that was running, and her great breadth - some 62 feet - will prevent any of that rolling which is so distressing to most landsmen who venture on a sea trip. The greatest care has been taken to study the comfort of the passengers, and some very novel features have been introduced. The main saloon is a very comfortable room, with lounge seats covered with blue plush. Instead of the usual portholes a striking improvement has been introduced in the shape of small windows which can easily be opened. The room is exceptionally bright and homelike. The smoking-room has been built after the style of a smoking-room in a first-class hotel, with a bar attached. The seats are upholstered in

Gwalia setting off from Barry Pier. Very few pictures exist of the first few weeks of operation of the Barry steamers, in April and May 1905, before repainting into the lighter hull colour with red funnels. After her maiden voyage from Barry Pier for invited guests, *Gwalia* entered public service the following day, on Thursday 20th April, 1905, running from Cardiff to Weston and back before taking the main morning sailing down-channel to Ilfracombe, prior to daily service over the Easter weekend. *Lionel Vaughan Collection*

The new Clydebank-built sisters seen together at Barry Pier, probably in May or June 1905 shortly after *Devonia* had been delivered from her Clyde birthplace. *Brian Luxton Collection*

green morocco. Among other evidences of the foresight of the Directors are a tearoom, a fruit-stall, an open engine-room (so that the passengers can see the entire working of the engines), a saloon for fore-deck passengers with bar attached, and an upper bridge-deck, which will be reserved for special parties, while electric light has been fitted up everywhere. The dining room will hold 120 persons . . .

Start-up of regular services, 'Devonia' arrives

Whilst the tone of these two newspaper articles, which were, after all, published for a Barry local readership, was neutral on the subject of Cardiff, the mention of connecting train services was relevant but not quite complete. Subsequent advertising fleshed out the details of what was being offered to Barry folk: on each day, from 1st May, two trains from Cardiff would run through to Barry Pier, the first being an all-stations stopping service leaving Grangetown at 9.24 am, thence calling at Cogan, Dynas Powis, Cadoxton, Barry Docks, Barry and Barry Island. Hard on the heels of this would be the express boat-train from Cardiff (Riverside) leaving there at 9.35 am (it had left at 9.30 during April), running non-stop to Barry Pier. But for Cardiff residents a choice existed on most days, between whether to catch the train and then join the steamer at Barry Pier departing at 10.10 am daily (10.00 during April) for Lynmouth and Ilfracombe, or to board the steamer at Cardiff Pier Head whence - on days when the tide permitted - departure was usually at 9.30 am, for Penarth, Barry and away down-channel.

The Barry Railway Company operated regular passenger services on a number of other routes, and times from Bridgend and Vale of Glamorgan stations on these, as well as from Porth via their own 'main line' through Wenvoe, were quoted. A change of trains at Barry station was necessitated for passengers from the Vale, but the Barry Railway Company 'Operating Notice for the Re-Opening of Barry Pier Station and Commencement of Steamboat Service' stated that, if there were boat-passengers on board, then the 8.38 am from Porth could be extended beyond Barry Island station through to Barry Pier. In the reverse direction, departure from Ilfracombe was initially usually set at 4.15 or 4.30 pm, depending on the tides, in order to connect into a set departure-time evening boat-train from Barry Pier to Cardiff, at 6.33 pm, calling only at Barry and Grangetown, and it was stated that this connection would be held to await the steamer's arrival. Passengers for all other stations were obliged to change at Barry.

It was to be another couple of weeks before *Gwalia* was joined in the Bristol Channel by her sister vessel *Devonia*, probably on or shortly after 3rd May, 1905. The pattern of services provided in May and early-June in 1905 required one vessel on the virtually fixed-time 'railway run' duty daily (except Sundays), leaving the other available for a variety of excursion services principally from Cardiff, or spare. On some occasions the Ilfracombe 'railway run' vessel might complete an early morning round trip between Cardiff and Weston-super-Mare before leaving Cardiff, or carry out a Weston-super-Mare round trip, calling at 'The Old Pier' as Birnbeck Pier was frequently referred to, in the evening after returning to Cardiff from Ilfracombe. One such advertised Weston trip seems to have been an evening one from Cardiff on 19th May, and such Weston 'ferry' trips were only offered occasionally at this early stage in the season. There were a few days where the second ship ran Cardiff-Weston trips if tides were such as to warrant these being offered in the middle part of the day. Alternatively, Cardiff-Minehead runs were sometimes advertised at this early, interim stage of the so-called Barry & Bristol Steamship Company undertaking, as well as odd appearances at Clevedon, typically running up the Somerset coast at low water after a Cardiff to Weston crossing had been made. Weston-super-Mare 'ferry' runs were not necessarily provided every day or to any set pattern: for example, on Saturday 10th June, 1905 both vessels were to be found on runs to Ilfracombe, the second vessel departing from Cardiff early in the afternoon whilst the first stuck to the rail-connected timetable.

As if to rub salt into the wounds of P. & A. Campbell Ltd, whose newest steamer *Britannia* was now almost 10 years old, no opportunity was lost to remind excursionists and others in Barry of the good performances being put in by the two smart Clydebank-built vessels, and healthy passenger carryings. On 2nd June, 1905 Mrs Grundy could jubilantly declare that 'The Barry passenger steamship *Gwalia* made a record passage to Ilfracombe last Saturday, leaving Cardiff about 2.40, and arriving at her destination between 4.45 and 4.50. The vessel had her full complement on board'.

What is unclear from surviving Barry Railway Company records is just what was intended in respect of a third vessel, in terms of whether this had long been envisaged or was simply a reaction to initially encouraging traffic levels at Cardiff - which were only being achieved by taking passengers away from the ships of the White Funnel Fleet, as P. & A. Campbell Ltd would probably have seen it. On the face of it, the new capital amount of £60,000 authorised for the construction of steamships in the 1904 Bill had already been spoken for, but later Barry Railway Company Minute Book evidence suggests that this constraint was deemed irrelevant as it was assumed then - at least by the Barry Directors - that by registering the two new ships at the Port of Cardiff in the names of the four gentlemen as the designated owners, then the Bill had effectively not been necessary for the railway company. Another explanation is that the railway company could if it chose simply argue that it had assigned its hard-won Parliamentary Powers to the syndicate. One wonders whether, back in the 1890s when a Bill was first promoted, those that drafted it believed that a capital limit of £60,000 would actually be adequate for a three-strong fleet given that *Westward Ho* had cost P. & A. Campbell Ltd around £20,000 in 1894, and that the slightly lower specification *Lady Margaret* had been purchased, when only one year old, for around £15,000. At these prices £60,000 should have been ample for two main-line ships and one for ferry duties - and this theme was indeed to be picked up soon enough after the excitement of the establishment of the new order in the Bristol Channel had started to wane.

It is reasonable to assume that the confidence of the Barry Railway Company, shortly after the two new paddlers had settled down to the daily Ilfracombe 'railway run' duties and the various excursions, plus a limited number of Cardiff to Weston trips, was such that the decision to go for a third vessel was taken. In the first half of May 1905 a rumour appeared, in Mrs Grundy's Jottings in the *Barry Dock News*, that a charter of the paddle-steamer *Greyhound* had been arranged, which was then stated to be running on the Clyde. This rumour proved unfounded, added to which *Greyhound*, an earlier Clyde-built steamer from the yard of J. & G. Thomson in 1895 (prior to the John Brown & Co. Ltd take-over) was then in service at Blackpool and elsewhere on the Lancashire Coast. The rumour had substance in that she did change hands around that time, but remained based in the North. She would have doubtless made an excellent fleetmate to the new John Brown & Co. Ltd-built pair, but this was not to be.

Only a week later, on 26th May, 1905, Mrs Grundy was able to state with greater conviction that the Barry & Bristol Channel Steamship Company had engaged an additional paddle-steamer which was expected to '. . . arrive next week from the Clyde . . . and ply exclusively between Barry and Weston. The Company intend running occasional trips to Bristol . . .' This information proved to be slightly more accurate and was followed by a formal statement on 9th June, 1905 that the services of the North Wales passenger steamer *Rhos Colwyn* had been secured, which would be renamed *Westonia*, and was then undergoing overhaul in Dublin. Regarding the rapidly growing popularity of sailings from Barry Pier, she also cheerfully claimed that the most popular trains on the Barry Railway every day now were those of the 'Atlantic Express' running to and from the passenger boats every morning and evening. It seemed that, finally, success had greeted the new venture and that if Cardiff folk so wished they could catch a Barry steamer to Ilfracombe at Cardiff or - if that did not suit - they could catch a Barry Railway Company train from Cardiff to Barry Pier, and join the down-Channel steamer there. For the moment Mr Thompson and his colleagues could ignore the protests from Bristol, and contemplate the third phase of expansion that acquisition of *Westonia* would permit as she was destined to run not between Barry and Weston - as Mrs Grundy had alleged (possibly to deceive the Campbell brothers) - but between Cardiff and Weston, where most days already saw two substantial White Funnel Fleet vessels in intensive service on the busy 'ferry' route.

What were the new steamers like?

Gwalia and her sister ship *Devonia* were distinctly handsome, well-proportioned vessels and fairly typical of their era with an almost completely uncluttered promenade deck given over to plentiful open seating capacity without deckhouses, other than that which served as the Captain's cabin underneath the exposed bridge, forward of the funnels. A larger construction was situated abaft the funnels, which sheltered the companion way down to the main deck. The forward part of this second deckhouse was designated as the chart-room, and behind it was the ticket office, whilst a reserved deck (officially described as the aft bridge deck) sat atop this structure, accessed by stairs at the aft-end. As two class ships, forward was allocated to second class passengers whilst saloon class passenger facilities were concentrated aft. Three lifeboats were carried, one aft on each sponson, port and starboard, and a third athwartships at the stern.

An early 'official' postcard view of *Gwalia,* taken after her first repainting into G&SWR colours. She is seen from the classic position at Ilfracombe Harbour, looking up the North Devon coast.
Lionel Vaughan Collection

A postcard view of *Devonia,* taken after repainting, manoeuvring alongside the unusually-shaped pier at Ilfracombe. This was the usual end of the daily 'railway run' voyage down-channel from Barry except in the high season when extension to Clovelly was common.
Lionel Vaughan Collection

The main deck layout was straightforward with much of the stern portion given over to a capacious first class saloon, with alcove seating. Four smaller rooms were fitted in between this area and the engine-room surrounds, namely a ladies room and a ladies cloak room (to port) and a first class smoking room & bar and a ladies tea room (to starboard), it doubtless being assumed that ladies did not require access to bar facilities in the same way as these were provided for gentlemen who wished to smoke. A writing table and two chairs were provided athwartships at the aft end of the first class saloon. The boiler was forward of the engines, and forward of the boiler room lay the second class saloon with mostly sparred seating around the perimeter. Accommodation for 10 deckhands was forward of this saloon, separated by a main bulkhead, and accessed from above rather than through the passenger accommodation. Gates to segregate the first and second classes were provided on either side of the engine & boiler room at the bulkhead which separated those two compartments, and were situated immediately above the coal shoots.

The lower deck astern accommodated the large first class dining saloon, reached by a stairway from the lounge above. To service this area the bar was situated on the port side, and the pantry to starboard, itself serviced by the galley above and forward on the starboard sponson, some distance away for the carriage of hot food relative to modern standards. The lower deck forward was similarly allocated to the second class dining room. Positioned between this area and the boiler room bulkhead was a group of four officers' cabins, one provided for the mate, one for the chief steward, one for the two engineers and a fourth for two pursers. A sizeable area led off the chief steward's cabin and was designated as being for stewards' stores.

The remainder of the crew naturally enjoyed the traditional location of the forepeak for their accommodation, divided by a bulkhead, with bunks for eight firemen right forward, and 12 stewards abaft of the partition. The general arrangement drawings suggest that the ladies stewardess would have berthed up on the main deck, on a bunk tucked in with the ladies cloak room, at a discreet distance from the remainder of the crew. Finally, most lavatories were provided on the sponsons, along with other areas such as those for engineers' stores, and a lamp-room.

Operations step up before all-out war is declared [sic]

An odd feature of the first couple of months of operation, in April and May 1905, was that after the maiden voyage of *Gwalia* and associated junketings, little or no specific mention was made in the newspapers of the entry into service of sister vessel *Devonia*. It may have been a deliberate ploy to avoid undue attention being focused on what was about to happen next, as the fleet went on to expand from two to three vessels, and acquired a drastic change of appearance. The late H.G. Owen of Swansea, when researching the history of the Barry steamers, ascertained that the two new vessels were repainted after 17th May, 1905, into a colour scheme that very closely resembled that used by the Glasgow & South Western Railway fleet, namely French grey hulls with white saloons and a striking shade of red applied to the funnels, and a deep black top. This repainting activity may well have taken a week at least for each vessel, and schedules from the late-May and early-June period in 1905 are such that on many days only one vessel was needed in service. Equally, there does not appear to have been any suspension of the daily new regular 'railway run' advertised, which is consistent with the assumed repainting activity at this time leaving only one or the other of the new Barry fleet available for traffic. Thus, traffic would have been confined to the daily Ilfracombe run and the odd morning or evening Weston round trip if tides were favourable and permitted the latter. It is not recorded what colours were worn by *Westonia* when she arrived in the Bristol Channel from Dublin, nor indeed whether the overhaul that she had received there included the repaint, in order to project a new image.

This was a fascinating and expansive period in which it seemed as though the Barry Railway Company was being deliberately provocative, in terms of sending its new vessels to ports and piers where the Campbell brothers might have thought they were protected - by the hard-fought 1904 Act - from such blatant competition. Birnbeck Pier at Weston-super-Mare had already received calls, and what appears to have been the first trip to Bristol took place on Thursday 1st June, 1905, when the Barry and Bristol Steamship Company advertisements referred to a sailing at 2.45 pm from Cardiff to Clevedon and Bristol, returning at 6.15 pm from Bristol and at 7.15 pm from Clevedon.

A few days later, the first excursion was advertised from Bristol by the Barry and Bristol Steamship Company, described in the *Western Daily Press* as 'The Opening Trip of the Season' by either of the new saloon steamers *Gwalia* and *Devonia*, on Monday 5th June, 1905. Billed to leave the Hotwells at 8.30 am this was a more or less identical trip to the normal P. & A. Campbell Ltd offering, for Clevedon, Cardiff, Penarth, Lynmouth and Ilfracombe, returning from the North Devon resort at 3.30, Lynmouth 4.05, Penarth 5.40, Cardiff 6.00 and Clevedon 6.45 pm. A trip like this offered plenty of different opportunities to an afternoon in Ilfracombe, and interested parties were referred for further particulars to the local Agent B.F. Fry at 9, Broad Quay, Bristol. As a White Funnel Fleet excursion was offered on the same day at the same time, 8.30 am from Bristol, returning at 4.00 pm from Ilfracombe, one can visualise the possibilities for some competitive steaming. To my great regret the Bristol papers appear not to have condescended to mention the start-up of Red Funnel Line steamer excursions from Bristol, and were content to just accept advertising fees. As at Ilfracombe the Campbell steamers were still those preferred by the newspaper commentaries in Bristol, as a few days later the numbers of passengers carried on the Whitsun bank holiday were described but with no recognition that the South Walian company vessels had ventured up the winding Avon Gorge.

As if to annoy the Campbell brothers still further, an 8.45 am departure on the following day Tuesday 6th June from Cardiff to Ilfracombe, making the customary Minehead and Lynmouth calls, was advertised as calling at Weston-super-Mare too. By cunningly extending a Cardiff-Weston 'ferry' sailing in this manner, the Barry steamers were seeking to encroach on the trade from Weston to Ilfracombe as well, something which P. & A. Campbell Ltd definitely looked on as its own preserve. The 'raiding' did not just stop there either - on that day the vessel was booked to return at 4.00 pm from Ilfracombe to Lynmouth, Minehead, Weston and Penarth, with another evening cruise then offered at 7.10 from Penarth and 7.30 pm from Cardiff to the Bell Buoy, returning to Cardiff at 10.00 pm. This really was making the most of a favourable tide!

According to Mrs Grundy in the *Barry Dock News* on 9th June, 1905, *Westonia* was due to arrive at Barry in time to run her first trip on Saturday 10th June, 1905 and would '. . . take her place on the Cardiff and Weston route . . .' accordingly. This was a subtle change of message from what had been said just a fortnight earlier, and doubtless the Campbell brothers were getting even more annoyed by now at what they would have regarded as the deceitful behaviour of their enemies in Wales, as formal direct communications with the Barry Railway Company had ended the previous year, and were now only made indirectly, through lawyers. The style of newspaper advertising used to market the Barry steamers now changed in style, and from June onwards the term 'Red Funnel Line' appeared prominently. A simple explanation of the change of image and name was that the railway company wished to indicate that a separate undertaking really was now responsible for the red-funnelled vessels which, clearly, were very much based on Cardiff as the centre of traffic and operations, and were competing head-on with P. & A. Campbell Ltd in the absolute sense, on routes and on price, and with what could have been projected as slightly superior - and certainly newer - vessels.

There was little that P. & A. Campbell Ltd could physically do to vent its frustrations as the company did not control access to any of the piers from which its new competitors sailed, i.e. the Pier Head at Cardiff, Penarth Pier and the down-channel destination piers of Minehead and Ilfracombe. The boatmen at Lynmouth would doubtless have been happy to ferry passengers out to and ashore from any passing excursion steamer, irrespective of what funnel colours it might have carried. To make matters worse, fare-cutting was to be an almost immediate consequence of the full introduction of *Westonia* to the Cardiff-Weston-super-Mare ferry route.

Midsummer 1905

In the week after *Westonia* entered regular service on the Cardiff-Weston 'ferry', an interesting excursion programme was offered from Cardiff on Tuesday 13th June, 1905. Scrutiny of the advertisements in the *Western Mail* newspaper referring to that day makes it plain that all three steamers were already in operation by then even though the names of steamers boldly listed at the top of the block still only mentioned *Gwalia* and *Devonia*. The Port of Cardiff registry records that *Westonia* came into the ownership, from 10th June, 1905, of one Charles Edwards Evans, Merchant, of 56 Mount Stuart Square, Cardiff. She had been transferred from the Liverpool port registry, and Board of Trade sanction to the name change having been granted on 5th June, 1905. The schedules for Tuesday 13th June, 1905 (the day after Whit Monday) showed that

This was what caused the controversy - *Devonia* setting off from the Pier Head at Cardiff, probably during the 1905 season, when P. & A. Campbell Ltd regarded Cardiff as its exclusive territory and argued that the Barry vessels should adhere to the limits prescribed by the Barry Railway (Steam Vessels) Act, 1904. *Lionel Vaughan Collection*

A rare view of *Gwalia* on the River Usk at Newport, taken some time before completion of the impressive Transporter Bridge which opened in September 1906. *Lionel Vaughan Collection*

the 'railway run' would leave Barry at the usual time, with the customary train connection from Cardiff (Riverside) at 9.35 am. High water was later in the day, and 'ferry' departures from Cardiff to Weston, generally via Penarth Pier, were advertised at 11.20, 11.40 am, 1.15, 3.15 and 5.30 pm. Return departure times from Weston were at 12.15, 2.15, 4.05, 5.10 and 11.30 pm. But a particularly interesting feature was the special excursion offered to Chepstow, leaving Cardiff at 11.40 am and calling at Weston and at Clevedon *en route*, giving a short time ashore before a return departure from Chepstow at 3.45 pm, from Clevedon at 4.40 and Weston at 5.10 pm. Whichever vessel was on the 'ferry' roster that day was not idle during the period of low water at Weston in the evening that day, as the 5.30 pm sailing from Cardiff to Weston was also advertised as going on from Weston to Clevedon, the pier there being accessible at pretty well any state of the tide. Departure from Clevedon was at 10.30 pm back to Weston to then pick up the last 'ferry' departure from Weston at 11.30 pm back to Cardiff.

Evidence from the Ilfracombe newspapers of the time corroborates the conclusion that *Westonia* must have entered service just in time for the Whitsuntide period, on Saturday 10th June, 1905, the Saturday preceding Whit Monday. On Whit Monday both of the larger steamers were recorded as having visited Ilfracombe, implying that Red Funnel Line 'ferry' duties up-Channel were solely in the hands of the newly-commissioned *Westonia* that day. Imagine the busy scene at Ilfracombe harbour, which the year before would only have embraced Pockett's *Brighton* from Swansea as the sole non-White Funnel Fleet paddler. In less than two months after *Gwalia* had made her maiden voyage, here was not one but two brand new interlopers, as the Campbells would have seen it, where seven vessels brought over 3,000 passengers into the North Devon resort, but only four of which were theirs. In the words of the *Ilfracombe Chronicle* which, unlike the rival *Ilfracombe Gazette* newspaper, did actually acknowledge the existence of the competitors:

> From Swansea *Brighton* (which has just begun her trips for the season) had about 800 passengers . . . the *Gwalia* brought 112, and her sister ship *Devonia* 506 from Cardiff and Barry. The *Westward Ho* took a small number up to Bristol at 7.30 am, and returned with 418. The *Gwalia* also made a day-trip to Bristol, with a good complement of passengers. The *Cambria* had 431, the *Britannia* 370 and the *Albion* 198, from Bristol, Cardiff, Weston, Penarth and other places. Several of the boats made trips during the day. The *Brighton* took about 100 to the Mumbles, and the *Cambria* had a fair number for Clovelly. The *Devonia* had 232 for a Channel trip, and the *Albion* nearly 200.

An editorial item in the same journal entitled 'Ilfracombe Snapshots' nicely illustrated the importance of all of these very welcome steamships to the local economy, taken together with the traditional coach and four that still ran on the road to Lynton:

> . . . a holiday crowd is certain to enjoy itself wherever it may elect to spend its leisure hours and here, besides the 'Severn Sea' . . . is all inducement to a time of pleasure that is health-giving to tired brain and body. What strikes the new arrival in Ilfracombe is the facilities for seeing the district, taking this as a centre . . . across the water lies the picturesque

principality of the Welsh, down towards the mouth of the Channel is Lundy, and Clovelly - whilst up where sea narrows into river, stands Bristol with its buzz of commerce. In daily communication with all these is Ilfracombe through the splendid lines of passenger steamers that ply here, and because other places of note are thus easily reached, folks like to visit us. Every excursion organised for Whitsuntide was well patronised, and a sight to be remembered was the coming and going of the boats at the pier on Whit Monday. From early morn till dewy eve their traffic was continuous . . .

The numbers quoted above constitute a key piece of evidence in piecing together and understanding the background to the complex legal proceedings against the Barry Railway Company that were shortly to be commenced at the instigation of P. & A. Campbell Ltd. Not only were the Barry boats running from starting points other than Barry, in defiance of the provisions of the 1904 Act, but they were now, as a three-strong fleet, able to run excursions to the Campbell heartland of Bristol, also expressly outside the Act other than if originating at Barry. This Whit Monday excursion appears to have been the first excursion by Red Funnel Line steamer starting down at Ilfracombe to voyage up the River Avon, Bristol having been visited earlier in the season from Cardiff. From the above, we can infer that *Gwalia* had gone down-channel earlier in the morning than her sister *Devonia* which would have taken the fixed-time railway run, not arriving at Ilfracombe until around lunchtime. Just for good measure, the short afternoon cruise, or 'Channel Trip' (as these were often described), offered by *Devonia* during her normal Ilfracombe layover time 'stole' the custom of over half of the pleasure-seekers at Ilfracombe that might otherwise have patronised *Albion*, doubtless the Newport boat on that day. It should be added that the Campbell brothers had no issue with Pockett's of Swansea, whose presence in the Bristol Channel was long-established, and whose control of the Swansea & Mumbles excursion trade - and the link between Ilfracombe and Lundy - was unchallenged from their base of Pockett's Wharf in the heart of Swansea.

As the midsummer of 1905 approached, Red Funnel Line (as they were now clearly branded, under the banner of The Barry and Bristol Steamship Company) services got fully underway and the hours operated and the nautical miles steamed each day stretched out as the days grew longer. Wednesday 21st June, 1905 was particularly busy and two steamers ran down to Ilfracombe, an 8.45 am departure from Cardiff supplementing the usual 9.30 am 'railway run', and which was scheduled to call additionally at Minehead, and go through to Clovelly. The tides were such that the ferry steamer was scheduled for four round trips between Cardiff and Weston, two in the morning and two in the evening. After the 'railway run' steamer was back in Barry at around 6.10 pm or so on the flood tide, her day was not over as she proceeded via Penarth to Cardiff in order then to offer an evening cruise to Clevedon and Portishead and back. A lot of new ground was being covered by the Barry steamers, as this day was probably the first on which Minehead passengers were given the opportunity to sail to Clovelly for the day, and it may also have been the first occasion of a Red Funnel Line vessel calling at Portishead. Truly the Barry steamers were reaching all around the Bristol Channel now - and there was still more to come!

Further to put into context the concerns of P. & A. Campbell Ltd, the overall excursion fleet situation in the Bristol Channel now was that the total passenger carrying capacity had gone up by more than half than that which they had offered in the preceding season of 1904. Two units of the White Funnel Fleet, *Brighton Queen* and *Glen Rosa* were away on the South Coast, but the remaining seven ships were Bristol-based in 1905, namely *Waverley*, *Ravenswood*, *Westward Ho*, *Cambria*, *Britannia*, *Albion* and *Bonnie Doon*. Pockett's had their *Brighton* based at Swansea, which played a large part in the excursion trade at Ilfracombe. Even allowing for the fact that the latest arrival *Westonia* was a ship with a troubled history, nonetheless she had been built (as *Tantallon Castle*) as recently as 1899, and so all three of the Red Funnel Line fleet could be presented as new or quite new, and certainly newer than the white-funnelled opposition. The P. & A. Campbell Ltd presence on the busy Cardiff-Weston route tended to depend on two of the older, less speedy vessels, advertisements often alluding to *Waverley* and *Ravenswood* but not specifically mentioning the second-hand *Bonnie Doon*. *Albion* was a newer vessel, and often associated with the Newport station at this time. Whilst two 'ferry' vessels sufficed for much of the time for P. & A. Campbell Ltd, this capacity would often need to be supplemented on busier days, and it is not hard to see why the Barry Railway Company, through its steamship operation - whether or not one conceded it was in-house as opposed to provided by a separate company - felt that it wanted a share of this buoyant market.

For a steamer built in 1899 to have changed hands three times before coming to the Bristol Channel in 1905 was distinctly unusual by the standards of the day, and suggestive of the extreme dissatisfaction of her first owners, for whom she clearly had not been up to scratch. Ordered in 1898 by the Galloway Saloon Steam Packet Company for their Firth of Forth traffic, and built by John Scott & Company of Kinghorn, *Tantallon Castle* had only run there in the 1899 and 1900 seasons before being disposed of. She was an attractive looking vessel, with twin funnels, albeit of a more old-fashioned profile than the two Clyde-built steamers she was destined to later join, and of lesser dimensions at 210 ft by 25.1 ft by 8.4 ft, and slower at 16½ knots. Her bridge was situated aft of the funnels. There seems little doubt of the extent of her failure to match up to expectations, being deemed light in the bow and therefore of a lively motion, and unresponsive in steering. According to Thornton, she had a forecastle deck added during her second season, in an attempt to improve her seagoing qualities.

She passed to Captain Lee for use in his Sussex Steam Packet Company fleet in 1901, and was registered at Shoreham. She entered service as *Sussex Belle* in May of that year, providing a range of trips out of Brighton to destinations as far afield as the Isle of Wight and Southampton. Her registered ownership changed in 1902 although she continued to sail from Brighton. The competitive situation there was changing rapidly as the P. & A. Campbell Ltd empire expanded, and *Sussex Belle* was sold after the end of the 1902 season to the Colwyn Bay and Liverpool Steamship Company, thus acquiring Liverpool registry. Her third owners quite naturally changed her name to something more fitting for her new duties in 1903, namely *Rhos Colwyn*, and evidently ran her on a service connecting Liverpool, Llandudno and Rhos on Sea.

Thus it was that *Rhos Colwyn* was available to be acquired by a Barry Railway Company nominee in 1905, after only two years of service on the North Wales coast. Later Barry Railway Company Reports and Accounts, published around the time of the major Chancery hearing in 1907, revealed that her cost had been in the region of £13,000. Two possible explanations exist for the fact that *Westonia* was registered in the name of a private individual rather than that of the Barry Railway Company, or even the same four gentlemen declared as the owners of *Gwalia* and *Devonia*. One is that the two new vessels had been so much more expensive than had been anticipated that no funds were left (relative to the £60,000 capital prescribed in the 1904 Act) for the purchase of a third vessel if that capital limit was to be adhered to. The other is that by adopting this ploy of supposedly different ownership from the outset, the Barry Railway Company could claim that this third vessel was nothing to do with them directly, and was thus free to ply wherever it was wished, without being obliged to the limits prescribed by the 1904 Act. This latter reasoning is consistent with the earlier statement that had been made in the Barry newspaper that trips were about to be run to Bristol once the additional vessel arrived, a place specifically barred to the Barry Railway Company (unless the voyage commenced at Barry) by the 1904 Act.

Fare cutting

Shortly after *Westonia* had entered service at Cardiff, an advertisement appeared on Wednesday 21st June, 1905 in the *Western Mail*, boldly headed 'FARES REDUCED'. It had been placed there by P. & A. Campbell Ltd and explained that fares by its steamers had been reduced with effect from 17th June, 1905. It did not actually say that this had happened in order to bring its fares into line with those charged by the Red Funnel Line, but prompt action by the Bristol company had been necessary to contain the loss of passengers to the opposition. Fares for regular services by P. & A. Campbell Ltd steamers were not normally quoted in the regular daily newspaper advertisements for Excursions, but to give a comparison of the scale of reductions now made we can compare the newly reduced fares in 1905 with those that were advertised in the Ilfracombe newspapers in 1898 when those still carried comparable advertisements. By 1899 such informative adverts had ceased and people were merely referred to the office of the Agent at Ilfracombe to pick up a bill for actual sailing times and fares details.

In 1898 the single fare between Cardiff and Ilfracombe by White Funnel Fleet steamer was three shillings in foredeck class, and four shillings in saloon class, the equivalents of third class and first class respectively. After the Red Funnel Line steamers had started the corresponding fares (in 1906, the oldest data to hand) these had had to be reduced to 2*s*. 6*d*. and 3*s*. 6*d*. respectively, a drop of some 15 per cent, to bring White Funnel fares into line. It has already been explained that an inherent feature of the early operation of steamers which called at Barry Pier was that P. & A. Campbell Ltd could only charge the same amount from Cardiff to Ilfracombe whether passengers went throughout by boat, or caught the train from Cardiff to Barry Pier. The apportionment of part of that fare to the Barry Railway Company in respect of the Cardiff-Barry railway segment had been the cause of much commercial uneasiness by the Campbells, for obvious reasons, as their steamer costs were not reduced commensurately.

In 1905 the Barry boats were not regularly competing with P. & A. Campbell Ltd for Bristol to Ilfracombe traffic, but it is significant that whereas a tourist return saloon ticket in 1898 between the two places cost 7*s*. 6*d*. it was still at the same price in 1906. Bristol fares clearly had to have some proportionality to Cardiff ones, and so the ability of the Bristol company to increase its Bristol fares was inhibited by the scale of reductions forced on them for the Cardiff traffic. This problem was not going to go away, and formed an important part of the legal action: P. & A. Campbell Ltd was to seek compensation for loss of earnings in addition to opposing the very existence of the Barry Railway Company vessels. This would be both directly, for the absolute loss of traffic to the competitor and indirectly, for lower fare yields from those passengers that remained loyal to the White Funnel Fleet steamers.

In any event by the summer of 1905 the enterprise that had given birth to the red-funnelled paddle-steamers running in connection with the Barry Railway Company had come a long way, and the variety of destinations to which excursions were offered grew as the summer progressed. On occasions Cardiff itself was the attraction for Devon folk, notably on Wednesday 28th June, 1905 when

> . . . nearly 1,400 passengers journeyed on board the Barry and Bristol Channel steamer *Gwalia* to Ilfracombe last Wednesday evening, including 500 Barry evening trippers, the remainder being passengers from the other side, who had come over early in the day to witness the visit of the Prince of Wales to Cardiff.

Shortly after this, it was reported in the *Barry Dock News* that on Saturday 15th July, 1905 the Barry flagship had again had a particularly long and productive day:

> The Barry and Bristol Channel Steamship Company's passenger steamer *Gwalia* accomplished a good day's work last Saturday. Leaving Barry Island Pier at 10.30 am she conveyed a large number of passengers to the Mumbles. From the Mumbles a trip was made to Newport, where 1,000 men of the South Wales Borderers were taken across to Minehead to camp. The *Gwalia* then steamed across to Barry, and back to the Mumbles, returning to Barry with a full complement of passengers.

For good measure, a special excursion to another new location by Red Funnel Line steamer was advertised for Friday 28th July, 1905, with a departure from Cardiff at 12.15 pm for Weston-super-Mare, Clevedon, and Sharpness, at a fare of two shillings and sixpence. And just to cap it all at this time, rumours started to appear that the success of the Red Funnel Line enterprise was such that two new steamers were going to be acquired, one of them a turbine steamer! But the next part of the story is concerned with the initiation of the complex legal proceedings that were ultimately to undo the apparently successful Red Funnel Line venture and whilst, on the face of it, the excursion programme offered continued to develop and expand, very few of the public would have known what was going on behind the scenes as P. & A. Campbell Ltd fought to claw back the ground it had lost to the insurgent Welshmen of Barry.

One can see how competition on the Cardiff-Weston 'ferry' may have caused tension: *Westonia* backs away from the Pier Head at Cardiff in company with a Campbell steamer already underway, which it will follow outwards and past Penarth Head in the distance.

Mitchell Library

Gwalia going astern from Barry Pier, probably 1905. *Lionel Vaughan Collection*

The legal challenge

Much of the detail of the legal proceedings that were to stretch over more than two years has been obtained from newspaper reports, which fortunately were relatively thorough in the coverage they gave, particularly at Ilfracombe. The Minute Books of the Barry Railway Company are largely silent on what took place as the legal proceedings unfolded, and very little can be gleaned from those of P. & A. Campbell Ltd either. As there was, ultimately, no actual judgement then no definitive report exists of what would have been the precise ruling of the Court of Chancery which presided over the case which was heard by Mr Justice Swinfen-Eady.

We have already heard that from the moment the Barry steamers started running the concerns of P. & A. Campbell Ltd were such as to warrant its seeking the opinion of Counsel, to establish whether a case existed to be pursued, the essence of which was that the steamer operation was *ultra vires*, i.e. outside the terms of the 1904 Act which had been so hotly contested. The motion that was instigated by P. & A. Campbell Ltd first came before the Chancery Division of the High Court of Justice during the first week of August 1905, where the plaintiff sought to restrain the Barry Railway Company from running its steamships other than within the limits of the 1904 Act. It was alleged that the Barry and Bristol Channel Steamship Company did not really exist, and that the term 'Red Funnel Line' was merely an alias of the Barry Railway Company, for whom in effect Messrs Symonds, Radford, Lewis and Jones were merely employees. Mr Thompson, as a Director of the company, was named as another defendant.

The report in the *Barry Dock News* of Friday 11th August, 1905 was succinct and to the point, and is worth reproducing here in full:

BARRY AND BRISTOL CHANNEL PASSENGER BOAT SERVICE
HIGH COURT ACTION AGAINST THE BARRY RAILWAY COMPANY

On Friday last, a motion in the action of the Attorney General versus the Barry Railway Company by which it was sought to restrain the defendants from running steamers in the Bristol Channel outside the limits of the Act of Parliament was mentioned before Mr Justice Swinfen-Eady in the High Court of Justice. The hearing was, however, adjourned until Wednesday for the purpose of completing the evidence. It was contended by the plaintiff that under the Barry Steam Vessels Act the area to be served by the steamers is distinctly defined, and that the Barry vessels should not be allowed to run beyond Lundy. It is understood that the defence is to the effect that those limitations, if prescribed by the Act, do not apply to the Barry steamers, as they are now run as a private trading concern.

Mr Miclin [*sic*] KC, for the Attorney-General, on the resumption of the case on Wednesday, said his motion was to restrain the Barry Railway Co. and various defendants from running certain steamships - *Devonia, Gwalia* and *Westonia* - in the Bristol Channel. The case made by the Attorney-General and the relation of the parties was that the railway company acquired statutory powers; that under these powers they purchased two of the steamships mentioned; that shortly afterwards they handed them over to a syndicate and began to run these ships as the Barry and Bristol Channel Steamship Company. The allegation was that in fact the ships were being run on behalf of the company *ultra vires* to the Act. Two affidavits had been put in on behalf of some of the defendants, which directly contradicted the allegations made - they did not

contradict all, but some. Under the circumstances he thought it was reasonable to determine the motion with the consent of the other side. There would be no order made on the motion, and the costs of it would be costs in the action.
The motion was, therefore, not proceeded with.

Although the words used in the Barry media understandably made light of this issue, it should be emphasised that the action was to continue as the case was not yet resolved. But the actual outcome of this first appearance, which amounted in effect to an adjournment, was that nothing really happened that affected the working then of the three Barry steamers, and operations continued throughout the remainder of the 1905 season. It was not until almost a year later that the case finally came up in Court, in the last week of April 1906, and only two mentions of the beginnings of this momentous legal challenge are recorded in the Barry Railway Company Minutes of Directors Meetings, the first being that dated 28th July, 1905. A letter had been received from Mr Bliss, the lawyer acting for P. & A. Campbell Ltd, and the Company Secretary was instructed to 'tell him that he was under a misapprehension, and to take all steps to protect the Company's interest'. It is easy to infer from this that the Board believed that they would brush off the challenge from the Bristol company, and that their method of registry of the vessels in the names of other individuals would suffice in law. The second mention, on 11th August, 1905, was to the effect that a writ of summons from P. & A. Campbell Ltd had now been received, via Mr Bliss. In terms of hard, minuted evidence the trail then goes almost silent . . .

Thus it was 'business as usual' and with the 1905 season now at its height, the basic pattern of traffic was for one vessel to carry out the daily 'railway run', one to maintain Cardiff-Weston 'ferry' sailings and the third to provide additional sailings on these routes. In addition, all manner of other excursions to a wide variety of Bristol Channel destinations had been offered, and which continued to grow in variety during August 1905. Lundy did not yet feature in the Red Funnel Line range of excursions, but Mumbles had been added, and on Tuesday 22nd August, 1905 a trip was advertised at 9.15 am from Cardiff to Minehead, Mumbles and Tenby, possibly the first to venture so far west along the Welsh side of the Channel. This mirrored very closely P. & A. Campbell Ltd trips that were often carried out during the high season by a Cardiff-based White Funnel steamer such as *Cambria*. Clevedon was a popular destination, and advertisements for Wednesday 23rd August, 1905 noted the added attraction there of Clevedon Regatta.

The normal practice (in July and August) seems to have been for the 'railway run' boat to extend to Clovelly, which meant a slightly later return departure time up-Channel from Ilfracombe in the afternoon than had applied in May. This necessitated later connecting trains from Barry Pier station: an express to Cardiff calling only at Grangetown would leave immediately after the arrival of the boat, followed by a 7.50 pm stopping train to Cardiff Riverside. Passengers for Vale of Glamorgan line stations could change at Barry for a 8.16 pm departure to Bridgend, whilst a 8.20 pm departure for Porth took the passengers bound for the Barry's Pontypridd (Graig) route. It was also normal practice to send a second boat down to Ilfracombe on Saturday afternoons, useful for those who worked on Saturday mornings.

Now that legal proceedings had been instigated, it was perhaps not too surprising that at the 42nd half-yearly meeting of the Barry Railway Company, in mid-August 1905, no mention whatsoever was made of the success of the steamships venture. Lord Windsor was unavoidably absent and so Mr Thompson chaired the meeting, who one might have expected to make a positive mention of the shipping venture into which he had expended so much personal effort. But it was more important, then, to keep up appearances and continue to maintain the claim that the Barry steamers were separate from the railway undertaking.

The 1905 season ends

Towards the end of the season, possibly not content with the adventurousness of running as far west as Clovelly and Tenby, the Red Funnel Line special excursion advertised for Friday 25th August, 1905 was a mammoth affair, and exploited the low-water availability of Barry Pier and a train connection from Cardiff into a 6.45 am departure (from Barry) to Ilfracombe and Newquay in Cornwall. One wonders at the reaction there of the first arrival of a large red-funnelled vessel, as White Funnel Fleet trips venturing that far had only ever been offered on rare occasions, and then primarily at times of day which suited Ilfracombe passengers as a special event. By now there were few calling-places of consequence in the Bristol Channel served by the White Funnel Fleet where the Red Funnel Line were not also making appearances.

A 'Splendid Long Day at Bristol' was had by the staff of the *Barry Dock News* on their annual outing on Saturday 2nd September, 1905 when they travelled at 5.45 am from Barry to Penarth, Cardiff, Clevedon and Bristol on *Gwalia*, which endured rough conditions crossing the Channel. Some of the party were ill but in the River Avon it was noted that the '. . . serenity of water was acting as a restorer to those who had been taken ill . . .', the party arriving at Hotwells shortly after eight. In the evening all returned to the pier and

> . . . several choruses were well rendered to the delight of a large number of Bristolians and others waiting the arrival of the Cardiff and Barry boats. Shortly before nine o'clock the *Gwalia* loomed in sight, and 'all aboard' being sounded, we bade adieu to Bristol and comfortably seated ourselves . . .

The Barry flagship reached Barry Pier shortly after midnight, the party proceeding thence on a special train home.

Services from Cardiff Pierhead and Barry Pier were cut back a little in September, as the 'railway run' boat did not now proceed to Clovelly and terminated at Ilfracombe, allowing reversion to the earlier departure time from there to Lynmouth (where calls were made 35 minutes after departure from Ilfracombe) and thence to Barry Pier (and on to Penarth and Cardiff on suitable tides) permitting the stopping train departure time from Barry Pier to be brought forward to 6.55 pm.

Another glimpse of how sailings were enjoyed then was given in the *Barry Dock News* for Friday 15th September, 1905:

> The voyage by the Barry passenger boat *Devonia* to the Mumbles last Friday was made in tempestuous weather, and the seagoing qualities of those on board were tried to the utmost. When off Mumbles Head, one of the passengers, a Barry gentleman, driven to desperation by *mal de mer*, clambered to the foot of the bridge, and with one hand on his stomach and the other across his forehead, asked the Captain whether the boat was to proceed to Tenby. Captain Denman replied in the negative, when the passenger, already spent with sea-sickness replied in the ecstasy of gratefulness 'if you had, I would have gone overboad'.

Fun and games were had shortly before this rough voyage experience when, on Thursday 14th September, 1905 it became apparent that two of the Barry vessels, *Gwalia* and *Westonia,* were due in at Cardiff at the same time, where the Red Funnel Line only enjoyed the use of one berth. Evidently a telephonic communication was sent to Penarth to instruct the Captain of *Gwalia* to meet *Westonia* in mid-Channel to take off her passengers and bring them to Cardiff. This was 'done without a hitch', in weather that was recorded as being 'delightfully calm'. The following day, *Devonia* had a temporary breakdown whilst running to Mumbles and Tenby, and her passengers were transferred to *Gwalia,* then taken to Ilfracombe.

The season drew to a close, and the appreciation of the public for the services of the Barry boats was evidenced at a complimentary dinner for the crews under Captain James (of *Gwalia*), Captain Denman (*Devonia*) and Captain Ryan (*Westonia*) given at the Marine Hotel at Barry Island, where 'through the generosity of the season-ticket and coupon-book holders' 100 men and boys were dined. This was doubtless much appreciated and, a couple of weeks later after sailings had completely ceased, a further dinner for the Captains and Officers was given on Tuesday 10th October, 1905 at the same establishment. Alderman P.W. Carey of Cardiff presided, and the three 'Agents' of the Red Funnel Line were named as being present on this occasion, Mr J. Charlton (of Weston-super-Mare), W. Jones (of Ilfracombe) and James Wedlake (Minehead). The Officers of the Red Funnel Line were toasted, and there was talk of

> the remarkable growth and development of facilities for steam passenger traffic in the Bristol Channel during the past few years, facilities which have reached a degree bordering on perfection through the enterprise and public spirit of the Red Funnel Line company (cheers).

Dr Mullins responded, and described the occasion as a 'red funnel day in the history of the red letter line'. W.T. Symonds (one of the four nominal owners of the first two Red Funnel Line vessels) deprecated misinterpretations in the media regarding small mishaps that the fleet had suffered and his syndicate colleague H. Rees Jones went on, in the words of the old song, 'we've got the ships, we've got the men, we've got the money too' (cheers).

Had Peter and Alec Campbell read a copy of this report, they would doubtless have been horrified at the brazen admission this amounted to, which was that the burgeoning Barry Railway Company had funded an opposition fleet to their own, and were seemingly prospering. So although the legal challenge had been instigated, the 1905 season had run its course and now all sailings of both fleets had ceased. The *Ilfracombe Gazette* newspaper wittily noted that on Tuesday 2nd October, 1905 it could be said that 'The Campbells are going' as the last representative of the White Funnel Fleet of the year finally left the North Devon resort for Bristol - but studiously still declined to actually make reference to the red-funnelled interlopers.

The 1906 season

The three vessels of the Red Funnel Line would have doubtless wintered in what was known as the Basin at Barry Dock, adjacent to the main lock into the No. 1 Dock, and it is reasonable to assume that dry-docking and other maintenance work would have probably been carried out at Barry which was well equipped for such tasks. As the 1906 season approached Mr Thompson, his fellow Barry Railway Company Directors and the four gentlemen that comprised the Barry and Bristol Channel Steamship Company syndicate must have contemplated the next phase of litigation that lay ahead at the instigation of their adversaries P. & A. Campbell Ltd of Bristol. They can only have assumed that their tactics would defeat the Campbell brothers, and that the pretence that the Red Funnel Line was indeed something distinctly separate to the railway undertaking would prevail. An early season advertisement in the Cardiff *Western Mail* newspaper, on Tuesday 3rd April, 1906, mentioned that *Westonia* had been refurbished and - tantalisingly - that in the season there would be trips to Lundy and to the Isles of Scilly.

The mention of Lundy at this point turned out to be a false alarm: talks had evidently taken place between the Red Funnel Line syndicate and Mr George Taylor of Abbotsham (near Bideford) who had taken on a lease of Lundy, since 1899, from the Heaven family who owned it. It was envisaged that excursions operated by *Gwalia*, *Devonia* and *Westonia* would run to Lundy from South Wales as well as from Ilfracombe and Bideford, the latter in connection with train services from Barnstaple. Regrettably this plan came to nought, but Lundy was to feature in the arrangements of the Red Funnel steamers in 1906 - albeit in a wholly different manner to that envisaged here.

Unusually, compared with the White Funnel Fleet sailings which had generally only commenced a day or two before Good Friday in previous years, Red Funnel sailings in 1906 commenced on Monday 2nd April although Good Friday did not fall until 13th April. An early manifestation of the competitive climate that was to prevail during the the second season of the Barry boats can be inferred from this *Western Mail* item from Thursday 12th April, 1906. It was doubtless included because P. & A. Campbell Ltd were good customers of the paper inasmuch as their daily advertisements were always carried in the Excursions section throughout the season, and which were a primary means of informing the public what was on offer as sailing times in the Bristol Channel differed with the tides every day.

The 'aft bridge' deck as well as the rest of the promenade deck of *Devonia* is busy with passengers in this postcard view produced by Harvey-Barton of Bristol.
Lionel Vaughan Collection

THE WHITE FUNNEL FLEET
RECORD PASSAGE BETWEEN CARDIFF & ILFRACOMBE

Messrs P. & A. Campbell's well-known and favourite steamer *Cambria* commenced their down-Channel service on Wednesday and she accomplished a very fast and record passage. The down journey from Cardiff to Ilfracombe, calling at Penarth, was done in two hours and two minutes, and on the return journey she took one hour and fifty minutes from Ilfracombe to Penarth, and was alongside the Cardiff pontoon in exactly two hours. The latter passage constitutes a record between Ilfracombe and Cardiff and vice-versa. As in past seasons, the public may depend on Messrs Campbell doing everything in their power to study in every way the comfort and safety of their passengers.

The down-Channel service by the Red Funnel Line steamers evidently started the day before with the operation of a complimentary trip which conveyed 'between 350 and 400 representative gentlemen from Cardiff, Barry and Penarth' to Ilfracombe on *Gwalia*, and it is clear that the battle to influence the travelling public to patronise the locally-owned vessels was again now on as it was Mr J.A. Jones, the President of the Cardiff Chamber of Commerce, who proposed the vote of thanks to the proprietors of the Red Funnel Line. The guests heard how the vessel had undergone 'extensive repairs and renovations' since the last season, which seemed odd for a new vessel unless the publicists were simply exaggerating the virtues of obligatory annual refit and certification procedures.

The Ilfracombe newspapers recorded that the Easter weather was particularly fine, and if taken at face value their comments could mislead the innocent into thinking that only the White Funnel Fleet steamers operated at that port. The numbers brought down by *Cambria* on each day before Easter, Wednesday to Friday, were dutifully recorded, and she brought a further 350 on the Saturday preceding Easter whilst on Easter Monday *Albion* brought 565, *Westward Ho* a remarkable 762, with *Albion* taking an equally remarkable 600 to Clovelly. No Red Funnel Line passenger numbers were mentioned. As the *Gazette* put it:

> . . . if any proof was necessary as to the popularity of the celebrated White Funnel Fleet of P. & A. Campbell Ltd, it was amply provided by the way in which they were patronised during the Easter season. The travelling and pleasure seeking public of today know a good thing when they see it and that accounts for the largeness of the numbers who patronised this favourite line.

It was also noted that the crowds had been well behaved and that the police had not had to deal with a single case of disorderly conduct. After Easter there was a period when the down-Channel steamers ceased running before the main start of the season in early May, and in late April it was noted that the island of Lundy was for sale. Much more would shortly be heard of what some then referred to as 'Lonely Lundy', but this would be in a very different light.

The following month saw the resumption of the legal action and it is worth pointing out that at this time the Directors of P. & A. Campbell Ltd were on record as considering that the state of their action against the Barry Railway Company was now 'very satisfactory'. They were, however, to be disappointed at the turn events took and, again, it seems worth presenting the exact words in which the *Barry Dock News,* on Friday 4th May, 1906, described the proceedings:

> BARRY v. CARDIFF RIVAL STEAMERS
> THE RED FUNNEL LINE STILL TRIUMPHANT
>
> The action of the Attorney-General v. the Barry Railway Co. and others came before Mr Justice Swinfen-Eady on Friday last in the Chancery Division as a motion by the Attorney-General at the relation of P. & A. Campbell Ltd, by which it was sought to restrain the defendants from running steamers on the Bristol Channel outside the limits prescribed by the Act of Parliament. The principal cause of complaint was that the defendants were running steamers from Cardiff, competing with Campbell and Coy., and Cardiff was one of the places outside the prescribed limits. The defendants denied that the steamers, which were run as the Barry & Bristol Channel Steamship Company, were run by them. It was submitted that the agreements between the two sets of defendants were *ultra vires*, the railway company merely paying for services rendered within the Act. The second defendants offered not to receive anything from the Company pending the trial but contended that they were entitled to go on running the steamers. His Lordship granted an injunction until the trial restraining the defendants from carrying out the provisions of the agreement between them, and the Railway Company from applying any of its funds for the purpose, the injunction however not to prevent the second defendants from doing anything they might lawfully do outside the agreement.
>
> The effect of the decision is that an injunction is granted restraining the Barry Railway Company from subsidising the Red Funnel Line, and the Red Funnel Line, as a private undertaking, will continue to run its fleet of steamers from Barry and Cardiff, as heretofore.

Thus for a second time it might have been inferred - at least from this piece of reporting - that those running the Barry steamers were right, and the Campbells were wrong. Almost a year after the first court hearing here was a second, and again it could be seen that the Red Funnel Line steamers could apparently continue to operate, unfettered, if one ignored the detail of the words of His

Lordship or failed to read into them that here was a case which in fact remained undetermined. My interpretation of these happenings is that merely being ordered not to apply its funds towards the running of the steamers would have made no actual difference whatever to the day-by-day steamer operation, given that the vessels had already been purchased with railway company money. All that was needed was for the syndicate to nominally purchase coal and catering supplies and suchlike, and pay the crews after pocketing the takings which - subsequent Reports & Accounts of the Barry Railway Company make quite clear - were such as to make the venture profitable, and somewhat more so if no burden of depreciation was being shouldered by the Profit and Loss accounts.

There was no suggestion that the Barry Railway Company could not continue to provide the train services to Barry Pier, on its own account. This, it could be argued, scarcely amounted to subsidy, in the context of the injunction. Sailings from the Pier Head at Cardiff continued normally. The Red Funnel Line would not have been charged anything for the use of Barry Pier, and there is no reason to suppose the injunction changed this. At the other places called at by Red Funnel Line steamers the landing-fees would have been paid just as if from any other operator. Mr Thompson must have been relieved that he now had a period ahead of him in which his steamers could prosper, but he certainly must have had some trepidation at what might happen next on the legal front. This was not, however, to come to a head until the summer of 1907.

The Campbell brothers must have been bitterly disappointed at the further delay in getting their case resolved. They still considered that the railway-owned boats were operating illegally, and that the syndicate was a device to circumvent the law. Still unable to afford any new vessels themselves, they saw their opponents picking off the cream of the Bristol Channel traffic, and they had been forced by the unwelcome competition to lower their fares. But it was to be the lawsuit that would define the future shape of Bristol Channel passenger steamship services, and without wishing to labour the point regarding seemingly tedious legal matters, a little more clarification is needed before describing the operational features of the 1906 season. Thus far, I have quoted Barry newspaper sources, and it is now timely to put the case as it was seen on the English side of the Bristol Channel. The full text of a letter from the solicitor to P. & A. Campbell Ltd, Herbert W. Bliss of Carlton Chambers, 8 Regent Street, London carried in the columns of *Ilfracombe Gazette* on 11th May, 1906 set out in admirable detail the case as seen by the plaintiff's side, and was intended to put matters straight in Ilfracombe, where the prosperity of the steamers closely correlated with that of the town.

Mr Bliss recited the past hearings and crisply set out why it was felt that his clients were suffering an injustice:

> . . . the Barry Railway Company acquired . . . the steamers *Gwalia* and *Devonia*, and throughout the year 1905 these steamers (though they had nominally been sold and transferred to four gentlemen in whose names they are registered) were being run under secret agreements, which we say amounted to this: . . . the steamers remained the Barry Railway Company's steamers, and the four gentlemen were only figure-heads and paid servants of the Company . . . and the Red Funnel Line was merely an alias of the Barry Railway Company.

Describing the injunction against the Barry Railway Company, he concluded:

> . . . this checkmates for the present the second attempt to use the Barry Railway Company's money to get the command of the Bristol Channel - unless they are prepared to face the consequences of disobedience to an order of the Court; but of course it is not surprising that the persons concerned put as good a face as they can on the matter . . .

What happened next can be seen on two very different levels as Red Funnel Line operations continued seemingly as before. Much later in the year, however, the recognition that the law might eventually see through the subterfuges they had adopted would lead to actions being taken by the Barry Railway Company Directors that were ultimately to lead to the guilt of the defendants being proven. But this is to jump ahead a little, chronologically, as the summer of 1906 was to be an exciting one as the competition continued apace, and a major new attraction for excursionists in the Bristol Channel was shortly about to come to prominence as a result of a serious and expensive navigational error by a major naval vessel, which gripped the attention of the nation.

The HMS 'Montagu' incident

The island of Lundy, in 1906, would usually enjoy weekly visits by excursion steamer from Ilfracombe. Since the 1860s the Pockett steamers from Swansea had run from that major South Wales port across to Ilfracombe, more or less daily during the summer season, and other ports around the Bristol Channel had seen Pockett vessels calling in on cargo runs too. After 1894 *Velindra* had been superseded by the newer *Brighton* on the Swansea to Ilfracombe run, which the older vessel had undertaken for over 20 years, and in the summer the Pockett's steamer would generally make Lynmouth, Clovelly or Lundy the destination of her afternoon cruise from Ilfracombe. On occasions she would run back across the Bristol Channel to give a cruise from Ilfracombe to the Mumbles, where a smart new pier had opened in 1898.

Pockett's monopolised, in a manner of speaking, the Swansea excursion trade from their well-sited berth at Pockett's Wharf, in the heart of the city. There was an amicable co-existence at Ilfracombe between the solitary Pockett's steamer and the various vessels of the White Funnel Fleet which, after running down to the North Devon port from Bristol, Newport or Cardiff, would either lie alongside the pier or outside the harbour, or sometimes run to Clovelly or Lynmouth, or occasionally cruise further afield towards the Cornish coast or just offer a short Channel trip. It was only *Brighton* that had the rights to land passengers at Lundy, and Friday was the regular day for these trips, although they might be provided twice-weekly in high summer. Only exceptionally had the Campbell steamers visited Lundy, and there is evidence that the Heaven family of Lundy tolerated rather than welcomed excursion passengers at this time, but naturally found steamship sailings a welcome facility at least for their own use, and that of their guests, to supplement the mailboat sailings to the island provided from Instow with less certainty by the sailing cutter *Gannet*. Despite the positive sounding statements earlier in the year, no regular Red Funnel Line sailings had actually started to serve Lundy.

HMS *Montagu* was a first-class twin-screw battleship, of the Duncan class, launched at Devonport in 1901, and carried a complement of 750 officers and men, with 16 guns, at a speed of 19 knots. She had been carrying out manoeuvres to the west of Lundy on 29th May, 1906, and a dense fog developed that night. In the small hours of 30th May she ran aground, on the south-west corner of the island, and it is probably fair to say that it was initially assumed that she would be relatively easily recovered. For those that know the coastline of Lundy, this area is a forbidding one, and the grounding of such a prestigious and relatively new ship there was instantly the subject of major media attention, on a national as well as a local level. Inevitably the spectacle prompted the excursion steamship operators to run cruises to view the stranded battleship, and it was an easy matter for both P. & A. Campbell Ltd and the Red Funnel Line to send whichever of their paddlers might have been lying at Ilfracombe during the afternoon for a couple of hours over to Lundy instead, and still adhere to their published schedules, as well as lay on extra trips to satisfy public demand and cash in on this novelty. The White Funnel Fleet appear to have been first off the mark, with *Westward Ho,* and on Friday 1st June, 1906 it was recorded in the *Ilfracombe Gazette* that three further excursions to 'would be run by P. & A. Campbell Ltd, one that day at 3.30 pm and two on Saturday 2nd June, at 2 pm and at 3.30 pm, at a fare of 1*s.* 6*d*.' Many other naval vessels had hurried to the scene of the disaster, and excursionists would have been able to see the wholly unprecedented sight of half a dozen battleships and destroyers milling around Lundy as well as various salvage and Admiralty vessels, and sundry tugboats. To put this incident further into context, the cost of building HMS *Montagu* was quoted in the newspapers then at being around 1¼ million pounds, a staggering amount indeed. The *Ilfracombe Gazette* newspaper still chose to ignore the Red Funnel Line presence at the port but the excursions were sold from a kiosk at the harbour anyway irrespective of formal advertising.

The loss of the battleship HMS *Montagu* immediately preceded Whitsuntide in 1906, and this gave rise to all-time record numbers of visitors being counted through the turnstiles at Ilfracombe harbour. A week after the *Ilfracombe Gazette* had documented the grounding, the report in that paper entitled 'Whitsuntide by the Silver Sea' proclaimed

> . . . never has such a brisk Whitsuntide been known here . . . The beautiful weather together with the fact that a million and a quarter of their money was piled up and in danger of being altogether lost near Ilfracombe, were probably the chief reasons of the unusual rush, but whatever it was visitors came in their thousands and the pier presented an animated scene at all hours of the day . . .

The *Ilfracombe Chronicle* gave some visitor figures for Whit Monday, 4th June, 1906:

> The boats began to arrive in good time, the *Brighton* bringing about 300 passengers from Swansea and Mumbles. The *Britannia* came with her full complement - over 800 - from Bristol. The *Westward Ho* came down in the late afternoon, bringing many from Bristol, Weston, Newport and Clevedon. The *Gwalia* arrived at two o'clock from Bristol, Barry, Cardiff, Penarth and Lynmouth, with her full load of 1,030. Of these, about half landed, and the rest, with as many more from the town, went down to Lundy at 2.30 to see the *Montagu* and the other battleships. The sea was very smooth, and the trip delightful.

The date of this rare view is almost certainly the summer of 1906, after the grounding of HMS *Montagu* at Lundy, which prompted the running of many excursions from Ilfracombe to view the wreck. *Lionel Vaughan Collection*

The attraction of the wreck continued throughout the 1906 season with numerous non-landing trips to Lundy provided by both the Red Funnel Line and P. & A. Campbell Ltd, with the latter advertising non-landing excursions from Bristol and from Newport as well as the more frequent ones from Cardiff. The fact of the wreck may have reminded the Red Funnel Line management and Mr Taylor (tenant of Lundy) of the discussions that had taken place in the spring about planned Lundy landing trips by Red Funnel Line steamer, and revived the commercial prospects in an unforeseen manner. Early in June 1906 the Revd Heaven, in a letter to his niece, stated that in addition to frequent non-landing trips the Red Funnel steamers were calling at Lundy on Tuesdays, and that the island was 'swarming with photographers' as a result. A little later on, an advertisement in the *Western Mail* newspaper on Saturday 14th July, 1906 referred to Red Funnel Line landing trips to Lundy to view the *Montagu* on Monday 16th and Wednesday 18th July at a fare of 4*s*. 6*d*. (fore-cabin) and 5*s*. (saloon), including landing and embarking. The departure time quoted from Cardiff (Riverside) was 9.35 am, i.e. that of the regular Ilfracombe 'railway run', and the return from Lundy was quoted as 3.50 pm. In a sense, the Red Funnel Line was now ahead of its White Funnel Fleet rivals.

Whilst the grounding of HMS *Montagu* provided the basis of worthwhile - and unexpected - earnings for the Red Funnel Line steamers, the syndicate was not content to simply sit back and run its steamers within the bounds that had been set out by the 1905 season, and other developments enabled a wide range of excursion opportunities to be marketed in parallel with that which was on offer from the numerically much larger White Funnel Fleet. A presence had been established in 1905 by the Barry boats at practically all places of consequence in the Bristol Channel, but a new destination for 1906 was represented - as far as the author has been able to determine - by Porthcawl. White Funnel steamers also appear to have started calling there in 1906, typically whilst on passage between Penarth and Mumbles. The first Red Funnel Line call at Porthcawl traced was advertised for Friday 10th August, 1906, with an 9.30 am departure from Cardiff to Porthcawl, Mumbles and Tenby. Return departure times were Tenby 5.15, Mumbles 7.00 and Porthcawl 8.00 pm. This must have been an exciting day in the Bristol Channel: high water at Bristol was at 10.56 am, and the P. & A. Campbell Ltd advertisements offered a sailing from Bristol at 8.30 am for Cardiff, Penarth, Mumbles and Tenby, with return departure times of Tenby (4.30), Mumbles

(6.15), Penarth (8.00) and Cardiff (8.30 pm) for Bristol. One wonders if these times meant that racing would be attempted, or whether the Barry boat left Tenby earlier than advertised to chase her white-funnelled adversary!

Over on the English side of the Bristol Channel, things had not gone quite to plan in Weston-super-Mare, either for the owners of Birnbeck Pier (the 'Old Pier') or the developers behind the more centrally-sited Grand Pier. It will be remembered that, in 1904, the latter had opened to the public, but without its steamer landing-stage having been completed. Equally, the attempts by the Weston-super-Mare Pier Company to construct a low-water extension at their Birnbeck Pier had faltered, and in 1906 there was no sign that this was yet anywhere near complete. The tidal limitations at the north jetty of Birnbeck Pier thus defined the times at which the ferry steamers of either the Red Funnel Line or the White Funnel Fleet could make calls, and when low water prevailed the normal practice was for steamers (arriving from Cardiff on the last of the ebb) to offer the alternatives of a cruise round the Holm islands, or a run up the Somerset coast to Clevedon Pier, where calls could be made at virtually any state of the tide. An advantage possessed by the Barry Railway Company was that its vessels could run back to Barry for time ashore there at low water, (when Cardiff was inaccessible) or maybe offer a Glamorgan Coast cruise from Barry Pier. Vessels of both fleets might instead merely lie at anchor, depending on the time of day, which day of the week it was, and the size of the tide. A contemporary guide-book - the Ward-Lock 'Red Guide' - for Clevedon and the surrounding region painted a glowing picture of what was in store for holidaymakers at Weston-super-Mare when works at the Grand Pier were complete, entitled 'The Front':

> But it is of course by its 'front' that a seaside resort must stand or fall. A glance at a map will show that Weston is situated on a spur of the Mendips, forming the northern horn of a spacious and finely-curved bay at the point where the Severn estuary broadens into the Bristol Channel . . . the curve of the bay is broken near the middle, at the foot of Regent Street, by the new Grand Pier, and slightly further north by the Knightstone promontory, on which stand the Pavilion and the Baths. At the extreme north of the town, round the bend of the headland, is another, older pier - the Birnbeck - not seen from many parts of the front. This is at present used by the steamers, but when the Grand Pier has attained its destined length the boats will be able to land and embark passengers independently of tides.

There was another, alternative destination for cruises from Cardiff and Weston when tides were the other way round, so to speak, and that was for the steamer to instead head down-Channel from Weston on the flood, and call for a short while alongside the slip at Burnham in Somerset. The slip at Burnham was of considerable vintage, dating from attempts by the Somerset and Dorset Railway in the mid-19th century to establish a maritime link between Cardiff and Burnham to feed passengers onto their railway line to Poole and Bournemouth. The P. & A. Campbell Ltd steamers occasonally called at Burnham, nearly always simply as an end-destination rather than as a pick-up point, and indeed one of the longest day-excursions ever offered from Cardiff was that by boat from Cardiff to Burnham on an early morning tide thence by special train from there to Bournemouth for the day, returning (after about three hours or so at Bournemouth) by train to Burnham and boat back across to Cardiff on the evening tide. But Burnham was waning by 1906 as the slip silted up and although trips *to* Burnham were still advertised by White Funnel steamer, the Bournemouth option had by then been replaced by the running of special trains from Weston-super-Mare to Bournemouth, via Highbridge. The year 1906 seems to have been the last one for Burnham calls, one notable epic excursion being that offered on Tuesday 24th July from Cardiff at 7.30 am calling at Penarth and then at Burnham, Watchet, Minehead, Lynmouth and Ilfracombe - this was veritably the Bristol Channel marine equivalent of the all-stations train!

I have found no evidence that Burnham represented a destination for the Red Funnel Line steamers in 1905 or 1906, but the possible redevelopment of the slip into a fully-fledged Burnham Pier was to become a key part of the outlook of the Barry Railway Company the following year. Further along the Somerset coast, the commercial port of Watchet was comparable to Burnham inasmuch as it represented an occasional calling-point for the Campbell steamers, but seemingly not yet those of the Red Funnel Line, although this situation was also to change in due course.

A couple of extracts from *Mrs Grundy's Jottings* in the Barry newspapers in the summer of 1906 paint a light-hearted picture of what were undoubtedly serious incidents at the time, certainly to those involved. On Friday 29th June she wrote:

> During the violent thunderstorm last Saturday evening, the large crowd of passengers from Barry who went for a cruise on board the Red Funnel Line steamer *Devonia* sought shelter 'down below' - in the saloon and cabins. One man, anxious about his personal comfort, dared not to go on deck owing to the heavy rain, which was falling in torrents, and looking up the main gangway, with pathetic humour he exclaimed 'Well, if I must drown, I will drown down here in the dry!

About a week later she again commented on the plight of one on board a Barry steamer:

> Soon after the Red Funnel steamer *Gwalia* had left Bristol last Monday for Barry, one of the crew accidentally fell overboard, but he was able to swim and was soon aboard again. The affair caused much excitement amongst the passengers.

A few days later, she noted that a party from C. H. Bailey's engine works at Barry Docks had been over to Weston on *Devonia* and proceeded to Cheddar, where some members of the party had purchased Cheddar cheeses and brought them back to Barry to sell at a profit!

There is no doubt that business was good for the Red Funnel Line steamers in 1906 whilst they were able to sail around the Bristol Channel without restrictions, and the figures of August Bank Holiday traffic recorded at Ilfracombe give a vivid indication of the popularity of excursion steamer sailings at that time. Noting that by 2 pm the railway had already brought over 3,000 passengers into Ilfracombe, in the item 'Bank Holiday Doings' the *Ilfracombe Chronicle* recorded the following:

> The steamers brought their thousands. The *Brighton* came from Swansea with 700, and the *Normandy* from the same place had 690. From Bristol and Cardiff the *Britannia* brought 760. From Bristol the *Westward Ho* brought 800. The sister ship *Cambria* came from Cardiff with 820, while the *Devonia* from the same place brought 720, and took 300 down to Lundy to land. From Newport came the *Albion* with 200.

Devonia proudly showing off her handsome appearance in Red Funnel Line colours after the short-lived early period when she wore a grey hull. *Lionel Vaughan Collection*

From the advertisements in the *Western Mail* on Friday 3rd August, 1906 I have pieced together the full workings of the Barry boats for that Bank Holiday Monday 6th August, 1906 (*see page 93*), the only assumption being that *Westonia* was the 'ferry' steamer and that *Gwalia* ran to Chepstow as we know from the *Ilfracombe Chronicle* (*above*) that *Devonia* ran to Lundy.

A couple of days after all this busy activity, another involuntary immersion was to occur from a Barry steamer, but this time it was a member of the crew valiantly rescuing a member of the public. The account in the *Ilfracombe Chronicle* was interesting in that it stated that, on the afternoon of Wednesday 8th August, 1906, the occupants of a small boat crossing Ilfracombe Harbour were all precipitated into the water and a lady became pinned beneath the overturned boat. Fully clothed, an 'attendant of the SS *Westonia*' dived in and rescued her, being loudly cheered for his heroism in effecting the rescue as she had got into an exhausted condition. Other boats arrived on the scene, and the other unfortunates were all rescued too. Mentions of *Westonia* running down-Channel are rare, and this may perhaps have been an occasion when traffic was lighter and her lower capacity was all that was needed if one of her bigger sisters was due a day off, and greater numbers were expected on the Cardiff-Weston ferry workings.

A number of longer trips by Red Funnel Line steamer, to Newquay in Cornwall, were promoted in 1906. These mirrored trips that the established Campbell steamers had already been providing from Ilfracombe and, to a lesser extent, from Cardiff and even occasionally from Bristol. Unusually, one such trip by Red Funnel Line steamer was actually advertised in the Ilfracombe press, and a good deal of publicity ensued on a later occasion in August when trips by both operators to Newquay were programmed to take place on the same day, on Wednesday 15th August, 1906. The weather was not perfect, and different versions of what happened were carried in the rival Ilfracombe newspapers. *Gwalia* and *Cambria* were reported to have both left Ilfracombe at 10.00 am, the latter having been advertised to have started at 6.00 am from Cardiff. By the time *Gwalia* was off Bude, seas were breaking right over the vessel, and the passengers evidently enreated Captain James to turn back, which he did. *Cambria* however went on, and reached Newquay at about 3.00 pm, it being alleged that some passengers were landed there in a deplorable state and unable to return to Ilfracombe by sea, or even by train that day.

Various letters giving different interpretations of this day were published in the two Ilfracombe newspapers in the ensuing weeks, but whatever the facts the message conveyed was that the White Funnel vessels were, on balance, superior: Captain Livingstone of *Cambria,* according to the *Gazette,* won on determination even if Captain James of *Gwalia* won on the grounds of chivalry, in the eyes of the *Chronicle,* in a narrowly-balanced contest under admittedly difficult circumstances.

Barry and Bristol Channel Steamship Co.

RED FUNNEL LINE

The New Steamers

GWALIA, DEVONIA, and WESTONIA.

The Largest, Fastest, and most luxuriously appointed Steamers in the Bristol Channel.

Sailing from ILFRACOMBE and LYNMOUTH

(Weather and other circumstances permitting).

MONDAY, JULY 16TH,

SPECIAL GRAND TRIP TO

NEWQUAY

IN CORNWALL,

Leaving Lynmouth 8-15 a.m., Ilfracombe 9-30 a.m.; returning from Newquay 4-30 p.m., allowing 3 hours ashore.

Return Fares from Ilfracombe 4/-, Lynmouth 5/-

NOTE.—This Trip affords Passengers an opportunity of Viewing the Grandest Scenery in the neighbourhood, passing through Bideford Bay, along the Coast to Bude, Boscastle and TINTAGEL CASTLE, the traditional Birthplace and Home of King Arthur.

N.B.—If time permits the homeward journey wlll be *via* Lundy to view the wrecked Battleship MONTAGU.

LUNCHEONS, TEAS, &c., provided on Board at Moderate Charges.

Tickets for this Trip may be had of Mr John Jones, Bootmaker, Broad Street; Mr A. Johnson, Tobacconist, opposite Royal Britannia Hotel; at the Red Funnel Office on the Pier, or on Board the Steamers. Further information of Captain Tom Pugsley, Agent, Mars Hill, Lynmouth; or from Wm. JONES, Agent, Red Funnel Office, Pier, Ilfracombe.

A rare advertisement for a Red Funnel excursion from Ilfracombe, published in the *Ilfracombe Chronicle & North Devon News,* Saturday 14th July, 1906. The event generated considerable newspaper coverage. *Ilfracombe Museum*

Either *Devonia* or *Gwalia* together with the P. & A. Campbell Ltd regular Newport boat *Albion* alongside the landing stage on the River Usk in the heart of Newport.

Lionel Vaughan Collection

Either *Devonia* or *Gwalia* off Penarth Pier when that structure had a very different appearance to the present day. *Lionel Vaughan Collection*

Workings of the Barry Railway Company 'Red Funnel Line' steamers, Bank Holiday Monday 6th August, 1906

Westonia (ferry duties)			
Weston		8.15*	*am*
Cardiff		8.55	
Weston		9.35*	
Cardiff		10.55	
Weston	a. 11.45 *am*		
to anchor			
Weston		4.00*	*pm*
Cardiff		5.10	
Weston		6.00	
Cardiff		7.10	
Weston		8.00	
Cardiff		9.10	
Weston		10.00	
Cardiff		(finish)	
Devonia (railway run)			
Cardiff		9.30	*am*
Penarth		9.40	
Barry		10.10	
Minehead		(11.xx)	
Lynmouth		(12.xx)	*pm*
Ilfracombe		(1.xx)	
Lundy	a. 2.xx *pm*		
(to land)			
Lundy		4.15	
Ilfracombe		5.30	
Lynmouth		(6.xx)	
Minehead		6.50	
Barry		(7.xx)	
Penarth		(8.xx)	
Cardiff		(8.xx)	
Gwalia (third vessel)			
Cardiff		9.35*	*am*
Weston		10.20*	
Cardiff	a. 11.xx *am*		
(idle at low water)			
Cardiff		4.20	*pm*
Weston		5.xx	
Clevedon		6.xx	
Chepstow	a. 7.xx *pm*	(short time ashore)	
Chepstow		8.45	
Clevedon		9.45	
Weston		10.15	
Cardiff		(finish)	

Notes
* denotes steamer not calling at Penarth *en route* between Cardiff & Weston, or v.v.
xx - minutes past the hour unknown where not specifically mentioned in advertisements

Westonia at Birnbeck Pier, Weston-super-Mare, doubtless backing out for another ferry run to Cardiff. *Lionel Vaughan Collection*

The 1906 season was now drawing towards its end, and one of the last special trips by the Red Funnel Line steamers was that on Tuesday 25th September, when either *Gwalia* or *Devonia* was advertised to leave Cardiff at 8.45 and Barry at 9.40 am, at a fare of 3*s*. 6*d*., to follow the Bristol Channel Pilot Cutters Race, from Cardiff to Ilfracombe then back to Sully Island, for a first prize of £50. Which steamer carried out this duty was unrecorded, but the winner was a Barry pilot-cutter, *Hope*, and it was also noted that *Cambria* had been 'chartered for the subscribers and followed the race throughout'.

'Adieu to the Barry passenger steamers till next summer' was the last utterance of Mrs Grundy on the subject in the *Barry Dock News* on Friday 28th September, 1906, who noted that the last trips of the season were being run that week. According to the Ilfracombe papers the honour of being the last White Funnel Fleet boat of the season to depart from the North Devon resort fell to *Cambria*, which left Ilfracombe on the afternoon of Wednesday 3rd October, 1906 for Cardiff and Bristol, to the accompaniment of the firing of rockets from the shore and from the boat, and the mutual dipping of flags. Shortly afterwards *Gwalia* took her departure and similar compliments were bestowed on her, as the season of 1906 ended at Ilfracombe.

Devonia at sea, with a good crowd on board, and a Bristol Channel pilot cutter in the background. *Lionel Vaughan Collection*

Chapter Three

The Barry Steamships must quit Cardiff

Phase Two: Climax and Crisis, into 1907

. . . the passenger bookings on the Barry last Saturday were larger than any previous day in the history of the railway . . . one of the leading London dailies this week describes Barry as 'The Silvern Gem of the Severn Sea'. Another, more prosaic, as the 'Biarritz of the Principality'. Next week we shall be looking out for 'The Paradise of the Bristol Channel'. The numbers of visitors to Barry Island this week are estimated at nearly 50,000 . . .

Mrs Grundy's Jottings, in the
Barry Dock News, 12th July, 1907

The next phase of expansion is planned

What had been achieved by the Barry Railway Company after its first two years of operating steamships in the Bristol Channel? A primary goal of bringing the Barry Pier extension railway and landing-stage back into regular use had clearly been of fundamental importance, although more use was actually being made of Cardiff Pier Head from where Red Funnel Line 'ferry' operations to Weston-super-Mare had been initiated. The two purpose-built vessels had been supplemented by a third, lesser vessel. Whereas the first two steamers were fully occupied on the 'railway run' and other 'main line' duties, the third sustained the more mundane Cardiff-Weston 'ferry' station. According to statements made by the railway company Directors to shareholders at twice-yearly meetings all was well, and worthwhile additional passenger traffic was being handled over the Barry Railway network in bringing passengers directly to Barry Pier. The range of regular sailings and excursions offered by the Red Funnel Line steamers in the Bristol Channel closely emulated that of the white-funnelled fleet of P. & A. Campbell Ltd, and herein lay the problem: a substantial lawsuit was underway at the instigation of the Bristol company, who sought to show that the Barry Railway Company was trading illegally, and demanded that its operations be brought into line with the terms of the 1904 Act. The full hearing was yet to come but, in late 1906, the stated position of the Barry Railway Company was that the Red Funnel Line was independent, and could thus do as it wished. Despite the initial court hearings and having had an injunction served on them, it was seemingly business as usual in Barry.

Looking ahead, there was every reason for continued optimism on the Welsh side of the Bristol Channel despite the continuing legal drama. The Red Funnel Line steamers were now a significant presence, Lundy calls had been added to their range in 1906 after the dramatic grounding of HMS *Montagu*, and a new pier at Weston-super-Mare with low-water landing capability was expected to be ready in 1907. For good measure another new venture to link with the Somerset & Dorset Railway on the opposite shore of the channel at Burnham

A Barry Railway Company vessel, either *Devonia* or *Gwalia*, lies off the slip at Burnham whilst boatmen bring her passengers ashore. The 1907 proposal to build a big new pier on this site never materialised in the manner envisaged, but occasional calls by both White Funnel Fleet and Red Funnel Line concerns took place, and until around 1906 the P. & A. Campbell Ltd trips from Cardiff occasionally ran in conjunction with special through trains to Bournemouth, over the Somerset & Dorset Railway, from the nearby station at Burnham-on-Sea. *Lionel Vaughan Collection*

was being assembled, with year-round services in prospect between Barry Pier and a completely reconstructed pier adjacent to the railway station at Burnham, which lay at the end of the railway line from Bournemouth. It is worth considering this visionary undertaking a little further before coming back to the more mundane and immediate legal issues with which the parties had to grapple. The year 1906 seems to have been the last one during which occasional excursion calls at Burnham were advertised by P. & A. Campbell Ltd, and landing facilities at the old slip were silting up. There is evidence that some calls at Burnham were actually by small boat, with the paddlers anchored a little way offshore rather than going alongside the actual slip. Though the attractions at Burnham were on nothing like the scale of nearby Weston-super-Mare, there was some determination locally that the quieter town should expand as a seaside resort, and having a rail-linked pier seemed like an obvious way forward if the tidal constraints could be overcome.

Burnham and its rail-connected pier could be seen as a sort of 'mirror image' in Somerset of what had already been created in Glamorgan at Barry Island, with the Barry Pier extension railway and its associated landing-stage facility. If the initial vision of the Barry Railway Company had been to forge the maritime link from its corner of South Wales to the opposite shore of Somerset, via Weston, then this was a logical next step, to get right across Wessex by rail to the south coast at Bournemouth in conjunction with the Somerset & Dorset Railway. There had been earlier attempts by that railway company, from 1858 onwards, to establish such a through route, from Cardiff through to France. This involved a Poole-Cherbourg sea crossing, but these endeavours were somewhat overtaken by events. The operation of railway-connected boats between Burnham and Cardiff, with lapses in service, spanned 30 years or so, but the opening of the Severn railway tunnel in 1886 had rather changed things. Although surely aware of these past failures, the Barry Railway Company was still keen - almost 20 years later - to make a fresh attempt. The words of the Ward-Lock Red Guide for the Clevedon district again sum up the situation on the front at Burnham neatly:

> In place of the ramshackle old landing-stage, it is proposed to construct a handsome new Pier, 780 feet long, with a Pavilion about 300 feet from the Esplanade. There will be three or four stages, approached by easy stairways, so that steamers can land and embark at any state of the tide. The fact that the River Parrett and the smaller River Brue find their outlet to the sea near this point ensures always a deep channel of water in the midst of the flats. It is curious to watch the tugs and small trading vessels making for Bridgwater and Highbridge apparently floating on an ocean of sand.

Very substantial sums of money were envisaged to be necessary to fund such a sizeable construction project, quite apart from the legal expenses associated with the use of Parliamentary Agents to handle the processes which statutory undertakings such as the Barry Railway Company had to adhere to in order to secure the requisite Powers. These were necessary if one wished to build harbour works, in addition to which the Barry Railway Company had the complication of being a railway undertaking which was obliged to seek further Powers to enable it to become involved in something other than just being a railway company running trains. Thus by 1906 legislative processes had already been initiated to enable the pier at Burnham to be transferred from its original local railway ownership to that of a new syndicate, who would take it over in order to effect the reconstruction. The Midland Railway Act of 1905 had paved the way for transfer of the pier to Burnham District Council, and a Pier & Harbour Order Confirmation (No.3) Act of 1906 set up the syndicate.

More legislation was still being prepared to enable the Barry Railway Company to secure the Powers it needed to increase its capital in order to then invest in the syndicate. A crucial point about this endeavour was that the Barry Railway Company, for all its financial might, was not seeking to finance these new works all on its own. What would today be called 'partnership funding' was what it had in mind, and a substantial local contribution was sought to match what it was prepared to put up. An item in the *Western Mail* newspaper in January 1907 stated that the Barry Railway Company was offering to find the first £15,000, and the shortfall of the other half of the capital would have caused those in charge of such matters in Burnham at the time some soul-searching. As 1907 unfolded, therefore, much was uncertain. The Burnham (Somerset) Pier Bill went before a House of Lords select Committee in March 1907 and, despite the representations of P. & A. Campbell Ltd who feared that the Barry Railway Company might become involved in what it saw as unfair competition, the Bill was nevertheless passed. At this point, then, Burnham folk could look forward to a new era, or so they thought.

More legal manoeuvring

This brief résumé of the situation in Somerset is necessary better to understand just what happened next in the development of the Red Funnel Line. Although the Minute Books of the Barry Railway Company are not absolutely explicit on this point, the Parliamentary evidence, in various legislative forms, is quite clear, and it was distinctly understood by the shareholders that Powers to become involved at Burnham Pier were being sought. It was surprising, therefore, when researching this book, to discover the exact reasoning that lay behind the decision of the Barry Directors in late 1906 to procure a fourth ship. Burnham was not mentioned at all, but rather a different reason for making the order was advanced by the Company Solicitor. That gentleman would have been mainly concerned with the Parliamentary and legal processes which had granted the Barry Railway Company the rights to build railways, operate docks undertakings and of course run passenger steamers. The meeting of Directors that took place at the Westminster Palace Hotel in London on Friday 7th December, 1906 was chaired by The Earl of Plymouth, and attended by Messrs Thompson, Cory, Jenkins, Hood, Davies and three others. The following was Minuted:

> Barry Steamships Act. The Solicitor reported . . . (the) necessity for bona fide exercising of the Powers before the month of August 1907. It was resolved that in order to get rid of any doubt as to whether the company had not already exercised their Powers in accordance with the Act that a steamship be purchased at a cost not exceeding £25,000

with the view of putting on a service in accordance with the Companies Act and that it be left to the General Manager either to advertise in the name of the Company or in the name of a broker with the view of ascertaining whether a steamer suitable to the requirements of the Company could be bought.

This amounted to an admission that the Powers granted to the Barry Railway Company by the 1904 Act had been either blatantly disregarded, or that the Directors actually believed they had assigned them to a separate undertaking - a move of questionable legality. The Powers themselves had a validity of three years from the date the Act had received Royal Assent, defined in Clause 4. Unfettered by any consideration of another part of the Act, Clause 6, which restricted their expenditure on ships to £60,000 (in the region of £75,000 had already been spent!), here were the Directors deciding behind closed doors that perhaps they had better now get another new ship in order to finally shake off the Campbell brothers and that £25,000 should do the trick. This was, indeed, a sizeable capital exposure even for a company with the resources of the powerful Barry concern. It might be noted that, a couple of years earlier, the Burnham folk had appealed to P. & A. Campbell Ltd to subscribe to the proposed new Pier undertaking, which approach had been declined. Thus, the Campbell brothers could scarcely begrudge the Barry Railway Company their wish to develop a Barry-Burnham link, and the only surprising thing when the order for a fourth ship became public knowledge was that nothing had yet physically happened at Burnham to lead anyone to think that new pier construction was imminent. Just what a fourth ship was going to do in the interim was therefore something of a mystery.

The year of 1906 ended, and early in the following year the knowledge that the Barry Railway Company had ordered a new ship became public. At the same time the court hearing was continuing, and although very few details of which way the litigation was going were apparent then, the press statement in the *Barry Dock News* on Friday 25th January, 1907 alluded to it:

MORE PASSENGER BOATS FOR BARRY
NEW TURBINE STEAMER BEING BUILT

In connection with the controversy relating to the running of the local passenger steamers in connection with Barry Docks . . . the Barry Railway Company have under construction by Messrs John Brown and Company, Clydebank, Glasgow a fine turbine steamer which is to ply between Barry and places on the other side of the Bristol Channel. The Company, it is understood, will run the vessel themselves, and as the service is to be a winter as well as a summer one, the steamer is being built so as to be able to face all weather conditions, and is to be delivered by June next. It is also believed that the steamer, which will have a speed of about 20 knots an hour, will be followed by others.

This particular court hearing led to an adjournment until July 1907, during which period the defendants were ordered to produce affidavits as evidence of ownership, and many issues remained unclear at this point in the proceedings. The reference to running the new vessel themselves tied in precisely with the (private) recognition by the Barry Railway Company Directors that this action was legally necessary to adhere to and execute their Powers under the 1904 Act, and would obviously have created further suspicion in the minds of the plaintiff

An endearingly amateurish multi-image card of *Gwalia* and views of her 'home port' of Barry Pier. *Lionel Vaughan Collection*

A stern view of *Gwalia* at sea, possibly around 1907, with a crowded promenade deck and a handful on the aft bridge deck too. *Lionel Vaughan Collection*

in the lawsuit, P. & A. Campbell Ltd. If not exercised, the Powers would lapse. Dubiety still existed, as the trading name of Red Funnel Line had been established over two summer seasons - so why this new development? A few weeks later the Barry Railway Company let it be known locally that a new company had now been created, but there was no overt admission that this was because the earlier one - that is, the so-called Barry & Bristol Channel Steamship Company - was in any way a deception. As Mrs Grundy neatly put it, in the *Barry Dock News* on Friday 22nd February, 1907: 'The private partnership which has hitherto carried on the well-known Bristol Channel steamships, known as the Barry Red Funnel Line, has just been converted into a Limited Company with a capital of £30,000'.

This might very well nowadays be described as being economical with the truth - which was that no actual Red Funnel Line company had ever existed up until that point. There is no obvious reason why the amount of £30,000 was decided upon, as this was clearly nothing like as much as the book value of the three steamships already being operated. The exact status of the Barry and Bristol Channel Steamship Company remained questionable too. But it was still some months before the Court of Chancery proceedings were due to come to a head and in the meantime, as the 1907 season approached, the outlook for the Barry Railway Company continued to appear promising and they must have felt assured of victory. Clearly satisfied with their two-purpose built ships from the Clydebank yard of John Brown and Company Ltd, Mr Thompson doubtless had no qualms in returning to Glasgow to open negotiations for a third ship from that yard. It had already become apparent that his other purchase, *Westonia*, continued to prove herself as unsatisfactory in Bristol Channel service as she had been for the three earlier owners who had run her and passed her on in rapid succession, and significant expenditure was required during the winter of 1906/07 to bring this vessel up to scratch. But money was perhaps was not then really seen as the problem as the belief persisted that rich dividends were there to be had, and a successful outcome to the fight with the Campbell brothers over the water in Bristol was confidently predicted.

The building of 'Barry'

The John Brown & Co. records make an interesting comparison with the press-release that had mentioned turbine-driven rather than paddle-steamers. Quotes for two vessels were submitted to the Barry Railway Company, which in retrospect are quite fascinating in the insight they give to what was going on in those days, in terms of competition and what might now be described as 'best practice'. The Glasgow and South Western Railway had, in 1906, taken delivery of a turbine steamer from John Brown & Co. which was named *Atalanta*, and joined the emerging fleet of smart, mostly Clydebank-built paddle steamers operated by that railway such as *Jupiter*, *Juno* and their latest acquisition *Mars* delivered in 1902. It was also the case that at the time they tendered to the Welsh railway company, John Brown and Co. had provided another tender to the G&SWR for a second turbine-steamer, at a price of £21,000. But the intriguing aspect of the two quotes submitted to Mr Thompson was that one of them exceeded the ceiling of £25,000 that had been set by his Board - this was for a steamer to be modelled on *Brighton Queen*, with arrangements similar to those of *Gwalia* and *Devonia*, capable of a speed of 18½ knots, i.e. rather slower than their first two vessels, at an 'approximate cost' of £26,000.

At 240 ft in length, *Brighton Queen* had been built in 1897 by the Clydebank Engineering and Shipbuilding Co. (who were subsequently acquired by John Brown and Company) to the order of the Brighton, Worthing and South Coast Steamship Company, and which after only three seasons in service for that body had been acquired by Alec Campbell. He promptly rebuilt her into a singularly attractive, sleek vessel of classic profile with one funnel, fully plated forward and in keeping with Campbell's own three 'flyers' *Westward Ho*, *Cambria* and *Britannia* built between 1894 and 1896. *Brighton Queen* had a good turn of speed and was the principal vessel used on the long cross-channel day excursions from Brighton, Eastbourne and Hastings to Boulogne in France. The quote now being offered to the Barry Railway Company for such a style of vessel was significantly less than that which had been paid for either of the 1905 pair, reflecting a less heavy type of build.

One wonders just what Mr Thompson actually specified as his requirements, as the other quote from John Brown & Co. was for an altogether less grand type of paddle-steamer, to be based on the design of *Mars* which had been built to a length of 200 ft. A slower and thus more economical vessel was what was being offered here, with a speed of 16½ knots, at the very much lower price of £20,500. The choices thus being put to Mr Thompson for the Barry Railway Company to ponder over were somewhat extreme, but speedy delivery was of the essence, and a guarantee was needed that the new ship could enter Bristol Channel service before the August 1907 deadline in the Act expired. The tender documentation was dated 19th September, 1906, suggesting that Mr Thompson must have opened discussions with John Brown & Co. well before his Board recorded its decision to place a ceiling of £25,000 on the purchase.

One can only speculate at the arguments for and against the two alternatives on offer, but what actually emerged must have been the result of a good degree of compromise. It had to be something based on a proven design, in order that the keel could be laid more or less straightaway. The Clydebank yard seems to have had a broadly similar level of other work on at this time as when construction of *Gwalia* and *Devonia* had commenced in 1904: the Cunarder *Lusitania* had been launched earlier in 1906 and was fitting out, and so out of the nine building berths only four were now occupied. One assumes that the yard was hungry for work, especially the initial steel fabrication and assembly of the framing, and had no worries that they could turn out a paddle-steamer in well under six months. However, the ship that was to emerge as the new *Barry* was neither a straight copy of *Mars*, nor was it truly a shortened version of *Brighton Queen* or, indeed, of the Barry Railway Company's own pair from 1905. In final appearance the new ship was to resemble, to some extent, yet another John Brown product: this was *Greyhound* belonging to the North Pier Steamship Company (Blackpool) Ltd, which we met earlier as a Blackpool-based vessel, and which could perhaps have been a better bet than the one time *Tantallon Castle* had she been purchased in 1905 instead.

In terms of general arrangements, strong similarities did nonetheless exist between *Barry* and her older sisters, but this time her bridge was placed forward of just a single funnel. Second class facilities were located forward, on the main and lower decks, and first class astern. One notable difference at promenade deck level was a slightly greater degree of provision of covered space as the aft-bridge deck (above the Purser's office and companionway) was carried out over the promenade deck, to the point where the sponsons stretched out from the main hull plating.

A comparison of the principal dimensions of the three respective paddlers makes interesting reading. Both *Greyhound* and *Mars* had their bridges abaft of the funnel:

	length *ft*	*breadth* *ft*	*depth* *ft*	*grt*	*machinery*
Greyhound (1895)	230	27	10	542	Compound diagonal, 2-cylinder 21 in., 45-48 in.
Mars (1902)	200.4	26.1	8.6	317	Compound diagonal, 2-cylinder 28¼ in., 53-54 in.
Barry (1907)	225.6	26.6	8.7	471	Compound diagonal, 2-cylinder 25½ in., 54-54 in.

Little time was lost by John Brown & Co. in starting work on hull No. 379, at building berth No. 5 in the main yard at Clydebank; it will be recalled that *Gwalia* and *Devonia*, hull Nos. 368/369 respectively had commenced life in the west yard a couple of years earlier. It seems surprising nowadays that work started in earnest so quickly then, and before contractual niceties had been dealt with. According to John Brown & Co. production records, the keel blocks of hull No. 379 had been laid by January 1907, and yet it was not until Wednesday 17th April, 1907 that its Minute Book records that the contract with the Barry Railway Company had been sealed! By February her frames were three-quarters completed, and work had commenced to build up the bulkheads. By mid-March the deck plating, stringers and keelsons had been completed, and a start made on the shell-plating. As early as mid-April, progress was such that she was almost fully plated, laying of wooden-decks was underway, and preparations for her launching were being made.

Start of the 1907 season

Briefly returning from the Clyde to the Bristol Channel, then, the forthcoming season beckoned and as early as Friday 22nd March, 1907 Mrs Grundy noted that the first trip by Red Funnel Line boat to Weston-super-Mare would be run the following Thursday, 28th March, by *Westonia*, and that the first trip to Ilfracombe would run the next day, Good Friday. From hereon one needs to read between the lines a little, as the *Barry Dock News* newspaper report on Friday 29th March describing the first trip that season by *Westonia* might have allowed folk to infer that all was well, whereas the truth was rather different. The piece was entitled:

TRIAL TRIPS OF BARRY PASSENGER STEAMERS

The Barry passenger steamer *Westonia*, which has undergone extensive repairs and alterations, left Barry Basin on Thursday last, under the supervision of the Board of Trade and owner's superintendents. After adjusting compasses, the course was adjusted to Weston Pier, which was reached in record time, the steamer being the first to land there this season. Another trial was made from Weston to Penarth Pier, where some of the company were landed, and thence to Barry Dock, where the steamer will receive her final touches for the summer service. Great satisfaction was expressed by all on board with the improvements on the steamer, which, as the trials proved, have contributed not only to the increased speed, but also to additional accommodation for the passengers.

The other steamers of the Barry and Bristol Channel Steamship Company, the *Gwalia* and *Devonia*, were submitted to similar tests this week.

The term 'extensive repairs' was perhaps euphemistic, in that later accounts were to reveal that the cost of these repairs had amounted to almost half of her purchase price, a remarkable amount to be obliged to spend in 1907 on a steamer built in 1899. In her first guise as *Tantallon Castle* her then owners had found it necessary to rebuild the ship after her first season with a new forecastle, before disposing of her after a second season. In her fourth phase of ownership by the nominee of the Barry Railway Company, it became necessary to rid the ship of this additional steelwork, and what emerged was arguably a neater looking vessel, which went on to carry out her duties less problematically for the next few years. But the Barry Railway Company had paid heavily to have her modified, and this haemorrhaging of money was not to go unnoticed by a vocal section of the shareholders.

At Easter Mrs Grundy noted that it was hoped that the new steamer *Barry* would be ready for service by the end of April 1907, but this view turned out to be a little premature. Immediately after Easter 1907 she declared that the start of the season had been a great success:

It is fully twenty years since the weather was so delightfully favourable for the Easter holidays as this year . . . at least 20,000 visitors to Barry on Good Friday and Easter Monday . . . Many took advantage of the Channel trips by the Barry steamers . . .

These Channel trips referred to would have been short cruises from Barry Pier at low-water, when the Cardiff-Weston ferry steamer ran out of water, so to speak, at Weston, and it became the practice to use the period of low-water to run across from Weston to Barry and thence offer a short cruise along the Welsh coast or around the Holms until the tide turned sufficiently to enable *Westonia* to be able again to get alongside at Birnbeck Pier and revert to running Weston-Cardiff services. Down-Channel services did not usually start up this early in the season, and in 1907 these commenced just before the begining of May.

In mid-April of 1907 the Barry Chamber of Trade expressed a wish that the steamers might be operated in such a way as to bring people to Barry, as the town was then significantly increasing its range of attractions as a seaside resort, and it was recorded that:

. . . the Chamber agreed to petition the Barry Red Funnel Steamship line to run day trips from places on the other side of the Channel to Barry in order that tradespeople in this district might benefit in the like promotion to those residing at Weston, Ilfracombe & c. . . .

The Chamber also went on to suggest that photographs of Barry be put in railway carriages of the Great Western and Great Central Railway companies. The response from the Red Funnel Line was that when they had tried such trips the previous year the results had been disappointing, although they undertook to attempt to satisfy the wishes of the Barry tradespeople.

The launch of 'Barry'

The new paddle steamer to the order of the Barry Railway Company had been speedily constructed, and the production records of John Brown & Co. state that she was launched at 4.30 pm on 4th May, 1907. In the official information disseminated in South Wales regarding the event it was still left to the imagination as to exactly what role this new vessel was intended to carry out. The Welsh newspaper articles on Friday 10th May, 1907 were careful to stress that she was indeed 'the first passenger steamer which is to be run by the Barry Railway Company' and the christening ceremony was performed by Miss Nesta Forrest, the daughter of Mr Robert Forrest, JP, DL, of St Fagans, a Director of the company. She bestowed on it the name *Barry*, the official description of the new steamer being as follows:

> The *Barry* is a steel paddle steamer, and her dimensions are as follows: length on waterline, 225 ft, breadth moulded, 26 ft 6 in., depth moulded, 9 ft. She will carry about 450 passengers for winter service, and about 1,000 for summer service. Her speed will be between 17 and 18 knots. She is fitted with compound diagonal engines, the steam being supplied by a multitubular boiler, which is constructed of an exceptional size with a view to economising fuel. This has a working pressure of 150 lbs. The promenade deck is about 213 ft in length, while the afterbridge deck has been extended to the ship's sides, thus giving a much larger space for passengers. It also provides a shelter on the lower deck for those people who prefer to remain on deck in rough weather. Other accommodation for passengers includes a dining saloon, main saloon, tearoom, cloakroom, a fruit stall, ladies cabins, and lavatories. A handsome feature of the two saloons is embodied in a new idea for ventilation. An artistic dome has been erected above the dining saloon. This goes through the centre of the main saloon and is terminated in a skylight on the promenade deck. Its woodwork is oak, and with an arrangement of plants inside it, it is a very effective ornament indeed. The boat has been built with extra strengthening for the winter service, and every consideration has been taken for the comfort and safety of the passengers. The boat is expected at Barry shortly, and will commence running early in June. She will be easily recognised by her funnel, which is red, with a narrow white band and black top.

After the launch at Clydebank, the new paddler *Barry* went down the river for her preliminary trials on 24th May, 1907. Further trials were conducted on 29th May, after which *Barry* returned to the Govan graving-dock. She undocked from there on 31st May, and was then taken back to Clydebank, before leaving there for her official trials at 12.20 pm that day. A few more days were spent in Scotland, and the John Brown & Co. Ltd official records state that on 4th June, 1907 Barry left her birthplace on the River Clyde at 10.30 am, for Cardiff. She was a decidedly handsome and purposeful looking vessel, as befitted being a

A trials photograph of *Barry* (the original was embossed with the name of the shipbuilders, John Brown & Co., of Clydebank, just visible here). *Mitchell Library*

One of the very few calls by a paddler at Weston's Grand Pier that did take place was by *Devonia*. This view may date from shortly after the first call had taken place in May 1907, by a rival White Funnel Fleet vessel *Ravenswood*. *Lionel Vaughan Collection*

product of a shipyard where she had taken shape alongside world-class Cunard ocean-liners, and her railway company owners would have been flushed with pride at the appearance of what turned out to be the last ship in the Barry fleet.

The importance of this event was such that it was publicised in Somerset as well, and the *Weston Mercury & Somersetshire Herald* had more or less the same take on it, stating that the vessel would ply

> . . . between Barry and all the seaside resorts in Somersetshire and Devonshire. We understand that that it has been built for winter as well as summer service, and it is quite probable that we shall very shortly have an all the year round time table service between Cardiff and Weston and Barry. Weston-super-Mare will thus become a suburb of the Welsh metropolis.

It is to this same newspaper that we turn to for the next episode in the exciting events for excursionists that were taking place in 1907. After a certain amount of delay, the new landing-stage of the Grand Pier at Weston-super-Mare was finally ready to be opened, but whilst the climax of events for the Red Funnel Line steamers was fast approaching, it cannot truthfully be said that Weston's Grand Pier was quite what its promoters hoped it would be. The full account of the opening can be found in the columns of the *Weston Mercury & Somersetshire Herald* for Saturday 18th May, 1907, but insofar as the Barry steamers were concerned the so-called pier opening did not actually involve a Red Funnel Line vessel going alongside the new structure. On the evening of Thursday 16th May, a 'goodly assemblage of Westonians' gathered on the structure only to see *Westonia*, which had already called at Birnbeck Pier, standing off at a distance of about one hundred yards from the landing-stage. The honour therefore fell to P. & A. Campbell Ltd's *Ravenswood* under Captain Chidgey to be the first steamer to call at the Grand Pier and land some 400 or 500 passengers after a bottle of champagne 'launched' by Mrs Stevenson (the wife of the pier's new Manager) had christened the pier. At this point it was hoped that regular calls at the pier would be made from the following Monday, Whit Monday, but ominously reference was made in the opening report to a need to carry out major dredging works - for an astonishing distance of 2,000 feet to seaward - so that '. . . by these means boats will be enabled to call at the Pier at low water neap tides'.

A whole book could be written about pier developments at Weston-super-Mare, but it suffices to say here that only very occasional calls were ever made at the new landing-stage at the Grand Pier, either by Red Funnel Line or Campbell steamers, a few occurring later in the season in 1907, and a few more in 1908, after which the relevance of the Grand Pier to steamers sadly ceased. Around the bay at Birnbeck the Directors of Birnbeck Pier were continuing with their low-water extension, and this properly joins the story later, in 1909.

Over on the Welsh side of the Bristol Channel, a new pier opened at Chepstow on 23rd May, 1907, and the honour of being the first steamer to call here again fell to P. & A. Campbell Ltd when the splendid *Cambria* came alongside, on an excursion from Cardiff, Weston-super-Mare, Clevedon and Portishead. Trips by Red Funnel Line steamer to Chepstow again took place occasionally during the 1907 season, the new pier actually being in effect a new, improved facility at the site of the original pier on the River Wye.

The Grand Pier landing-stage extension opened in 1907 was a huge affair, yet did not stretch out far enough into deeper water to be considered safe to use by the excursion steamer operators of the day. There was however an impressive pavilion structure in which visitors could be entertained.

Author's Collection

This view from Anchor Head emphasises the enormity of the Grand Pier extension. Had it been successful, the story of the Barry steamers may well have turned out quite differently.

Author's Collection

WESTON-SUPER-MARE.

Grand Pier . .

and Pavilion.

SUMMER SEASON COMMENCING

May 20th and ending Sept. 29th, 1907.

Thrice every week day and twice on Sundays, with special Vocalist on Saturday and Sunday Evenings. Re-engagement of

HERR JULIAN KANDT'S FAMOUS

AUSTRIAN BLUE BAND.

High Class Entertainments,

CHANGED EVERY WEEK,

For Particulars of which see bills. Concluding each Evening with the

PAVILION BIOSCOPE.

Season Booklet forwarded on application to

JOHN H. STEVENSON, Manager.

TELEGRAMS: "GRAND PIER," WESTON-SUPER-MARE.

Telephone: National 24 & 24A.

For Particulars of Steamer Sailings, see following Pages.

As the season of 1907 unfolded, it was expected that the Grand Pier at Weston-super-Mare would open its long-awaited landing-stage extension for steamers, either those of the Red Funnel Line or the P. & A. Campbell Ltd White Funnel Fleet. This advertisement appeared in the 1907 timetable booklets produced by the latter, but the steamer sailings referred to were very few, during 1907/08. Thereafter the Grand Pier concentrated on more straightforward musical and other entertainments, and subsequent advertisements ceased to mention steamer trips.

Author's Collection

Whitsuntide at Ilfracombe 1907

Through study of the Ilfracombe newspapers from the 1880s into the years just before the Great War one can see how through the eyes of 'Combeites a sort of barometric indication was portrayed of what the Bristol Channel excursion steamers were doing year by year. Bigger and better vessels were successively introduced, and the resort expanded its accommodation and offerings in correlation with ever-growing visitor numbers, by sea and by rail. The weather played a large part in visitor numbers on a day by day basis, but the underlying trend was distinctly upwards and the Barry Railway Company was, perhaps, doing no more than seeking a share for itself of this healthy, expanding market. The *Ilfracombe Gazette*, the paper loyal to the Campbell cause, was able to report, practically every year from the 1890s onwards, that each one broke previous records, and occasionally quoted numbers of folk passing the pier turnstiles to prove the assertions made.

Whitsuntide in 1907 seems to have fitted the pattern, despite unexceptional weather conditions, being basically dry and mainly sunny, but cool. On Friday 24th May, 1907 the report of Whit Monday happenings was more than usually voluble, and after describing how the trains had brought in over 4,000 holidaymakers from London and 1,290 from Barnstaple, went on to describe how

> . . . the steamers simply poured people on the pier all day. The magnificent white-funnelled steamers of Messrs P. & A. Campbell, and the fine steamer the *Brighton*, belonging to Messrs Pocketts, being great favourites . . . during the day the steamers ran excursions to Lundy Island to see the wrecked *Montagu* . . .

On the Saturday of the Bank Holiday it was stated that ' . . . no fewer than ten boat-loads of holidaymakers landed on our Pier . . . naturally infusing a considerable amount of new life into the town . . .' There was still no explicit mention here of the part the Red Funnel Line steamers were playing in this buoyant economic activity in North Devon, of course, and it was only a matter of weeks before the same paper would be carrying lengthy reports, in minute detail, of how the great legal case was proceeding, there being little doubt whose side the *Gazette* had always been on. The picture was, naturally, painted rather differently in South Wales and especially so in Barry.

The summer of 1907

Spring was giving way to early summer and I make no apology here for including in full the most fanciful quote by Mrs Grundy which I discovered whilst researching this book. It seems to me to encapsulate the whole, brief climax of the steamship business of the valiant Barry Railway Company when it thought defeat of the Campbell brothers was imminent, as delivery of its fourth ship was awaited. These words were published on Friday 31st May,1907:

Last Sunday evening I sat on Friars Point at the Island, and gazed down Channel to the wide Atlantic. Suddenly, as if by magic, my hitherto clear view of the Devon hills became obscure, and a huge cloud of mist glided silently across the rippling waters. On and on it came till the Island, then the town, and the country to the north of Barry was enveloped. Sunday night passed and Monday morning arrived, but still we were enshrouded in nature's thick veil. However, not for long. King Sol broke through, and before many had rubbed their eyes we were in a world of sunshine, and the merry song of the birds told us that summer had really come.

A week later, the new steamer *Barry* had arrived at its eponymous home port and Mrs Grundy had reverted to her more usual, matter of fact style, stating that the ship had arrived on Wednesday 5th June and was berthed in the Basin on the following day for inspection. She added that the steamer would run summer and winter between Barry and 'places on the other side of the Channel', that it would run its first trip in the course of a few days, and that it had a red funnel with a white band and a black top. After considerable scrutiny of all the evidence, it is by no means clear that the Barry Railway Company exactly knew what to do with their new charge - there had been no start of work at Burnham, the new Grand Pier at Weston now appeared to be an operational impossibility, and their three other ships at Cardiff were handling traffic quite capably - and the hearing in the Court of Chancery was due to restart in a few days time. But the outcome of this was still unkown, so perhaps the climax for the Barry's maritime adventure was really still to come, when four vessels were in operation in the Summer of 1907 and before the outcome of the long-running legal saga was established.

But this is to jump ahead a little from the maiden voyage of *Barry*, which took place - from Barry rather than from Cardiff this time! - on Saturday 15th June, 1907. An advertisement in the *Western Mail* newspaper on the preceding day finally revealed details of the schedules she would offer which consisted, during her first week in service, of a variety of trips solely from Barry Pier but promoted as all being by connecting train from Cardiff Riverside. Oddly enough, the description of the maiden voyage of *Barry* carried in the *Western Mail* was more lucid than that in the *Barry Dock News*, so I have chosen to reproduce the former:

THE STEAMER *BARRY*
NEW WESTON & MINEHEAD SERVICE INAUGURATED

The Barry Railway Company's new steamer *Barry*, which is to ply between Cardiff, Barry, Weston & Minehead, made her first run on Saturday morning, during miserable weather. This fact explains the circumstance that the public was not strongly in attendance, but the few members of the press who were the guests of the company for the run had every occasion to be delighted with the accommodations. The boat is an improved *Gwalia*, with a length of 225 ft. and 26.5 ft. beam, and a speed of 17.5 knots, capable of being pushed to 22 knots in emergency. She has accommodation for 897 passengers for the local run, or 500 for Ilfracombe, and her saloon and dining-room equipments are the latest thing, and superior to those of any other steamer of her size in the Channel service. The catering is in the hands of Messrs Culley & Co. and in every way sustains the reputation of that concern.

The *Barry*, it may be explained in extension of the foregoing details, is one of the finest and fleetest vessels of her size and class ever constructed, it being entirely unusual to find a vessel of such necessarily light draft capable of acquiring such a speed; but she is a beauty from a builders' standpoint. In addition to racerlike lines of hull her sponson lines (those outside the paddle boxes) are very finely sheered, and this facilitates her getting alongside the piers and other landings without bumping. She has only one funnel, and her upper deck gives a clear promenade of 215 ft. Her spacious main saloon is sumptuously upholstered in bluey-green utrecht velvet, and her first-class dining-saloon, which is mechanically ventilated, and is as light and airy withal as a conservatory, is as sumptuous as that on an American liner. The second-class dining-saloon, without being quite so elaborate as its opposite number aft, is far superior to the first-class saloons on the majority of boats. The retiring accommodation, ladies saloons & c., are exceptionally well appointed, and the ship has no appreciable vibration. In fine, the *Barry* is a distinct acquisition to the Bristol Channel service.

The *Barry* was built by Messrs John Brown & Co. of Clydebank. Her engines, 1,500 i.h.p., are of the compound diagonal type. Her Commander is Captain G. Ayland (formerly of the *Devonia*); chief engineer, Mr J. Heathcote; chief steward Mr H. Frape.

The honours of the occasion were performed on Saturday by Mr W. H. Lake on behalf of his father Mr E. Lake, the general manager of the Barry Railway Company. Details as to the time schedule of the new boat will be found in our advertising columns.

The standard 'textbooks' which deal with the history of Bristol Channel excursion steamers have never provided what I regard as a sufficiently detailed explanation of just what it was that the new ship *Barry* actually did to earn her living when first introduced. Duckworth & Langmuir refer vaguely to a 'triangular' service between Barry, Minehead and Weston, and Grahame Farr does not really state anything explicitly about her duties other than noting that Burnham Pier never actually got built. It was thus rather odd to discover, on looking up in the aforementioned 'advertising columns' for excursion sailings from Cardiff in the *Western Mail* newspaper for Friday 14th June, 1907, to see that a new 'block' had been added, entitled thus:

COMMENCEMENT OF REGULAR SERVICE BETWEEN CARDIFF (RIVERSIDE STN.)
& WESTON, MINEHEAD & CLEVEDON via Barry Pier,
in connection with the passenger saloon steamer *BARRY*

	ex-Riverside	*Steamer leaves WSM*	*Minehead*	*Clevedon*
June 15th	6.25, 8.35, 10.20 *am* (M), 3.42 *pm*	8.10, 10.20 *am*, 6.10 *pm*	12.40 *pm*	
June 17th	6.25, 8.35, 11.05 *am* (W&M), 4.23 *pm*	8.10, 10.30 *am*, 2.45, 6.15 *pm*	1.15 *pm*	
June 18th	6.25, 8.35, 11.05 *am*, 1.05 *pm*	8.10, 10.30 *am*, 2.45, 6.15 *pm*		
June 19th	6.25, 8.35, 11.05 *am*, 1.52 *pm* (W&C)	8.10, 10.30 *am*, 12.45, 8.45 *pm*		7. 50 *pm*
June 20th	8.35, 11.05 *am*, 1.52 *pm* (W&M)	10.30 *am*, 1.00 *pm*	5.30 *pm*	
June 21st	8.35, 11.05 *am* (M), 1.52 *pm* (W&M)	10.30 *am*	12.45, 6.30 *pm*	

Notes
M - to Minehead, W&M - to Weston & Minehead, W&C - to Weston and Clevedon.
Other train departures from Cardiff (Riverside) for Weston only.

Wholly in addition to the range of Red Funnel Line sailings from Cardiff, here then was a mixture of additional trips between Barry and Weston, Barry and Minehead, and Barry and Clevedon, all promoted as an extension of (and in connection with) train departures from Cardiff (Riverside) station to Barry Pier, as an integrated rail & steamer service. The advertisement claimed that the services offered were regular, but a glance at the day-to-day variations rapidly confirms that there may have been a discrete number of train departure times from Riverside, but no two days were actually alike in that first week! Whilst the reason for this lack of regularity was simple - there was still no tidally-unconstrained berth at Weston-super-Mare - it is difficult to think that the travelling public would have been greatly impressed by this offering. Although regular services could have been offered to Clevedon and to Minehead, where both piers ran out far enough to cater for all but extremes of low water, there was not deemed to be sufficient demand to warrant those places commanding all the attention *Barry* could have given them.

Weston folk, if wishing to get to Cardiff, would still have no particular reason to go via Barry in order then to catch the train, there was simply no time or cost advantage. One can just about see where the notion of triangularity came from, as certain sailings proceeded from Barry to Minehead via Weston, and returned directly from Minehead to Barry, but there really was no discernible pattern whatever. Matters continued like this for a few weeks, and the promised Burnham Pier venture still did not take off. Events were, however, wholly to overtake these attempts by the Barry Railway Company to stimulate more rail traffic through Barry Pier station on to its own new paddle steamer *Barry*.

The climax comes

But before the climax of Barry Railway Company steamer affairs happened, another interesting development was taking shape. On the same day as the first advertisement for sailings on the new *Barry* was placed another stated that either *Gwalia* or *Devonia* would, on Friday 21st June, 1907 - Midsummer's Day - run all the way from Barry Pier to Penzance and the Isles of Scilly. Such ambitious enterprise points towards what might have been a new dimension in the Bristol Channel where the competition between White Funnel and Red Funnel interests spurred on more diverse trips of a different nature to basic day excursion opportunities, if only occasionally. A special train departure from Cardiff Riverside was to connect into an 11.00 am departure from Barry Pier to Ilfracombe and Penzance, with arrival there at around 8.00 pm. There would be a departure at 10.00 am on the Saturday to St Mary's in the Isles of Scilly, returning from there at 3.30 pm. Sunday was not mentioned (sailings in the Bristol Channel were still not normally offered on Sundays at this time), and the return time on Monday 24th June was fixed at 7.30 am from Penzance to Ilfracombe and Barry Pier, all for a return fare between Cardiff and Penzance of 20 shillings, not including meals or accommodation. Equally enterprising was the mention of an arrangement with the operators of the paddle-steamer *Normandy* (then competing for the Swansea excursion trade with Pockett's *Brighton*) for passengers to leave Swansea (West Pier) at 9.30 am on the Friday for Ilfracombe to connect into the Red Funnel Line steamer for Penzance, returning on the Monday at 5.30 pm from Ilfracombe to Swansea. It was later reported that this trip had been run very successfuly by *Gwalia*, and been blessed by particularly fine weather, which had not been commonplace during the 1907 season up to that point.

Whilst Penzance and the Isles of Scilly were exceptional destinations as far as the voyagings of the White Funnel Fleet were concerned (*Britannia* had visited

This view commemorated the Royal Visit to Cardiff in 1907, in connection with the opening of the new Queen Alexandra Dock, in which the Barry vessels played an important part. *Westonia* can be seen here, berthed prominently at Cardiff's Pier Head, alongside *The Marchioness* and probably *Gwalia* which, with the then newly-delivered *Barry*, accompanied the Royal Yacht.

Lionel Vaughan Collection

A delightful view of *Barry* proceeding along the River Avon close to centre of Bristol, and very much in the enemy Campbell heartlands. Possibly taken for publicity purposes when new in 1907, as she wears the distinctive white band on her funnel which unequivocally declared her Barry Railway Company ownership before the lawsuit had run its course.

Lionel Vaughan Collection

in her first year 1896, and again on occasions since then), the attractive little Cornish port of St Ives represented an occasional destination for a 'Special Excursion', as these were known, typically from Cardiff and Ilfracombe. The passage time from Ilfracombe to Newquay on the more commonplace trips to that North Cornwall port was around 3¼ hours, whereas it took rather longer from Ilfracombe to St Ives, more like 4½ hours. On occasions a P. & A. Campbell Ltd boat for Newquay might leave Bristol at three or four in the morning and pause for an hour or two at Ilfracombe, then to punch the tide to arrive in Cornwall with sufficient water to land passengers by launch. It was perhaps only natural therefore that the Red Funnel Line would seek to promote trips from Cardiff to St Ives as well. One such was advertised for Friday 19th July, 1907, and exploited the considerable advantage of being able to leave Barry Pier at the not too unconvivial time of 6.30, after the arrival of a 6.00 am connecting train from Cardiff Riverside. The tides could in this manner be overcome by the Barry Railway Company, as high water that day was at 12.09 am and 12.37 pm at Cardiff, rendering such a trip impractical if not actually impossible from there. This particular excursion was advertised to give 2½ hours ashore at St Ives, for a fare of 7*s*. 6*d*. Mrs Grundy duly reported that a good time was had by all:

> The passenger steamer *Devonia*, of the Red Funnel Line (Barry) with between 500 & 600 passengers on board, had a most enjoyable and successful trip to St. Ives last Friday, leaving Barry at 6.30, and after calling at Ilfracombe, reached St Ives about 2 o'clock. The run both ways was delightful.

A lot was going on for the Red Funnel Line at this time, and I think the true climax for the Barry Railway Company steamships venture can be said to have taken place in the second half of July 1907. On Saturday 13th July, 1907 there was the magnificient occasion of the opening of the new Queen Alexandra Dock at Cardiff, attended by HM King Edward VII and Queen Alexandra, who came to Cardiff on their Royal Yacht. This event attracted massive crowds and fulsome reports of the occasion are to be found in the *Western Mail* newspaper. One should not understate the enormity of this undertaking - works had commenced as far back as 1898, and around 52 acres of water were enclosed, the dock being designed for general import traffic as well as the staple export coal for which the most modern type of new coaling cranes were installed. A general holiday was declared throughout the city and it is recorded that over 100,000 spectators watched the event. I have extracted just one small but pertinent paragraph to convey the symbolic importance of this event insofar as the Barry Railway Company was concerned, when its new ship *Barry* did indeed occupy the prime position of importance and status. Here was a locally-owned ship, of a powerful local Welsh railway company, reigning supreme at what was a major event for Cardiff, and no Bristol-influenced interloper was going to wrest the crown on this occasion! The report emphasised that first the brand new *Barry*, and then *Gwalia* were in the forefront of the proceedings:

Another nice view of *Barry,* this time lying off Clovelly, on a day when she might well have taken the 'railway run' in high summer when it was customary to run down beyond Ilfracombe to the quaint little fishing village. Note the number of small boats needed to handle the hundreds of passengers which were common on good days on such excursions.

Lionel Vaughan Collection

It was a special occasion when, on Wednesday 24th July, 1907 the still new *Barry* made a visit to the historic port of Watchet in Somerset. This postcard was credited to Bert Hole, of Watchet. The port has a different appearance nowadays as commercial maritime activity has ceased, and a new marina has been constructed inside the harbour. Occasional calls by the preserved motor vessel *Balmoral* are, however, still made at the section of harbour wall illustrated here.

Ken Jenkins Collection

EXUBERANT WELCOME BY CARDIFF STEAMERS

. . . In the van of this maritime cavalcade the Barry Railway Company's new steamer *Barry* rode joyous in her pride of place. She was crowded, as all the other local steamers were, with loyal citizens of Cardiff and its environment, all hungering to be among the first to cheer and welcome to their rulers. Like all the other boats too, she was smothered in a dazzling display of bunting. (After *Barry* were *Gwalia*, then *Cambria* and *Ravenswood*.) . . . [The report continued - humorously in my opinion - by mentioning the catering arrangements on *Barry*] . . . they went below with appetites whetted by the sea breeze, and tucked into a menu which was so alluring in its excellence that many of them entirely missed the main item of the subsequent spectacle.

Mr Thompson would have been on board his new ship *Barry* that day, and rightly been an immensely proud man - he had brought the Barry Railway Company maritime vision to life, and here was the crowning glory for himself and his fellow Directors on a truly momentuous occasion. But he was not alone in his moment of triumph, for the Bristol enemy had naturally arranged its sailings that day so as to participate too, even reducing Cardiff-Weston ferry sailings to a single vessel to free *Ravenswood* to support *Cambria* so as not to be outnumbered by the Welsh rivals. Ominously, the legal proceedings had now restarted, and Peter and Alec Campbell, doubtless on board their vessels bringing up the rear at this admittedly Cardiff-centred event, were probably having very different thoughts to those of their Welsh adversaries; who was going to be proved right in the Court of Chancery?

But before dealing with this major event, it is worth briefly stating how the Barry Railway Company now utilised its four-strong fleet of paddle-steamers, three of which were billed as constituting the Red Funnel Line and offered excursions primarily from Cardiff, whilst the fourth and newest vessel *Barry* was clearly promoted as running rail-connected sailings from Barry unambiguously in the name of the railway company. Barry Pier was accessible at all states of the tide, but Weston-super-Mare still lacked this facility. Thus, during the week commencing on Saturday 20th July, 1907, the pattern was for *Westonia* to normally offer four or five round trips daily (Sundays excepted) between Cardiff and Weston, usually serving Penarth. It was customary for two round trips to operate between Cardiff and Ilfracombe on Saturdays, with an afternoon boat augmenting the fixed-time 'railway run' morning sailing. During that subsequent week, the Ilfracombe boat was extended to Clovelly on three occasions, and to Lundy on two occasions: the wreck of HMS *Montagu* was still attracting the crowds. Whichever of *Gwalia* and *Devonia* was not on the 'railway run' offered various trips to Clevedon, sometimes to Bristol, and when necessary augmented Weston 'ferry' runs. On Monday 22nd July, 1907 an afternoon cruise out of Minehead, passing Porlock & Glenthorne, was offered after a Cardiff-Weston-Minehead run. Down at Barry Pier itself, *Barry* would typically run two or three rail-connected Weston trips most days, some days crossing to Minehead too. Wednesday 24th July, 1907 was quite exceptional, as Weston was unserved by her that day, and after a second Barry-Minehead run *Barry* was then billed to proceed to Watchet, departing from there at 7.45 and returning from Minehead to Barry at 9.00 pm.

The great legal battle

Just days before this grand event, there is evidence that Mr Thompson and his fellow Barry Railway Company Directors had indeed been taking the impending court case seriously. Although the Red Funnel Line had been legally constituted back in February 1907, the Port of Cardiff registry records show that it was not until 8th July, 1907 that the supposed ownership of the three steamers *Gwalia, Devonia* and *Westonia* was transferred to that body from the four gentlemen - albeit mortgaged to the Metropolitan Bank - comprising the syndicate. One infers from this that Mr Thompson thought it likely that evidence would be called for by the Judge in the hearing, but it seems remarkable that he and his colleagues had left it so long to make these changes. The case was only to focus on these three vessels, as *Barry* had been quite openly registered in the name of the Barry Railway Company directly, with the Company Secretary Mr W. Mein designated as the managing owner. What was about to be tested in law was this - P. & A. Campbell Ltd asserted that the Barry Railway Company was the true owner of the three vessels, that the Red Funnel Line was bogus, and that the operation of the three steamers was therefore *ultra vires,* and that it was entitled to seek to have this illegality stopped. For its part, the defendant Barry Railway Company denied the deception, and claimed that the steamer operation was quite above board. What this meant in practice was that it hinged very much on whether the Barry boats were at liberty to trade out of Cardiff: this was where the traffic was, and where revenue was to be had. Barry Pier itself was, in one sense, an irrelevance, just somewhere to call at as a backstop when tides at Cardiff were adverse. The new *Barry* was another distraction for the time being, having been ordered in haste before it was clear that a proper role existed for her.

The hearings lasted through most of July 1907, with a number of adjournments. I have said earlier that the key feature which bedevilled the research for this story was the absence of an actual judgement which could simply be quoted here. But the newspapers treated it all seriously, none less so than the *Ilfracombe Gazette,* and over a period of three weeks in July 1907 their readers could ponder over the arguments and counter arguments as the adversaries and their expensive lawyers battled it out, all reported in detail. After the first two weeks it seemed that the case was evenly balanced between the anguish of the Campbell brothers at the loss their business was sustaining against the predictable Barry attitude that it was at liberty to trade through a linked organisation, the 1904 Act and its terms thus being deemed irrelevant.

In the third week of the trial, matters took a different turn and rumours circulated that an out of court settlement between the parties was going to be reached. Finally, after much to-ing and fro-ing, it looked like the Barry Railway Company was about to concede that it had lost the battle. Despite its protestations and posturing, it became apparent that the Welsh railway company agreed it would trade within the terms of the 1904 Act, having been obliged to admit that the three steamers were the Barry's - it had paid for them, the Red Funnel Line was indeed an alias, and so it had little choice but to capitulate. It had been a long drawn-out fight, but one key piece of evidence that may have swung the verdict was the admission that when John Brown and Co. had been pressing for payments for the construction of *Gwalia* and *Devonia*, it was the Barry Railway Company that had paid them, irrespective of any supposed existence of intermediaries. The Welsh railway company thus looked rather sheepish when the legal proceedings had ended, and the plaintiff P. & A. Campbell Ltd was awarded costs against it, just to make the point quite clear.

The practical consequence of all this was very simple: the Barry steamers were henceforth obliged to stick within the terms of the 1904 Act, and had to cease trading out of Cardiff. This restriction was to take effect at the end of July 1907. Some magnanimity was shown by P. & A. Campbell Ltd when agreeing to this date, around 10 days after the actual cessation of the legal proceeding, as handbills and other publicity material had already been published for the whole of that month. It is important to reiterate that no actual judgement had been given by Judge Swinfen-Eady, who had been involved in this case for around two years by this time. Perhaps he was glad it had ended, as it is clear from the newspapers of the time that he had been particularly annoyed at the delaying tactics of the Barry Railway Company when he had ordered the production of certain items of evidence. But a victory for the Campbell brothers it most certainly was, and Mr Thompson and his colleagues can only have been utterly dismayed at the prospect now ahead of them. This equated to the significant liability of a short piece of railway, a pier and four paddle-steamers that now had very little prospect of carrying worthwhile volumes of traffic if access to the Pier Head at Cardiff - and its huge hinterland - was now to be denied.

Handling the crisis

It is very probable that after this milestone outcome of the long-running legal battle neither side could immediately predict exactly how passenger demand would be affected - after all, if the services of the Red Funnel Line were really that popular surely some loyalty would enter the equation with Cardiff folk simply getting the train to Barry Pier instead to start their sea journey rather than embarking at the Pier Head at Cardiff? It is highly probable that there would have been confusion at Cardiff during the first few days of August, as the newspaper advertisements throughout the week commencing Monday 22nd July, 1907 still referred to the established arrangements, but also separately advertised services by *Barry* by rail from Cardiff Riverside - as it were - to join that vessel at Barry Pier. Mrs Grundy predictably made light of the great blow received by her local railway company, stating on Friday 26th July, 1907 that

> . . . the litigation which has been proceeding for some time between the Red and White Funnel Passenger Steamship Companies has been settled this week. The Red Funnel steamers will, of course, continue to run but from Barry, within the prescribed limits.

This statement presupposed that her readers were familiar with the terms of 1904 Act, which seems a little unlikely. A week later the *Barry Dock News* was somewhat more explicit, stating the following:

This shot of *Gwalia* in the River Avon nicely illustrates the threat to the P. & A. Campbell Ltd undertaking which was based at Bristol - another company, which could afford handsome, well-found new steamers was trading outside its legal limits, in prime White Funnel Fleet territory. Until the legal settlement in 1907, the Barry company was basically saying, we will sail our ships where we please! *Lionel Vaughan Collection*

In a similar vein, a well-laden *Devonia* steams away from the Pier Head at Cardiff, with a couple of White Funnel Fleet vessels visible at the other berths. The Red Funnel Line vessels were obliged to withdraw from Cardiff after the end of July 1907. *Lionel Vaughan Collection*

BARRY CHANNEL PASSENGER STEAMERS

The four steamers *Gwalia, Devonia, Westonia* and *Barry*, will in future ply between Barry, Bristol, Clevedon, Weston, Minehead, Lynmouth, Ilfracombe, Lundy, Tenby, Swansea, Port Talbot & Briton Ferry. All tickets will be available on any one of the steamers. Boat season-ticket holders can obtain 3rd class return tickets to Barry Pier at Clarence Road, Riverside and Cogan stations, free on presentation of their season tickets at the booking offices. Boat coupons will be honoured at Clarence Road, Riverside and Cogan stations as well as on the four steamers.

The *Western Mail* newspaper advertisements changed their format from Monday 29th July, 1907, boldly stating that there would now be a 'SPECIAL BOAT TRAIN FROM RIVERSIDE STATION via Barry Pier, at 9.35 daily, at same fares as from Cardiff Pier Head, Steamer leaves Barry Pier 10.10'. In reality this train had always run anyway, but doubtless now required a few extra carriages to cater for passengers who would have been accustomed to embarking at Cardiff Pier Head on those days - typically 11 or 12 out of every 14 - when the tides permitted the customary 9.30 am sailing time from there to Barry Pier and Ilfracombe. But this was clearly to be a transitional phase.

A couple of days later it was felt necessary by the Red Funnel Line to reassure passengers that the altered arrangements at Cardiff would not penalise them on fares. On Wednesday 31st July, 1907, the final day on which the Barry steamers sailed from the Pier Head at Cardiff as a result of the ban imposed by the Court of Chancery settlement, the established 'Excursions' advertisements section in the *Western Mail* finally ceased to refer to Red Funnel Line departures and it was instead announced that: 'THERE WILL BE NO INCREASE IN FARES BY THE RED FUNNEL STEAMERS. All sailings will be carried out from Cardiff Riverside by train . . .'

The timing of the legal settlement could scarcely have been more embarassing for Mr Thompson and his fellow Directors as the half-yearly shareholders' meeting took place on 2nd August, 1907. Whilst there could be no denial that things had changed drastically, yet it was too soon for satisfactory answers to be given to those difficult and vocal shareholders who could now rightly say that they had warned that the steamship venture would prove calamitous. An admission was made that *Barry* had just cost the railway company £24,300, and that £9,000 had been spent in connection with the promotion of the Parliamentary proceedings for the proposed Burnham Pier venture. This would all be lost, it was opined by one Mr E.P. Clarke, who was effectively told to shut up and to leave it to the Directors.

The Barry Railway Company defeated

To have been forced to reach this humiliating settlement with the plaintiff P. & A. Campbell Ltd was scarcely a satisfactory state of affairs for the defendant railway company. After an expensive legal battle lasting over two years, the origins of which went back almost a further decade when the Barry Railway Company initially sought its Parliamentary Powers, things did not now look good. The trial proceedings as published in the local newspapers allow one to infer that the reluctance of the Barry Railway Company to produce the evidence sought by the Judge was a factor in the eventual decision to settle rather than allowing the case to go to a ruling in the Court of Chancery. Both parties' lawyers must have been involved in heated discussions as the trial proceeded fitfully with adjournments, but it must be said that the Campbell brothers had never publicly wavered in their view that the Barry Railway Company was behaving illegally. Right was therefore on their side, the public would have perceived, but the actual details underpinning exactly how the settlement was arrived at are difficult to pin down precisely.

In the final analysis, the railway company had ordered and paid for the vessels and whether or not the Red Funnel Line truly existed in any practical sense was questionable. It will be recalled that this company had been set up as late as February 1907, well after the introduction of Red Funnel Line steamer excursions in the Spring of 1905. Perhaps the most damning actual evidence against the Barry Railway Company had lain in the Port of Cardiff ships registry documents; the 'transactions' sections for *Gwalia*, *Devonia* and *Westonia* which showed that it was very much a last-minute action, in July 1907, that these vessels were re-registered from the supposed ownership of the four gentlemen comprising the syndicate (effectively the nominees of the Barry Railway Company) to that of the Red Funnel Line Ltd, trading from the Merchants Exchange at Cardiff. Whilst in syndicate ownership, with Mr Symonds as the designated 'Managing Owner', the Port of Cardiff transactions referred to a mortgage from the Metropolitan Bank of London, which was discharged on 8th July, 1907, the date of transfer to the 'new' company which had been set up for the purpose earlier that year.

The newspaper reports were silent on such unglamorous details as those involving ships registry, but I think it reasonable to assume that it was not until the last phase of the legal battle was underway that Mr Thompson conceded that, finally, he would have to do something tangible as evidence was going to be demanded by Judge Swinfen-Eady. The Barry Railway Company thus virtually condemned itself by this eleventh-hour device - it practically amounted to an admission of deception. Down in Ilfracombe, there was little or no press comment about the way things had turned out, and ships of both hues of funnel continued to arrive at the harbour and disgorge large numbers of excursionists and holidaymakers upon whom the local economy largely depended. As the month of August passed, it might have seemed in South Wales that little had really altered and, on Friday 16th August, 1907 Mrs Grundy noted that:

> The recent decision of the High Court, in the case of the rival Bristol Channel pleasure boat services appears not to have greatly affected the Red Funnel Line. The boat trains are almost daily crowded, and the Barry boats are well patronised by the general public of Cardiff and the hill districts.

There had been buoyant traffic on the August Bank Holiday Monday, 5th August, 1907, the *Western Mail* stating that 10,000 passengers had been taken across the Channel that day. A variety of special excursions continued to be offered by the Red Funnel Line, one such being a 3.10 pm departure from Barry

Pier (with connecting train from Cardiff) to Porthcawl, returning from there at 7 pm, on Friday 9th August, 1907, for a fare of two shillings . Later in the month there was a trip offered on Friday 30th August, 1907 at 10.00 am from Barry Pier to Penarth Roads, to follow the Pilot Cutters Race to the finish. A subsequent report of this cruise said how pleasant the weather was, and that the nine competitors were becalmed - and regrettably failed to mention which steamer took the trip. Curiously there were a number of Red Funnel Line trips advertised from Cardiff Riverside (by train) and Barry Pier to the newly-opened Grand Pier at Weston-super-Mare, which offered only a very short time ashore there, mostly little more than an hour. One, on Saturday 21st September, was a little bolder with a 2.32 pm train departure from Cardiff (Riverside) and return from the Grand Pier at 8.15 pm: this possibly gave more like three or four hours at the lavish new pier. The tide predicted that day was the biggest of the month, 32 ft 10 in. at Bristol, at 7.05 pm, so by leaving Barry Pier at around 3.15 and arriving off Weston at about 4.00 pm the Barry boat could await the first opportunity gingerly to get alongside the new Grand Pier Landing Stage on the flood, and still be safe if it got away not much more than an hour into the ebb. No comparable White Funnel Fleet trips to Weston-super-Mare Grand Pier were offered at this time: but then the Barry Railway Company now had more steamers on its hands than it perhaps knew what do with outside of peak times.

The end of the turbulent season of 1907 was fast approaching and drama unfolded on board *Gwalia* on the evening of Saturday 21st September, 1907 as she returned up-Channel from Ilfracombe to Barry. Accidents on board Bristol Channel excursion steamers over the years had, mercifully, been few and far between and the heroic rescue of a would-be possible suicide naturally attracted very considerable press attention. The *Western Mail* headlines on Monday 23rd September, 1907 thus read as follows:

CLUNG TO THE ROCKS
BRISTOL CHANNEL SENSATION
BARRY MAN LEAPS FROM A STEAMER
GIVEN UP FOR LOST, BUT FOUND ALIVE

The article went on to decribe how the passenger, George Archibald Wood, aged 24, employed as a painter with the Barry Railway Company, deliberately jumped overboard, after a day spent at Ilfracombe, leaving there at dusk. Drink was not explicitly mentioned but a number of unruly men on board had given cause to the Captain for concern. Wood was said to have semi-stripped, and then jumped overboard. The aft jolly-boat was lowered, and the ships searchlights were used for 40 minutes. Meanwhile *Gwalia* drifted down channel 1½ miles. Everyone assumed that Wood had been lost, and the Red Funnel Line Managing Director W.T. Symonds said that this was the first Red Funnel boats' fatality. It became apparent in Barry, however, on Sunday morning from a telephone call that Wood had been rescued at Lynton, unconscious. Wood's widowed mother had been informed and naturally was tearful. The Foreland lightkeeper had heard yells, but had been unable to descend himself to assist, and so alerted the Lynmouth Coastguard station. After his rescuers had rowed

A view of a well-laden *Barry*, after the white band on the funnel had gone.

Lionel Vaughan Collection

All four Barry steamers seen together in the Basin at Barry Dock, looking from the *Lady Windsor* entrance-lock towards Barry No. 2 Dock., possibly after the end of the 1907 season.

Brian Luxton Collection

round the Foreland, Wood was soon spotted. He had narrowly escaped being washed out to sea and, it was thought, and might have been caught in a backwash of ebbing tide. By Sunday afternoon he was said to be recovering.

In a further report on Tuesday 24th September, 1907 Wood recounted how he had swam from *Gwalia* and scaled the rocks off the Foreland. After coming home to Barry on Monday evening he evidently told his friends that 'there was absolutely no premeditation in his action in quitting *Gwalia*. He felt people were annoying him, and his sole desire for the moment was to get away from them. That was why he took the plunge'. When he hit the water he said he came to, and swam, and scrabbled up rocks to a ledge 60-70 feet up. This was precarious, and his rescue had been very difficult. There had been sterling work by Coastguard Wotton and Coxswain Crocomb, who had got him to Lynmouth at about ten o'clock on the Saturday evening. Wood had been handed over to Cecil N. Bevan (the local Agent to the Shipwrecked Mariners Society), of the Lyn Valley Hotel.

After this drama, the regular 'railway run' from Barry to Lynmouth and Ilfracombe only had a few more days to run until the end of the season, the final trip being on Tuesday 1st October, 1907. A handful of other trips ran during the next few days, during one of which - on Wednesday 2nd October - *Devonia* was reported as having come into contact with a piece of wreckage on passage from Ilfracombe back to Barry at night after an afternoon cruise, with about 200 passengers on board, and which delayed her by some five hours. Then it was practically all over for that year for the four steamships. The Barry Railway Company could now take stock of its maritime affairs, and it was clearly going to have to do some explaining to its shareholders. This had been skirted over at the beginning of August, but it was obvious that matters would have to be rethought. The most immediate manifestation of the great legal battle, in terms of the uncertainty it induced as well as undermining confidence in any further investments, was that there was no progress at Burnham towards construction of the grand new pier that had been proposed, and for which authority to proceed was now available. That it did not proceed at all was now not surprising - and so the rashness of having procured a smart new fourth steamer *Barry* for the purpose of linking Barry and Burnham was even more apparent.

A second phase had thus ended, and whilst the Barry Railway Company's affairs may have been seen to have been in the ascendant from the point in 1904 where John Brown & Co. Ltd of Clydebank had taken the order for two rather splendid paddle-steamers with which they could challenge the established Bristol operator, a peak had now been reached, and the trend was going to be inexorably downwards. What happened in 1908 is properly the subject of a third phase of the red-funnelled steamers, but for the moment there was little that Mr Thompson and his colleagues could do but lick their wounds, and perhaps pretend that still they could fight back.

Passengers on board *Barry*, with some of the catering crew visible. *Lionel Vaughan Collection*

Passengers on board *Barry*, with detail of the navigating bridge visible.
Lionel Vaughan Collection

Phase Three: Perseverance, 1908/09

If any firm of monopolists imagine that they are going to succeed in closing an important part of the Works and Undertakings of the Barry Railway Company, and that the Barry Railway Company are willing to allow the public to be placed at the mercy of any monopolists, so far as a Sea Passenger Service in this Channel is concerned, they have, in my opinion, formed a very improper estimate of the nature of the conflict which they have entered upon; and I shall be very much surprised, and disappointed, if any bona-fide Shareholder of the Barry Company will approve and endorse the treatment which we received throughout this business.

T.R.Thompson, Director, Barry Railway Company, 7th February, 1908

The stormy shareholders' meeting

One of the more remarkable pieces of evidence that shed light on what had really been going on in the early years of the Barry steamers was the transcript of what took place at the 47th half-yearly meeting of shareholders, which was held at the offices of the Barry Railway Company at Barry Docks on Friday 7th February, 1908. The Right Hon. The Earl of Plymouth was in the chair. Earlier copies of the Reports and Accounts for a number of half-yearly periods had said little or nothing about the 1899 Pier opening, the difficulties with getting P. & A. Campbell Ltd to service the new pier satisfactorily, and the build-up to the commencement in 1905 of the Barry's own shipping venture. This was not too surprising in view of the element of subterfuge in the steamships venture, yet here were four, closely-printed sides of A3 text which - with a fair amount of scrutiny and cross-referencing to other sources - suddenly seemed to explain most of the underlying story of what had truly been going on for the previous decade. The Chairman had opened the proceedings, and explained that Mr Thompson would give a full account of the steamships venture: he also loftily stated that the formal position of the Board then was that they were still considering the decision of the Court of Chancery - and that had been as long ago as July 1907!

They were still intending to make a success of the provision for passenger steamers at Barry Pier, and in a swipe at one Lieut Col E.P. Clark who six months earlier had sought detailed information on the running of the steamers, and been rebuffed by the Board, the Chairman described that gentleman's financial interest in the company as being of insufficient size to be of any real influence on whatever decisions they, the Board, might make. Lieut Col E.P. Clark persisted with his questioning on such matters as expenses connected with the promotion of Burnham Pier, and failed to draw any constructive response from the Board. The language was reasonably courteous, but the message was clear: the Directors of the Barry Railway Company knew best. Later on in the meeting, as the Lieut Col continued to protest, Mr Thompson interrupted him to scathingly silence his criticisms, thus:

> . . . I must compliment you on the keen interest you take, and if every holder of £175 Consolidated 4% preference stock would pay such close attention to the affairs of this Company we should be materially assisted.

After Mr Thompson rose to address the shareholders the essence of what he had had to say described the rationale by which the Barry Railway Company had got involved in a steamship operation in the first place. The original expectation had been that if they built the pier facility at Barry then, surely, an operator of steamships would come forward to provide the services, thus avoiding any capital exposure of the railway in purchasing ships themselves. It is fair to recall that at the time the idea of Barry Pier was conceived, there were two big operators at Cardiff, with the locally-owned Edwards, Robertson 'Yellow Funnel Fleet' competing with the growing P. & A. Campbell Ltd presence in South Wales. But the former had rapidly succumbed to the latter and so, when Barry Pier eventually opened in 1899, there were only really the ships of the White Funnel Fleet to serve it - a monopoly force, as Mr Thompson put it, and which he had feared from the outset. The substance of his present argument to the shareholders was that they should wait longer to let the business become properly established because, in the six seasons from 1899-1904 inclusive, the arguments with P. & A. Campbell Ltd had meant severe disruption such that for three seasons there had been no service whatever, which had not surprisingly given the Barry route a poor reputation.

> These are the people [he said] who drove the Barry Company to create other steamers to develop the Company's Excursion and other traffic . . . during the three years they blackballed the Barry Pontoon and Railways their steamers never once utilised the unrivalled facilities of the Barry Company's Low Water Pier and Pontoon, although on scores of occasions their steamers passed close in to Barry, with plenty of room on board for passengers, and as they held the monopoly of the Channel, it was a duty which they owed to the public to do so.

This was emotive language, and he went on to quote the numbers of passengers who had used Barry Pier since its opening. The increase in 1907 over 1906 was quite striking, even allowing for the fact that a fourth ship had joined the original trio, and probably lent support to his recommendation to shareholders to persevere with the operation by the Barry Railway Company in 1908 of the full fleet of four steamers despite the block on trading out of Cardiff.

1899	45,936	1902	45,791	1906	77,969
1901	50,489	1905	86,787	1907	191,403

The recorded response from shareholders was that this was really the first time that their Board had ever been more open about the steamships enterprise, and much of a surprising nature was now being revealed. Mr Thompson stated that although (for the last period of the accounts) steamship expenses at £10,434 had exceeded receipts of £8,331, leading to an apparent loss, railway passenger receipts had risen by £4,000, which he maintained was principally attributable to the steamers. Opinion from the floor was basically divided between some who felt their dividends were being dragged down, and others who were inclined to give the Board the benefit of the doubt. The withdrawal from Cardiff had been imposed late on in the previous season, and so it was perhaps still too early to judge how much a whole season restricted to just what originating traffic through Barry Pier alone might generate. The Chairman, in his concluding remarks, wholeheartedly endorsed all that Mr Thompson had said, and advised those present to wait and see - a very substantial investment had been made, and he felt it would be quite wrong to give up now. This was how matters stood, then, after the steamship question had been aired.

One matter not mentioned at this meeting was that the three 'original' vessels - *Gwalia, Devonia* and *Westonia* - which since 1905 had been registered in the supposed ownership of the Red Funnel Line, had on 23rd January, 1908 been re-registered in the name of the Barry Railway Company. William Mein, the Company Secretary, was now named as the Managing Owner. This brought them into line with the newer vessel *Barry*, which had been registered in the name of the railway company from the outset. After the legal proceedings of the previous year there was no longer any point in maintaining the pretence of independent ownership and control, but although the re-registry put right a technical anomaly the name Red Funnel Line continued for marketing purposes. At this point it is reasonable to ask what had become of the so-called Barry and Bristol Channel Steamship Company, which name had been used prior to July 1907? As far as can be ascertained, this company never actually existed in the strict sense of having been registered under the Companies Act, but it had been frequently referred to from around March 1905 onwards (just before *Gwalia* and *Devonia* were delivered from John Brown & Co. of Clydebank to Barry), and appeared on many advertisements.

Records do exist of a company called the Barry & Bristol Steam Packet & Carrying Company Ltd which was registered in July 1890 with a nominal capital of £5,000, with an address at Barry Dock. The purpose of this business had been 'to carry on the business and businesses of shipowners, hauliers, Ore, Coal, Flour, Corn, Meal, Seed, Salt and Hay Merchants'. It only lasted one year until becoming amalgamated with another company called the Barry Cooperative Building Material Company, Ltd. Crucially, the first company was wound up in 1891, but not actually dissolved within the next 12 months as was normal practice. The Board of Trade files reveal that dissolution of this company was not effected until 15th March, 1907. Is it, perhaps, too much of a coincidence that this date was so soon after the Red Funnel Line company was actually formed? Although this is speculation, one does wonder if the Barry Railway Company had somehow acquired the dormant company, and thus its name, around 1905 as its new ships were approaching completion in Scotland. This would have enabled the railway company to refer to the first part of it, loosely, as a part of the pretence to deceive its enemies P. & A. Campbell Ltd. The name Barry and Bristol Channel Steamship Company does not appear in any formal, legal sense in those places that one would expect it, such as port registry documents, and one is obliged to conclude it never truly existed. Such a conclusion fits all that was said in the legal proceedings which reached their climax, as we saw, in July 1907.

The 1908 season outlook

Mr Thompson had clearly explained the belief of his Board that despite the legal setbacks, they were undaunted and intended to continue the passenger steamship operations from Barry Pier. This would be in conjunction with the two mainstream business activities of coal traffic hauled over the Barry network by Barry locomotives, from the valleys to Barry Dock, and running the now well-developed local rail passenger services radiating from Barry to the Vale of Glamorgan, the Rhondda valley and, most importantly, to the capital city of Cardiff. By this time the Barry Railway Company network had, in truth, ceased to expand and despite huge expenditure on Parliamentary proceedings for promotion of further legislative Powers that would enable the company to expand and venture further to the north-east into Monmouthshire, no further railway building was actually to take place. Another ambition, to invest in schemes promoted by others in the west, towards Pontardawe and Brynamman, was unfulfilled.

Without the ability to trade at Cardiff, the Red Funnel Line fleet (as it was still promoted in 1908) of four paddle-steamers was obviously somewhat excessive for the trade out of Barry alone. The two ventures in Somerset were still not happening, inasmuch as the investment to create the new pier at Burnham had not happened yet, nor had Weston-super-Mare acquired the new tide-free berth which had been in the minds of both pier companies for almost a decade now. Progress at Birnbeck Pier on the 'low-water extension', as it was known, was slow

After the 1907 legal settlement the Barry steamers undertaking for a couple of years lacked the ability to trade at Cardiff. Probably taken after this critical moment, in the period 1910-1911, one P. & A. Campbell Ltd steamer (*Ravenswood*) is seen at its berth at the pontoon structures at the Pier Head whilst another (*Britannia*) has backed out and is departing, possibly for Penarth and Ilfracombe on a down-channel run. A Red Funnel Line paddler (probably *Westonia*) can just be seen, on the extreme right. There were four berths at Cardiff. Note the arrangements for handling queues of intending passengers.
H.A. Allen Collection

and, round the bay in the centre of town at the Grand Pier, it seemed highly unlikely that its promoters could ever extend the pier to the length necessary to overcome the tidal constraints as they had already committed large amounts of capital to something that was still practically unuseable. Dredging was allegedly being undertaken, and a few odd excursion steamer calls did take place in 1908. One could argue that there was only really work for two steamers out of Barry itself, one for a shuttle service to Weston as the tides permitted, and the other to run down to Ilfracombe, on the now well-established 'railway run' at 10.10 am or thereabouts every day. Taking a more generous view of the wish to cover peak traffic days and allow for contingencies, then three steamers was all that was justified, yet all four were retained, so that the brand-new *Barry* had yet to really earn her keep at all. But pride was at stake here, and selling all or part of the fleet off was not seriously considered at this stage: it was more important, it seemed, to seek to hold on to a share of the market, to try new destinations and to try and pick up originating traffic from other sources, as we shall see.

As Easter beckoned, and the start of another season, one interesting development was at Barry Island itself, and which was consistent with the steady development of that place as a resort in its own right, with expanding promenade and other seafront facilities to cater for growing day-trip traffic from the Valleys and surrounding areas. As Mrs Grundy reported in the *Barry Dock News* on Friday 24th April, 1908:

> For the convenience of passengers by the Barry Railway Company's pleasure steamers a railway bridge has been erected over the line at Barry Island Pier Station; and a footpath to the station has been formed from Redbrink Crescent . . . During the Easter holidays the passenger pleasure boats of the Barry Railway Company were well patronised, the daily trips being both successful and enjoyable. [Also noted was a new marketing initiative:] An attractive feature of the Barry Railway Company's pleasure boat service this year is the fact that for a guinea a passenger may travel 1,000 miles either by boat or rail. This handy system of travelling is immensely popular on some of the great railway systems in the US and on the Continent, and is sure to prove equally popular on the 'Red Funnel'.

A glance at a map of Barry Island (in this case one issued by P. & A. Campbell Ltd to promote its own short excursions from Barry Island some five decades after the demise of the Red Funnel Line) illustrates the first point about passenger convenience nicely. This was logical if the Barry Railway Company were to seek to attract day-trippers to Barry Island (i.e. those who were already there) on to its steamers at Barry Pier with easy pedestrian access. Rather than assume that folk already at Barry Island for a day out would bother to join a train at Barry Island station for the three or four minute trip through the tunnel to Barry Pier station, the footpath referred to provided an alternative means of accessing the pier. All in all, positive efforts were to be made in 1908 to stimulate traffic despite the constraint on sailing from the Pier Head at Cardiff.

The *Western Mail* newspaper, on Friday 17th April, 1908, had carried an advertising 'puff' for Bristol Channel cruising opportunities that Easter, both by White Funnel and Red Funnel vessels, and also mentioned the other operator of a paddle-steamer at Cardiff whose services might have been over shadowed by the more glamorous passenger excursion steamers. The item gently reminded Cardiff folk that the Red Funnel steamers had now ceased to depart from the Pier Head at Cardiff:

> The Barry Railway (Red Funnel) line also advertise a large number of trips in addition to the daily service to Weston. The *Gwalia*, which has been overhauled and re-decorated, made a trial trip to Minehead this week, and the large and influential company on board were delighted with the passage, and expressed the opinion that the steamer would surpass her previous records both in speed and comfort. The trip was conducted by Mr W.T. Symonds, the Marine Superintendent who, by his courteous and genial manner, has won much popularity for the boats he represents. Special trains run from Riverside (GWR) station to the pier at Barry Dock, and meet the boats on their return. The steamer *Marchioness* also runs whole day, afternoon and evening excursions between Cardiff and Bristol.

The 1908 season progresses

Later on in the season an attempt to secure a toehold at Swansea was made, and H.G. Owen recorded that *Devonia* ran a trip on 14th July, 1908 from Swansea and Mumbles to Ilfracombe, followed by another trip by *Barry* from Swansea to Weston on 18th July, 1908. But Pockett's had exclusive use of their centrally-sited Swansea berth, and perhaps mindful of that company being a good tenant of theirs, the Swansea Harbour Trust were disinclined to reduce their charges for ships of the Barry Railway Company to come alongside their quay wall. This, combined with practical difficulties like arranging coaling without steaming back to Barry, rendered this attempt to seek new business short-lived. Calls at Mumbles Pier were not a problem, and of course had been featuring regularly either as a destination from Barry, or as a call *en route* to Tenby on occasions during the season.

Of minor significance, but interesting in terms of evidence of seeking out fresh attractions, a trip was advertised for Friday 10th August, 1908 from Cardiff Riverside (by express train at 9.37 am) via Barry Pier to Appledore in Devon. This was probably a variant on the 'railway run' which, as in earlier years, often went beyond Ilfracombe to Clovelly or sometimes Lundy in the high season. It may have been prompted by the opening, on 1st May, 1908, of the final section of the grandly-titled Bideford, Westward Ho! and Appledore Railway between the latter two places. This was in practice a remarkably short-lived light railway, with intriguing American-styled tramcar carriages, which ran alongside Bideford Quay and went a rather long way round to reach the picturesque old port of Appledore. A big Red Funnel steamer anchored off Appledore must have presented a striking sight in the River Torridge, opposite Instow which was then the home of the Lundy sailing packet *Gannet*.

Of rather more significance was another, different attempt earn new income, from a new destination, admittedly in a one-off manner. This came about because of events over at Avonmouth, and which resurrected the big argument with P. & A. Campbell Ltd about what was and was not legal within the terms of the 1904 Act. The Port of Cardiff had had its big day the previous year, with

Cardiff-owned vessels of the Barry Railway Company in pride of place at the celebrations marking the opening of its new dock with a Royal visit. Now it was the turn of the Port of Bristol formally to open its new Royal Edward dock at Avonmouth, again with a regal presence. This was a major event for P. & A. Campbell Ltd, being on its territory this time, and it planned extensive special excursions to run on the four days Tuesday 8th July to Friday 10th July, 1908. The escort cruiser *Æolus* and the Royal Yacht were expected to arrive in Kingroad (off Avonmouth) on the Tuesday. The tidal cycle that week fitted the events perfectly, as one would indeed have expected, and trips from Bristol (by the White Funnel Fleet) to view the Royal Yacht were thus offered on the Tuesday and Wednesday, and more trips were run on the Thursday to Avonmouth to land to enable people to observe the formal opening that day. Finally, trips were planned on the Friday to follow the departing Royal Yacht and her cruiser escort down-Channel, and it was only natural for the Barry Railway Company to also offer trips from its side of the Bristol Channel, both to view the Royal Yacht and to see the formalities, which it duly advertised for the Thursday. The latter trip was booked to land passengers at Avonmouth as well.

This seems to have touched a raw nerve with P. & A. Campbell Ltd and triggered its decision to go to the courts again: only the previous year it had succeeded in court in getting the Welsh company banned - or so it had hoped - from trading outside the limits of the 1904 Act, and yet already the Bristol company had had to think in terms of having recourse to the law again as it argued that running trips from places like Port Talbot and Briton Ferry (which the Barry had earlier been doing) was outside the prescribed limits. The same Act stated that passengers could only be brought back from Bristol by Barry steamers if those passengers had been conveyed to Bristol by a Barry steamer in the first place, and at a fresh court hearing on Wednesday 29th July, 1908 the Barry Railway Company argued in its defence that as Avonmouth was within Bristol it was at liberty to take passengers there. It is easy to see that a lawyer could think that now P. & A. Campbell Ltd was overplaying its hand rather, in purely legalistic terms and, this time, Mr Justice Swinfen-Eady took the side of the Barry Railway Company and ruled that the sequestration motion sought by the plaintiff P. & A. Campbell Ltd could not be allowed.

This judgement, especially as costs were awarded against the Bristol company, gave some satisfaction in South Wales, although the point had been passed at which the Barry Railway Company could hide behind the law after the July 1907 enforced withdrawal from Cardiff. The places at which the Red Funnel Line could legitimately trade were perhaps going to be insufficient to generate sufficient traffic volumes, and so what might have seemed like a beneficial judgement ultimately was not going to save the business. There was some talk of an appeal by P. & A. Campbell Ltd but little more was heard of the matter.

For the moment, it was still not established whether a sufficient market share could be carved by the Barry Railway Company out of the Bristol Channel. On the face of it there were still plentiful volumes of passengers to be had, and the overall numbers conveyed to Ilfracombe during Whitsuntide in 1908 might have stiffened the desire to press on in kind weather. As the *Ilfracombe Gazette*

Although the Ilfracombe newspapers regarded P. & A. Campbell Ltd as 'old friends' of the North Devon resort, during the comparatively short time that the Red Funnel Line steamers linked Ilfracombe with South Wales they brought in many thousands of visitors and boosted trade accordingly. This paddler is seen berthed at the 'Stonebench', still discernible a century later despite major harbour reconstruction works. *Lionel Vaughan Collection*

Either *Devonia* or *Gwalia* seen at anchor off Clovelly. To her stern can just be seen the whaleback bow of Pockett's *Brighton*, which would have come across from Swansea. Clovelly was a frequently-visited destination from Ilfracombe. *Lionel Vaughan Collection*

put it, the first steamer on Whit Monday, *Britannia*, arrived from Bristol at six o'clock in the morning and:

> . . . hour after hour steamers came and steamers departed till about half past eight at night . . . another proof was given of the well-worn saying that old friends are the best friends. Despite the huge traffic to be obtained from Cardiff to Weston on bank-holidays Messrs Campbell saw to it that Ilfracombe should have a good service . . .

This somewhat unfair 'dig' at the Red Funnel Line was based on there having been five arrivals at Ilfracombe from up-Channel by White Funnel steamers (two trips by *Britannia*, and one each by *Cambria*, *Westward Ho* and *Albion*, thus comprehensively dealing with demand at Bristol, Cardiff and Newport) which brought in about 2,300 passengers whilst *Brighton* brought 800 from Swansea and *Gwalia* 'came last' with 650 from Barry. It seems likely from the advertisements for that busy day that certainly two vessels of the Red Funnel Line, probably all of the other three in practice, did indeed handle up-Channel traffic, (i.e. between Barry and Weston, with practically hourly train departures from Cardiff Riverside to Barry Pier). This was scarcely surprising in view of the Red Funnel Line fleet being effectively shut out of those very three principal places up-Channel that generated such substantial volumes for the White Funnel Fleet, as well as at the Pockett's stronghold at Swansea.

The next development that caused concern at Ilfracombe was the receipt by the Harbour Master of a letter dated 27th June, 1908 from E. Lake, the General Manager of the Barry Railway Company, which innocently enquired whether it might be permitted to run steamers to Ilfracombe on Sundays. This, in 1908, was a taboo subject as the steamers most definitely had never run on Sundays there, and Ilfracombe prized its Sabbath observance highly, so highly in fact that for almost six weeks afterwards the correspondence columns of the local newspapers were almost entirely devoted to letters from Ministers of every denomination, and countless others, wholly denouncing this dreadful threat to the peace and quiet of their Sundays. A polite refusal was promptly transmitted to Mr Lake and the Barry Railway Company thus failed to find a new source of traffic by Sabbath-breaking. It was hardly necessary to point out, of course, that P. & A. Campbell Ltd would never have dreamt of such a shocking notion. It was not to be until well after the Great War that Ilfracombe appeared in the Sunday schedules of the Bristol Channel excursion steamers.

Weston-super-Mare's Grand Pier again attracted a small number of calls by Red Funnel Line steamers in 1908, and it is probably reasonable to speculate that the Barry company had more of an interest in seeing this develop than did P. & A. Campbell Ltd. During the June to August period four or five Red Funnel trips were advertised in the Cardiff newspapers, which tended to give a short time alongside there. That advertised for Monday 10th August, 1908, the day of Weston Regatta, involved a train departure from Cardiff Riverside at 1.52 pm, with an 6.45 pm return from the Grand Pier to Barry. High water was 5.43 pm that day, so two or at best three hours alongside was all that was offered. (Seemingly there was no advertised attempt to take people *from* the Grand Pier on cruises - even short ones around the Holms - in view of the restricted amount of water, although the possibility of trips 'Round the Bay', chalked up on a blackboard, using otherwise idle time, cannot be wholly ruled out if the weather was fine and plenty of people happened to be about. Scrutiny of the *Weston Mercury* newspaper did not, however, yield evidence of any such excursions.)

Things were moving forward slowly at Birnbeck Pier with the planned low-water extension but, in 1908, the Barry Railway Company still found itself unable to run the regular services it had once envisaged across the Bristol Channel between Barry and Weston-super-Mare, and its pier thus remained underutilised, as did its fleet. Having said that it is clear, from comments made in the columns of the *Weston Mercury*, that Weston folk were generally unimpressed with the notion of going to Cardiff at regular intervals if this involved being routed via Barry Pier by boat and train. What was really still needed, it was opined, was a low-water pier at Cardiff as Barry Pier represented simply too much of a detour, however good the interchange facilities provided there.

Marketing the Red Funnel Line steamers

In looking at traffic figures and accounts one can easily overlook the simple basics of what was being sold to the travelling public during this time. Excursion steamers, with their comparative comforts and attractive catering, offered the means of getting from A to B enjoyably where this was quicker and thus cheaper than a railway journey. In the Bristol Channel, Ilfracombe was a focus for staying passengers as well as day-trippers, whilst Weston traffic was more geared to the latter as the crossing was less than an hour's duration, and there was much at Weston to attract those with just a day to spare. But excursion steamers could offer travel just for the pleasure of being at sea, and an official 1908 City & Port of Cardiff handbook extolled the virtues of this, for its own sake, as a means of escaping the pressures of city life.

Describing the range of excursion opportunities from Cardiff by steamers of both the Red Funnel and White Funnel lines, the handbook declared

> . . . not only from Cardiff, but from the surrounding districts, are the pleasure steamers patronised. There is no more delightful sensation on a hot summer's day than to escape from the heated busy streets, and find rest and a cooling breeze on the saloon deck of a large paddle steamer. Many people spend their holidays in this way, combining the comfort of nights spent in their own homes with daily excursions up and down the Channel.

More specifically describing the arrangements for travel from Barry, the handbook went on:

> . . . passengers from whatever the point of departure are taken by rail, for a fare which includes rail and steamer, and carried to the head of the Pontoon, within a few yards of the boats. There is no waiting about, the steamer is alongside ready to start, and as soon as the train arrives and the passengers are embarked she leaves. Similarly on the return journey, the train is awaiting the steamer's arrival. The Pontoon is accessible to the Passenger Steamers at any state of the tide so that passengers can embark and disembark at any time. This provision is unique in the Bristol Channel . . .

The Barry Railway Company doubtless still hoped that its beliefs would be vindicated by the traffic returns if it persisted, and the August Bank Holiday Monday - like Whitsuntide that year - generated goodly numbers of passengers. This time the tides were a little more helpful and two steamers ventured down Channel from Barry on Monday 3rd August, 1908, depositing lots of people in Ilfracombe in order to spend some of their hard-earned cash. The figures seem astonishing nowadays, but this is what was recorded in the *Ilfracombe Gazette*, and which I think illustrates why the management of the Barry Railway Company felt justified in seeking to hang on to a share of the market:

> . . . from Cardiff the *Cambria* brought over 700 and took 450 to Clovelly. The *Devonia* from Barry had 780 and took 100 to Clovelly, whilst the *Westonia*, also from Barry, brought 600 and took 200 for a cruise. From Newport the *Albion* came with 450 and took 350 for a cruise, whilst the *Britannia* landed 880 from Bristol, and took 500 to Lundy.

These figures may have been uppermost in the minds of the Barry Directors later that week when the 48th half-yearly meeting of shareholders was held at Barry Docks on Friday 7th August, 1908. This was a less turbulent affair than the previous such meeting, but there were still calls from some of those present to cut loose from the steamships and stick to the business of running a railway. Compared to 1907, it appeared that overall passenger numbers on the ships were increasing. As it was not yet the season-end then not unnaturally the recommendation was to continue, in order to be able to gauge the whole-season result fairly in due course. Oddly, Mr Thompson appears not to have been present at this meeeting, and it does seem likely that he had said all he wished to say on the subject of the steamships venture, and had retired - gracefully or otherwise - from the ensuing unseemly debate. One surprising admission was that the Burnham venture now seemed to have been dropped by the Board. Despite having gained the means the year before to put capital into this, after much hard-fought advocacy, it now turned out that further opposition during the progression of the Act had led the Board to withdraw from its intention to invest in a new, revitalised Burnham Pier venture. Some economy with the truth was apparent here - having 'lost' the Cardiff battle to P. & A. Campbell Ltd in 1907, now was clearly not the time to be committing substantial capital sums to something so self-evidently marginal. But the gist of Earl of Plymouth's speech as Chairman was straightforward; he stated that the steamship carryings would be fully reviewed and told one vociferous opponent this:

> What we have undertaken to do with regard to the steamships is to profit, as well as we can, by this full year's experience. But I may say this much, Mr Ferrier, that we intend to fully consider the results as business men. We do not intend to inflict loss upon the shareholders because the Directors might have individual opinions as to whether there might be steamship traffic or not. But you may be quite certain that we will fairly consider the situation after the experience that has been gained, and if you will excuse the use of a homely expression, we shall not be pig-headed on the subject.

Whereas much of the foregoing has been extracted from the 'official' source of the published Report & Accounts, there was considerable newspaper coverage of the Shareholders' Meeting from which it can be inferred that it was a distinctly lively affair. That in the *South Wales Echo*, entitled 'Breeze at Barry

Promotional material for Cardiff in the early part of the 20th century generally extolled the virtues of sea-travel via the port of Barry and its well-found steamships, and this homely, composite view of aspects of *Devonia* nicely illustrates the comfort and catering on offer from a large and responsive crew, despite the mis-spelling! *Lionel Vaughan Collection*

Westonia in the River Avon, well-laden with passengers for this particularly scenic excursion run, with a White Funnel Fleet paddler in hot pursuit. *Ken Jenkins Collection*

Railway Meeting', portrayed Lt Col Clark as having effectively accused the Board of fraud! Another, the *South Wales Daily News*, laid emphasis on the concerns of shareholders at the large sums of money charged against railway earnings - and thus diminishing their dividends - for repairs to *Westonia* at around £8,000, and for the costs involved in the lawsuit brought by P. & A. Campbell Ltd, at a further £8,000. These were substantial sums, especially when considered in relation to her purchase price, and the problems of the steamships venture were clearly not going to simply go away. The number of occasions in 1908 when operation of all four steamers would have been necessary were few and far between, and two had probably been laid up in late August as traffic dwindled. Another season was drawing to a close, and after the end of September, Mrs Grundy was able to report with her customary brevity, in the *Barry Dock News* on Friday 2nd October, 1908, that:

> The Barry passenger boat service has closed for the season, the final runs taking place last Wednesday, when, attracted by the fine weather, there was a good muster of passengers both for the Ilfracombe and Weston boats.

1909: The last year of Barry Railway Company steamers

The steamers had run normally in 1908, and it is reasonable to suppose that the opinion of the Barry Railway Company Board remained divided as to whether a second season after being 'shut out' of the lucrative Cardiff traffic would see more satisfactory financial results than the first. The only real hope for improved traffic levels lay in the expected opening, in 1909, of the low-water extension at Weston's Birnbeck Pier when, at long last, a regular timetable with fixed departure times in either direction across the Bristol Channel could be promoted to link Somerset with the Welsh capital. The Minute Books of the meetings of Directors of the Barry Railway Company shed very little light on the exact thinking of the Board at that time, but one Minute (on Friday 22nd January, 1909) noted a recommendation from the Steamships Committee that *Westonia* should be sold. A further recommendation was that only two vessels should be operated that Easter, with a third later in the season, and a possibility of both the 1905-built vessels *Gwalia* and *Devonia* needing new paddle-wheels at a cost of £3,500 was noted.

The half-yearly meeting of Shareholders which took place on Friday 5th February, 1909 again featured much cross-examination of the Board by some of the more influential investors in the company as to how long it was intended to persist with the steamships venture. On this occasion David Davies was in the Chair rather than the Earl of Plymouth, and he spoke at some length on the matter. He conceded that operating expenses in 1908 had far outstripped revenues (£31,273 compared to £18,529) but said that the boats had carried 50 per cent more passengers in 1908 than in 1907. They had called in an expert to advise them, and it was expected that

> . . . the new pier at Weston . . . would shortly be completed, so that they would not be dependent on the tides. Hitherto they had not had much assistance from neighbouring railway companies, but with better facilities to enable the people from the coal districts

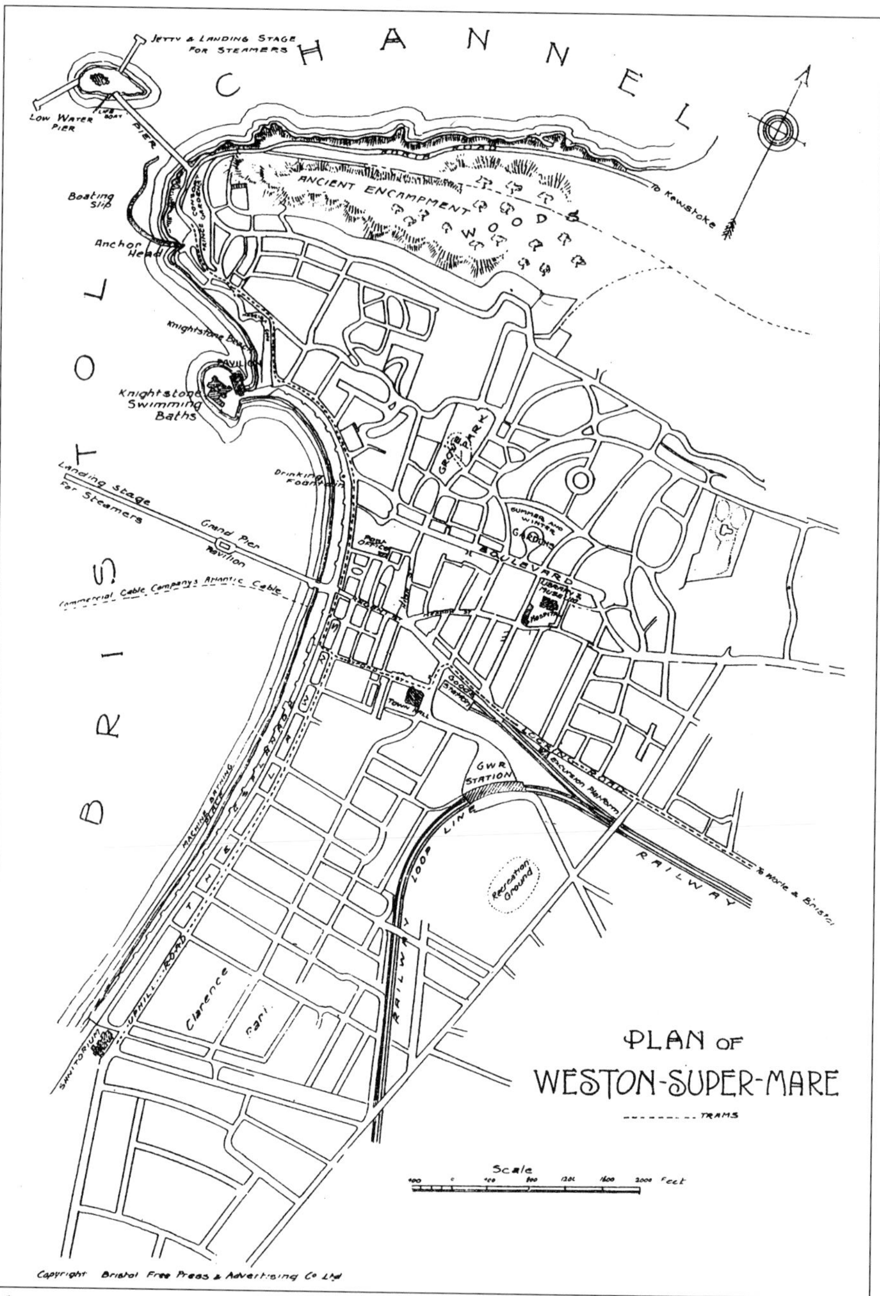

The attractions of Weston-super-Mare were a key feature in attracting passengers from South Wales by the excursion steamers, and this plan of the town usefully illustrated the relative positions of the two piers after 1909 at the time that the low-water extension at Birnbeck had finally been opened, as well as showing the tramway routes from there to the Great Western Railway station and along the seafront to the Sanatorium. The Kewstoke direction also represented an attractive walk for passengers arriving at Birnbeck Pier by steamer. (Published in the 1913 edition of the P. & A. Campbell Ltd Bristol Channel District Guide.) *Author's Collection*

to come to Barry and take advantage of the boat service, he hoped there would be a very considerable increase in the passenger traffic this year.

One can only imagine this reference to neighbouring railways meant sending more excursion trains down to Barry Island - the railways in question (the Taff Vale, the Rhymney and the Cardiff Railway companies) mostly had comprehensive through booking arrangements in place with P. & A. Campbell Ltd and the GWR, and maybe the Brecon & Merthyr Railway, to get South Wales folk across via Cardiff or Penarth to Somerset, Devon and beyond, and on the London & South Western Railway too, to practically any destination in the West of England. The notion may, thus, have been somewhat fanciful.

A little later on in the year, on Friday 2nd April, the Board approved the appointment of Mr D. Lean McIntosh as Marine Superintendent, at an annual salary of £200, with a bonus of £50 if the season's results were 'satisfactory' - although the term satisfactory was not there defined. Presumably his appointment was to relieve certain Directors of the burden of the day-to-day management of the operations of the steamers. Again, in the absence of the actual Minutes of the Steamships Committee, we are obliged to make deductions, but it appears that the resolution to economise on the the number of vessels which comprised the Red Funnel Line fleet was only partly heeded. *Westonia* was not disposed of in 1909, but on the other hand there seem to have been very few occasions when all four vessels were needed for the traffic mustered through Barry, and one wonders whether all four vessels were fully crewed that year. Once again, we are indebted to Mrs Grundy's Jottings in the *Barry Dock News* regarding the start of the season at Easter 1909, Good Friday being on Friday 9th April, 1909, and which suggested that two vessels were brought out for the Bank Holiday weekend: 'The Barry Red Funnel channel passenger boats began running for the season today (Thursday) the trips to Weston, Minehead and Ilfracombe being well patronised'.

After Easter a quiet few weeks ensued until the start-up of more regular operations in May. At long last, the low-water extension at Birnbeck Pier, at Weston-super-Mare was brought into use on the first day of May 1909. Now the Red Funnel steamers could finally advertise a daily, regular service (Sundays excepted) between Weston and Cardiff, via Barry Pier. For the period 1st May-31st May, 1909 this is what appeared in the columns of the *Weston Mercury*:

Leave Weston (Old Pier)	*Leave Cardiff (Riverside Station, GWR)*
10.55 am, 1.40, 4.05, 7.20, 9.25 pm	9.31 am, 12.00 noon, 2.27, 5.47, 7.45 pm

So here it was, a repeating daily timetable, after many years of waiting, during which the rival Grand Pier had eventually contrived to get its landing stage opened a couple of years earlier, in 1907, but which had effectively been boycotted by steamer operators on account of its severe limitations. The developments at Birnbeck must have put paid to any lingering ambition on the part of the owners of the Grand Pier to extend out to low water, although a few calls by Red Funnel steamers (but seemingly none by P. & A. Campbell Ltd) were offered in 1909. One imagines this early season timetable was sustained by the more economical vessels *Westonia* or *Barry*, and the next step-up of operations was just before Whitsuntide. On Monday 24th May, 1909 this announcement appeared in the *Western Mail* newspaper at Cardiff:

RED FUNNEL LINE BOAT SERVICE

The Red Funnel Line announce a daily service of excursions by their steamers from Barry to Weston and Ilfracombe this week, for which there are through bookings by rail from Cardiff, Porth and Bridgend. Weston may be reached by a frequent daily service, whilst the pleasures of Ilfracombe can be appreciated in a full day's trip, the last boat leaving Ilfracombe at 4.15 calling at Minehead on the 24th and 25th at 5.40 pm. On Wednesday there will be a cheap evening trip to Minehead, leaving Cardiff (Riverside) at 5.47 pm, for which the fare is only 1*s*. 6*d*. Excursionists to Ilfracombe have the opportunity of calling off Lynmouth to and fro.

A three-vessel operation was now getting underway and for Whit Monday, 31st May, 1909, the excursions offered overall were the usual, intensive 'ferry' service of six round trips between Barry and Weston, the 'railway run' to Ilfracombe, and an afternoon excursion to Bristol with train departure from Cardiff Riverside at 11.50 am, returning from Bristol at 5.15 pm, for a fare of 1*s*. 6*d*. The boat running to Bristol would doubtless have assisted on ferry runs too. At Ilfracombe it was recorded that the weather was 'fairly fine' but that a clash with Swansea Regatta probably diminished the overall numbers of visitors from South Wales to Ilfracombe. It was *Gwalia* that brought the substantial number of 900 passengers from Barry, and then took 270 on a cruise down-Channel. For P. & A. Campbell Ltd *Britannia* and *Cambria* brought the usual crowds from Bristol and Cardiff, and one very remarkable feature of that day was a 'double-run' by *Albion* from Newport, which unusually gave an opportunity for Ilfracombe folk to sail up to Newport and back in the day. Conversely, Newport folk could have a very long day in Ilfracombe if they wished, and the *Gazette* recorded that *Albion* brought 250 down from Newport and Weston before returning up-Channel.

This may have been fine for P. & A. Campbell Ltd whose profits were rising as those of the Barry steamers were declining, on account of being forced to stick within the provisions of the 1904 Act. But *Devonia*, a commodious steamship less than five years old, was laid up at the beginning of the 1909 season and thus earning nothing to offset her depreciation. As early summer progressed into high summer, a slight tweaking of the Barry-Weston timetable took place and for July a sixth daily round trip was added so that the timetable (as published in the *Weston Mercury*) now looked like this:

Leave Weston (Old Pier)	*Leave Cardiff (Riverside Station, GWR)*
9.15, 11.25 am, 1.45, 4.15, 7.15, 9.30 pm	7.12, 9.20 am, 12.05, 2.32, 5.48, 7.45 pm

Daily service (Sundays excepted) to Lynmouth & Ilfracombe, leaving the Old Pier at 9.15 am

The last sentence was evidence of an enterprising intention, although how many Weston folk took advantage of the offer to travel by Red Funnel Line steamer from Weston to Ilfracombe via Barry is questionable, for that is what was being offered. On many days in the season, the more or less daily P. & A. Campbell Ltd steamer from Bristol to Ilfracombe would call at Clevedon and Weston *en route*, plus Minehead on occasions, and generally at Lynmouth too by launch. The journey time between Weston and Ilfracombe on a White Funnel steamer was typically between two and a half and three hours, depending on whether a Minehead call was included, and could be described as a 'direct' service, in the strict sense, albeit not of a non-stop character. By comparison, to set off from Weston to Barry on a Red Funnel Line steamer, in order there to change steamers to get to Ilfracombe, was a little less obvious as an excursion opportunity, via an 'indirect' route. With the timetable quoted above there was little waiting around at Barry, as arrival there from Weston would have been about 10 or 15 minutes before the 'railway run' steamer departure time, after arrival at Barry Pier of the 9.37 am train from Cardiff Riverside. Summer passenger numbers must have meant that it was necessary to run two trains from Cardiff down the Barry 'main line', at 9.20 (for Weston) and at 9.37 am (for Ilfracombe), yet still the Barry Railway Company were only really deploying two steamers for core services, not three, and certainly not four. In the evening, departure back up-Channel from Ilfracombe was retarded to 5.30 pm, again providing the opportunity for the 'railway run' boat to be extended beyond Ilfracombe to Clovelly, or even Lundy. Only a brief wait at Barry Pier in the evening was involved for those changing onto the last Weston 'ferry' departure of the day at around 8.30 or thereabouts, after the 7.45 pm train from Cardiff Riverside had arrived.

Exactly when a fourth boat was commissioned in readiness for the high summer period of 1909 is unclear, but the August Bank Holiday Monday (then the first Monday in August, unlike nowadays) was a peak time of demand. Advertisements for Saturday 31st July, 1909 suggest that all four steamers may have been needed that day, as there was an additional departure from Barry Pier direct to Ilfracombe at 10.05, effectively a 'relief boat' to the 10.10 am 'railway run' boat, and doubtless two on the ferry to Weston, and providing some Minehead journeys as well.

An inference drawn by the *Barry Dock News*, in referring to the the customary Report & Accounts (for the six-month period ending June 1909) for the August 1909 half-yearly meeting of shareholders released just in advance of the actual meeting, after noting that there was a 'dark spot' in the accounts regarding the disappointing results of the passenger steamer workings, was that at that point *Westonia* 'has not been run at all this year'. This is certainly consistent with the 1908 season where three boats normally sufficed, and assuming that the Barry Railway Company could still muster a fourth crew it would have been reluctant to turn traffic away on a peak day. I therefore think that the last real peak day of Barry Railway Company steamer operation was probably the Bank Holiday, Monday 2nd August, 1909 when the excursions advertised required the availability of the entire fleet (*see overleaf*). With some clever scheduling, the six round trips by one ferry vessel between Barry and Weston appear to have been augmented by a further three round trips by what I have defined as the Minehead boat, which did three round trips to that port too. A neat feature of this was that the six basic round trips advertised on a daily basis were not retimed, but simply supplemented on that day, and a handful of Barry Island train services extended to Barry Pier to ensure all boats had rail connections to and from Cardiff. The 'railway run' boat proceeded to Clovelly, and the fourth boat went to Mumbles, and possibly even ran a trip from there too.

BARRY RAILWAY COMPANY
'RED FUNNEL LINE'
BANK HOLIDAY MONDAY 2nd August, 1909

Four vessel operation

Barry-Weston 'ferry' duties

Train dep. Cardiff Riverside	*Steamer dep. Barry Pier (est)*	*Steamer return dep. Weston SM*
7.12 am	(7.45) am	9.15 am
9.20	(10.00)	10.55
11.05	*(11.45)*	*12.30 pm*
12.05 pm	(12.45) pm	1.45
1.07	*(1.45)*	*2.30*
2.32	(3.15)	4.15
5.18	*(6.00)*	*6.45*
5.48	(6.30)	7.15
-	-	*9.00*
7.45	(8.30)	9.30
-	-	

NB Times shown above in italics represent additional round trips over and above the basic six round trips usually provided by the allocated ferry vessel, generally *Westonia.*

The 'Minehead boat'

Barry Pier	(9.00 am)
Minehead	10.15
Barry Pier	(11.30-11.45)
Weston	12.30 pm
Barry Pier	(1.45)
Weston	2.30
Barry Pier	(3.30)
Minehead	(4.15)
Barry Pier	(5.30-6.00)
Weston	6.45
Barry Pier	(7.30)
Minehead	8.45
Barry Pier	(10.00) finish

'Railway Run'

Barry Pier	10.10 am
Lynmouth	(12.xx pm)
Ilfracombe	(12.xx-1.xx)
Clovelly	(2.xx)-4.10
Ilfracombe	(5.xx)-5.30
Lynmouth	(6.xx)
Barry Pier	(8.15)-(light)
Weston	9.00
Barry Pier	(9.45) finish

Fourth vessel

Cardiff Riverside	(train dep.) 7.12 am
Barry Pier	(8.00 am)
Mumbles (cruise?)	(arr.10xx)
Mumbles	8.30 pm
Barry Pier	(10.xx pm) finish

Extracted from *Western Mail,* Red Funnel Line excursion advertisements, for Monday 2nd August, 1909.

1909 - other aspects of the season

An oddity of the 1909 season was that seemingly no reference was made on the Barry side of the Channel to this new regularity of connection with Weston, and one is tempted to conclude it was something of a non-event really. Rumours of a repeated attempt to gain a toehold for the Barry steamers at Swansea surfaced again in July, but came to nought. An outing of the Barry Conservatives Club to Weston on *Barry* in July involved a 'cavalcade of charabancs, brakes and waggonettes' for the journey on to Clevedon. The Barry Conservatives, in these numbers, out to enjoy themselves, must have been a formidable sight and the Hotel Bristol was again the venue for lunch, in a marquee during which a terrific thunderstorm broke. Some of the party returned on the Weston, Clevedon & Portishead Light Railway to Weston to cross the channel for 'an exhilarating trip home in the teeth of half a gale', as it was described.

Later in July another party outing was described in the *Barry Dock News*, this time the Barry Chamber of Trade having voyaged on *Westonia* to Weston and thence proceeded on the Weston, Clevedon & Portishead Light Railway all the way to Portishead for a dinner at Portishead's Royal Hotel followed by tea at Clevedon and a visit to Clevedon Court before getting the boat back from Weston at 9.30 pm, feeling naturally rather tired after such a full day. The Weston, Clevedon & Portishead Light Railway had only finally opened its extension beyond Clevedon to Portishead a couple of years earlier, in August 1907, and so offered something of a novelty, as there was nothing which quite compared with its rustic, even wayward, charms back in South Wales. Over the years this fascinating light railway offered a useful link between the three seaside resorts and their piers for passengers seeking a little diversity, and discounted rail fares were offered to holders of steamer tickets.

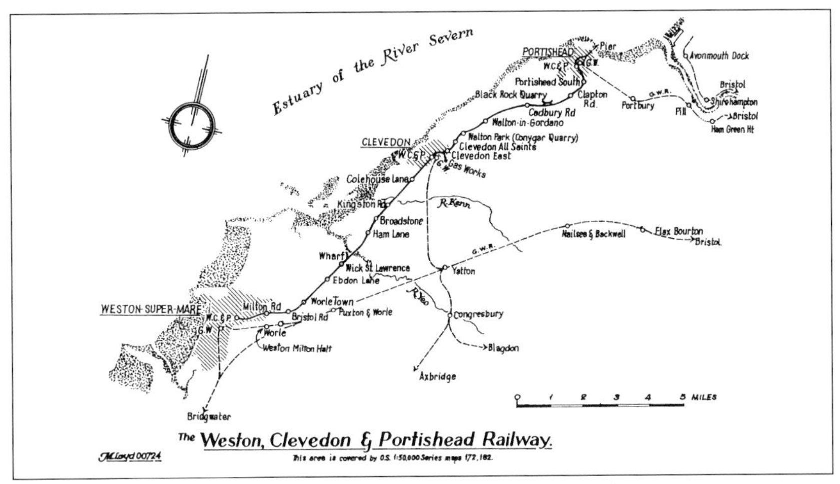

The more adventurous passenger from South Wales could use the Weston, Clevedon & Portishead Railway to link between the different places served by the steamers, and concessionary rail fares were offered on production of steamer tickets. The WC&P was an attractive light railway in its own right, and quite separate from the GWR local branch lines to Portishead and Clevedon, and the loop line through Weston-super-Mare. *M. Lloyd*

ASK FOR TICKETS BY THE

TAFF VALE RAILWAY & P. & A. CAMPBELL, Ltd.

EXCURSION TICKETS are issued daily (except on Sundays, and August 3rd and 4th) to **WESTON-SUPER-MARE**

Via PENARTH PIER. *For Steamer Times see page* [illegible]

FROM	THROUGH FARE (including the Pier Tolls at Penarth).
Cardiff (Queen Street)	2/-
" (G.W.R.)	
" (Riverside)	
Grangetown	
Penarth Dock	Children under 12 Half-Price.
Lavernock	
Sully	
Cadoxton	(NO LUGGAGE ALLOWED)

CLEVEDON.—Passengers holding tickets to Weston may, when conveyed by a boat which is running through to Clevedon, extend their journey to that place without extra charge, but they will not be allowed to break their journey at Weston either on the outward or return trip.

Tickets will be available by any train, also by any of P. & A. Campbell's Steamboats, which will enable holders to make the to-and-fro journey on the day of issue.

Holders of these tickets may return to Cardiff by any of P. & A. Campbell's Steamboats if they desire to do so.

NOTICE—The Company do not guarantee that there will be room on the Steamers, which are advertised in connection with their trains, and Through Tickets are issued and must be understood to be accepted subject to this condition.

The fare does not include conveyance between Railway and Steamboat, or Weston Pier Tolls.

If travelling from Cardiff to the Barry area, an alternative route to the Barry Railway Company direct trains via Dinas Powis was that offered by the Taff Vale Railway, via Penarth, and which had running powers into the Barry's Cadoxton station. Each season the weekly timetable booklets issued by P. & A. Campbell Ltd carried this advertisement, pointing out that its boats enabled people from the Barry area, in Cadoxton and further up the coast at Sully and Lavernock, to cross to Weston via Penarth Pier. Intending passengers were firmly reminded to 'Ask For Tickets By the White Funnel Fleet'. No mention was made of the walk from Penarth station to the pier, through the Dingle, delightful but steep in the return direction, and scarcely to be compared with the purpose-built arrangements at Barry Pier. *Author's Collection*

The half-yearly shareholders' meeting held on Friday 6th August, 1909 was again the scene of continued controversy regarding the steamers. Two gentlemen were particularly loud in their complaints, T.E. Morel pointing out yet again that dividends were being adversely affected by the steamer losses, and stating that '. . . if they could not make this boat business a success, the sooner they disposed of the boats the better . . .' J.B. Ferrier was also insistent in his concerns that, as if the operating losses were not themselves bad enough, the depreciation charged was worse, and he found it ludicrous that the Barry fleet, with an aggregate passenger capacity of some 4,000, was still sailing broadly at similar times of day to the Campbell boats from Cardiff, whilst Barry Railway Company trains typically conveyed 400 passenger seats - just where did they think the boats were going to be filled from? The Earl of Plymouth, in the chair, generally reiterated the remarks David Davies had made in February - but the resolve of the Board was now clearly weakening, and although the Earl said the hard-won Powers to operate steamers would not be given up lightly, it was starting to seem as though the game was almost over. Mr Thompson was present, but made no comment on the steamers.

During August a number of excursions were offered that provided a touch of variety to the normal fare, and one such was advertised on Thursday 19th August, 1909 when, after arrival at Barry Pier of the 7.12 am train from Cardiff Riverside, a steamer left for Watchet, Minehead. Ilfracombe and Clovelly. A week later another unusual trip was advertised, this time an afternoon outing from Barry Pier (in connection with the 2.32 pm train from Cardiff Riverside) for Minehead and Porlock, with time ashore at either place. The Campbell steamers had visited Porlock on occasions around the turn of the century, as it represented a logical short extension for, say, a Newport-Minehead boat when tides permitted landing at Porlock Weir by launch. Indeed, this Red Funnel visit may have been an experiment by Mr McIntosh which was prompted by the knowledge that P. & A. Campbell Ltd had advertised a Newport-Minehead & Porlock trip just a few weeks earlier in the 1909 season, on Tuesday 27th July. All that was needed was an arrangement with a local boatman.

Tenby was visited on occasions, and it seems that there may have still been an odd Burnham trip too. But nothing on quite the grand scale of 1907 - when far-flung destinations in Cornwall featured in the Red Funnel excursions programme - seems to have been offered in 1909. The size of the coal-bill for fuel-hungry big steamers like *Gwalia* and *Devonia* must have constrained the ambitions of the new manager, for it was an established fact that they got through considerably more than their White Funnel opponents.

The end of the Barry Railway Company steamships venture

As August gave way into September, in 1909, operations wound down, and it must have been apparent to some observers that an era was ending. For five years the Barry Railway Company had run its Red Funnel Line steamers but during the last two seasons, they had visibly struggled after being shut out of the Port of Cardiff. The simple truth was that not enough traffic could be channelled through Barry alone to make the ships profitable, however many destinations were tried, or however attractive the fares and facilities. Three boats continued in operation in the first half of September 1909, and for example Watchet and Minehead were visited on Monday 13th September, and twice on Thursday 16th September, with morning and evening calls at both Somerset ports. An afternoon trip from Barry to Porthcawl was offered on Wednesday 15th September, and one wonders just how many passengers this attracted. The Ilfracombe boat continued on its Summer schedule returning from the North Devon resort at 5.30, and from Lynmouth at 6.00 pm.

A tragedy struck on Friday 17th September, as a dead body was found in the paddlebox of *Devonia* that morning by Able Seaman Richard Fleming, which was thought to have been there since the ship had berthed alongside the pontoon at around 8.00 pm the previous evening. The body was that of Archibald Jones, of Pontypridd, who had travelled on *Devonia* on the Thursday and evidently missed his train home to the Rhondda, according to witnesses. An open verdict was returned, it being speculated that he had fallen in the water and, exhausted, clung to the paddle-wheel and floats all night, unable to escape any other way.

The 'last trip of the season' to Mumbles and Tenby took place on Friday 17th September, and the services were thinned out after Saturday 18th September, such that only two vessels were now required in service. After that day, the six round trips on the Barry to Weston 'ferry' were reduced to five, the last one of the evening being withdrawn, with the times advertised from Weston for the remainder of September 1909 as: 9.15, 11.15 am, 1.45, 4.15, 7.15 pm.

From Monday 20th September, 1909, the departure time from Ilfracombe of the boat returning back up-Channel reverted to the early season pattern of 4.00 pm. The connection at Barry Pier in the mornings off the 9.15 am crossing from Weston

A delightful 1905 view of the Cumberland Basin at Bristol, with either *Gwalia* or *Devonia* canting outside the lock prior to a voyage down the River Avon, with the Portishead branch line visible in the foreground. *Lionel Vaughan Collection*

A misleading early view of the first Barry Railway Company vessel *Gwalia*, seemingly retouched from a Clyde trials photograph, and declaring the vessel to be run by the so-called 'Barry & Bristol Channel Steamship Co.' She initially ran with this hull colour and black-tipped buff funnels for a few weeks before being repainted into a scheme akin to Glasgow & South Western Railway colours, that is, with a light coloured hull and red funnels. *Author's Collection*

BARRY RAILWAY COMPANY.

OFFICIALS' AND STAFF

(By kind permission of the Directors,)

WEDNESDAY, JUNE 19*th*, 1901.

The Committee request the pleasure of the Company of

....

R.S.V.P. by 13th June, to

THOS. R. ROBINSON, *Hon. Sec.*

This beautifully-produced invitation for a special excursion from Barry Pier was produced by the Barry Railway Company. Regrettably, the local newspaper did not state which White Funnel vessel ran the excursion, which was evidently most successful. *Miss Gwyneth White*

Paddlebox detail, *Devonia*. *H.A. Allen Collection*

for Ilfracombe was still possible. Some slick working in the evening was doubtless necessary to maintain the connection in the reverse direction between the returning 'railway run' boat due in at around 6.15 pm, and the last boat from Barry Pier for Weston which connected out of the 5.47 pm train from Cardiff Riverside. This needed to be away from Barry Pier not much later than 6.30 to maintain the last departure of the evening back across the Channel at 7.15 pm from Weston to Barry Pier. All would then go quiet after about 8.00 pm, and we can envisage in late-September 1909, perhaps, that *Westonia* and *Devonia* had already been withdrawn from traffic and were safely berthed just round the corner in the Basin, their crews already paid off after the end of their season of duty. This would leave ferry duties to *Barry*, and the 'railway run' to the larger *Gwalia*.

Services most years wound down after the last day of September,and, in 1909, the season actually went on for a couple of days longer, the final day of operation being Saturday 2nd October. Regrettably the end of season did not attract any comment from Mrs Grundy, nor the Ilfracombe newspapers, and so we do not know definitively to which vessels can be attributed the dubious honour of becoming the last to fly the colours of the Barry Railway Company that evening. A further reduction in Weston ferry services, from five round trips down to four, had been effected on Friday 1st October, with the first round trip in the morning from Barry to Weston and back being withdrawn on those last two days. Thus the 'railway run' boat would probably, after her arrival back at Barry Pier from Ilfracombe and Lynmouth at about 6.15 pm, have retired to the Basin to be prepared for lay-up. A couple of hours later, the last 'ferry' would have arrived from Weston, and likewise paddled the short distance astern from the pier and then gone ahead into the Basin to join the other three ships of the fleet. At this point, the officers, crew and indeed the Manager Mr McIntosh may well have had deep misgivings about what the future might bring but, unbeknown to them that late summer evening in October 1909, an era had just ended. The last sailings to run in the name of the Barry Railway Company had taken place.

Chapter Four

Bristol Channel Passenger Boats Ltd

. . . the Company has been formed for the purpose of acquiring and working Passenger Steamers in the Bristol Channel and elsewhere . . . the Barry Railway Company have had to bear the brunt of the heavy initial expenses incident to a new business . . . as a result of this expenditure a valuable business has been built up. This Company thus secures the immediate benefit of a large connection which it will be able to considerably develop in consequence of being free to run from any Port in the Channel.

Prospectus, Bristol Channel Passenger Boats, Limited, May 1910

An outsider view

In looking at how a company sought to run their steamships profitably, and in this case how the struggle to find new sources of income from limited traffic sources had perhaps been a distraction, the Barry Railway Company was obliged to remember shareholders were not a benevolent body, who graciously permitted Directors to take actions that were arguably reckless, or even obviously insufficient if dividends were slipping. Whereas individual shareholders may have given some latitude to the company in which they invested if they happened to enjoy certain privileges such as free passes on the steamers, or had simply expressed local pride through their investments, and reluctantly accepted diminishing returns on generally small shareholdings, bigger institutional shareholders were less tolerant. There was no room for sentiment, and no less an organ than the *Stock Exchange Gazette*, on 30th September, 1909, had felt it necessary to pass comment on the way in which the steamships venture seemed to be biting into the profitability of the Barry Railway Company, pointing out that dividends had fallen from 9.5 per cent in 1906 to 8 per cent in 1907, and 6.75 per cent in 1908. There were more than just rumours that the railway was poised to dispose of the steamships venture, as these remarks make clear, although the reference to the opposition of the Barry Railway Company to a 'fusion' between the Taff Vale Railway and the Rhymney Railway - which the Barry feared - was something quite separate, but which had been expensive in terms of yet more legal costs:

> . . . the decline in the distribution in recent half-years has been due to causes that now look like being removed . . . heavy legal expenses to defend against Taff Vale & Rhymney Railway fusion . . . moreover there are indications that the steamboat service, which has been run at a loss, is to be dealt with in the same way that will stop the drain on the company's revenue; the service has always been in disfavour with the stockholders, and at the last meeting the Chairman, in answer to criticisms, announced the matter was receiving the Board's consideration. It is quite on the cards that the vessels will be sold before the next summer service is due to commence.

We can here introduce a different, distant railway company as playing a part in the unfolding story of what was to be the end of the Barry steamships

Built in 1898 for the Glasgow & South Western Railway, the paddle-steamer *Juno* formed the basis of the design for the pair ordered in 1904 by the Barry Railway Company from John Brown and Company Ltd of Clydebank, which were delivered in 1905 as *Gwalia* and *Devonia*.
Ian Boyle Collection

Built in 1902 for the Glasgow & South Western Railway, the paddle-steamer *Mars* formed the contractual basis of the design for the third vessel ordered (in 1906) by the Barry Railway Company from John Brown and Company Ltd of Clydebank, which was delivered in 1907 as *Barry*.
Ian Boyle Collection

The former *Gwalia* looked every bit as impressive in her new guise as *Lady Moyra*, as portrayed in this Furness Railway advertisement which portrayed the Fleetwood-Barrow route, and the railways and lakes beyond to which she gave access for Blackpool holidaymakers.
Andrew Gladwell Collection

When P. & A. Campbell Ltd purchased *Lady Moyra* in 1922 she kept that name for around a decade, and was frequently used as the steamer based at Swansea. *Lionel Vaughan Collection*

Only three of the four-strong Red Funnel Line fleet of vessels passed to the new company in 1910. The fourth, *Gwalia*, was sold to the Furness Railway and renamed *Lady Moyra*, running for that concern until 1914. *Richard Clammer Collection*

One imagines that the new owners were well pleased with their acquisition from South Wales, and that this group of contented passengers enjoyed an excursion from Fleetwood to Barrow on *Lady Moyra* and thence around the Lake District. *Lionel Vaughan Collection*

venture. Since the turn of the century, the Furness Railway had - like the Barry Railway Company - been involved in the operation of coastal steamships which were seen as an adjunct to its own core business of railway operations. Like those of the Barry Railway Company, these were somewhat biased towards freight. An excursion steamer service had been maintained between Barrow-in-Furness and Fleetwood in Lancashire, primarily as a means of bringing tourists from Blackpool across Morecambe Bay to take a variety of railway, motor and launch trips around the Lake District. Its own steamer *Lady Evelyn*, dating from 1900, had been augmented by a familiar, second-hand vessel from the Bristol Channel, namely *Lady Margaret*, but the latter evidently proved unsatisfactory and was sold after the 1907 season. A former General Steam Navigation Company vessel, *Philomel*, filled the gap in 1908 and 1909, but she too was deemed unsatisfactory. Accordingly, an offer was made to the Barry Railway Company in November 1909 to buy *Devonia*, it then being known that offers for the Red Funnel fleet were welcome. This did not proceed as the Furness Railway evidently considered her condition, after an inspection, to be unsatisfactory. A report was published, in the *South Wales Daily News* on 6th December, 1909, that *Devonia* had been sold, and was on the point of leaving Barry for Barrow, but this did not happen. This uncompleted transaction left the Furness Railway still in need of a replacement vessel.

Early in 1910 the time for the 51st half-yearly meeting of the Barry Railway Company came round, on Thursday 12th February. The steamships were still a major cause of concern, and the Chairman was obliged to admit that things had not improved in the 1909 season as the Board had hoped. He stated that receipts of £19,317 (for the whole of the 1909 season) had been exceeded by expenses of £27,678. Even allowing for the fact that £5,000 had been charged for depreciation within the stated level of expenses, this was a pretty poor operating ratio. Again, two prominent shareholders were particularly vocal in their view that the time had come to get rid of the steamers and T.E. Morel, having estimated that the typical total annual loss was now approaching £15,000, urged the Board that they be sold quickly, and not laid up, as further losses would still then accrue. The view of fellow shareholder and local businessman J.B. Ferrier was broadly similar, and he went on to say that he believed that the steamships '. . . would pay their way as a speculation on the part of people who could run them under fewer restrictions . . .'

This was perhaps a more constructive notion than merely advocating that they be got rid of regardless, and the meeting closed with a confirmation from the Chairman that it was now decided that the steamers would be sold, having conceded that the selling-price would be adversely affected if the fleet were allowed to go into a protracted period of idleness. Subsequent events were to bear out this decision, and at a Barry Railway Company Board meeting on Friday 4th March, 1910 the appointment of John Conacher as their new General Manager was confirmed, at an annual salary of £1,000. Mr Conacher had been with the Cambrian Railways, and seemingly wasted little time in getting to grips with the steamships problem, as he doubtless saw it, unfettered himself by any past involvement or even sentiment. At practically the moment he took office, authority to offer *Gwalia* for sale to the Furness Railway for £22,500 was

FURNESS RAILWAY.

(CONISTON FROM BEACON CRAGS.)

20 Rail, Coach, and Steam Yacht

TOURS THROUGH LAKELAND

EVERY WEEK-DAY

From Whitsuntide to September 30th.

The following Tours embrace the chief places of interest in the Lake District.

No. 1.—**Outer Circular Tour,** embracing Windermere Lake, Furness Abbey, and Coniston.

No. 2.—**Inner Circular Tour,** embracing Furness Abbey, Coniston Lake, and Crake Valley.

No. 4.—**Middle Circular Tour,** embracing Windermere Lake, the Crake Valley, and Coniston Lake.

No. 5.—**Red Bank and Grasmere Tour,** *via* Ambleside and Skelwith Force.

No. 10.—**Round the Langdales and Dungeon Ghyll Tour,** *via* Ambleside, Colwith Force, Grasmere, and Rydal.

No. 13.—**Five Lakes Circular Tour, viz.—Windermere, Rydal, Grasmere, Thirlmere, and Derwentwater.**

No. 14.—**Wastwater Tour,** *via* Seascale, and Gosforth. Churchyard Cross, A.D. 680.

No. 15.—**Six Lakes Circular Tour, viz.—Windermere, Rydal, Grasmere, Thirlmere, Derwentwater, and Ullswater.**

No. 16.—**Duddon Valley Tour,** *via* Broughton-in-Furness, Ulpha, and Seathwaite.

No. 20.—**George Romney's Home (1742 to 1755), Walney Bridge and Island, and Furness Abbey Tour,** *via* Sowerby Wood.

For further particulars see the Company's Illustrated Tours Programme, to be had gratis at all Furness Railway Stations; from Mr. A. A. Haynes, Superintendent of the Line, Barrow-in-Furness; and at the Offices of Messrs. Thos. Cook & Son; also at the principal Bookstalls.

BLACKPOOL AND THE LAKES In connection with the Company's Paddle Steamers 'Lady Evelyn' & 'Lady Moyra.'

Every Week-day from Whitsuntide to September 30th.

THE OUTER CIRCULAR TOUR

(This Combination provides an ideal Day's Pic-nic Tour), by *Sea, Rail, Lake,* and *Coach,* embracing **Furness Abbey, Windermere Lake and Coniston.**

ALFRED ASLETT,
Secretary and General Manager.

Barrow-in-Furness, *April* 1914.

Lady Moyra was accompanied in her new trade by the older *Lady Evelyn,* and this Furness Railway advertisement in a Black's *Guide Book to the Isle of Man* listed the wide range of tours on offer, and mentioned the steamer service. *Author's Collection* given to Mr Conacher, who had joined the Steamships Committee. It must have hurt Mr Thompson to propose that '. . . the Committee be given a free hand to dispose of the boats, and if unable to do so to sail them during the coming season', but this he did, on Friday 1st April, 1910, seconded by Sir Clifford Cory.

The Furness Railway quickly decided to purchase *Gwalia*, for the sum of £21,750, doubtless after some tense bargaining had taken place. Furness Railway sources suggest that considerable monies would have had to have been spent on *Philomel* had that steamer been retained for the 1910 season, and perhaps mindful of this Mr Conacher negotiated what he doubtless saw as a keen price with Mr Aslett of the Furness Railway, who for his part ended up with an identical vessel to the one he had almost purchased the previous year, but ostensibly in better shape. His name duly appeared on the Port of Cardiff shipping register as Managing Owner of *Gwalia*, with effect from 13th May, 1910. My inference from the Barry Railway Company Board Minutes of the two meetings mentioned above, and a third on Friday 6th May, 1910, was that having decided to sell the ships, there was now felt to be no point in wasting any further time. Things moved very quickly, and the other three ships were rapidly sold to a local shipbroker who was prepared to act as an intermediary as no new operating company had at that point yet been constituted. The names of Joseph Davies and Claude Percival Hailey thus appeared on the Port of Cardiff shipping register, the former as Managing Owner of the vessels *Devonia*, *Westonia* and *Barry*, with effect from 12th May, 1910.

Now it was truly all over for the Barry Railway Company steamships venture, and its hard-won Powers as defined in the Barry Railway (Steam Vessels) Act, 1904 were no longer of any use or value. More embarassing would have been the effect on the books; when *Gwalia* was sold to the Furness Railway, the Barry Railway Company was not taking too much of a hit on its capital accounts, as the price received was not greatly apart from her initial purchase price of a little under £30,000 less five years worth of depreciation. Her new owners renamed her *Lady Moyra*, in honour of the wife of Lord Richard Cavendish, a Furness Railway Director, and she seemingly gave good service to her new owners. For the remainder of the fleet, the story was somewhat less favourable.

The new company

Messrs J.B. Ferrier and T.E. Morel had not been idle in the early part of 1910, and the former's comments at the 51st meeting gave the vital clue as to what happened next. The very same J.B. Ferrier, two years before, had been particularly outspoken regarding the steamships and this quote from the February 1908 shareholders' meeting nicely summarizes the frustrations he and others then felt with what was seen as the intransigence of their Board, in persisting with the steamships, when he addressed the Chairman:

> . . . I tell you frankly, my Lord, that, when I came here, I fully expected to hear from the Board that they had made a blunder in the matter. We have expended some £100,000 on

One of the 1905-built Clydebank pair brings another good load of passengers into Ilfracombe. Adequate profits had eluded the Barry Railway Company, and the new company hoped to do better by running three vessels without the restriction of being unable to call at Cardiff. Sights such as this must have made people believe that profits were there to be had, as demand had been growing since the 19th century. *Lionel Vaughan Collection*

these passenger boats, and with the Pontoon you may take it roundly at about a quarter of a million pounds. If it is for the purpose of continuing the use of the Pontoon that the boats should be worked, I would answer, personally, that the Board would satisfy me with a better prospect if the boats were sent out into the Channel and blown to pieces . . . the Barry Company tried to do the best they could for the pleasure community of the district by supplying pleasure boats, but the Barry Company is not a venture, a philanthropic concern, merely to cater for the pleasure of the general public . . .

Mr Ferrier expressed other concerns as well on this occasion, linked to his wider business interests, but clearly believed that the boats might have a commercial future if freed from the restrictions of the 1904 Act which effectively confined them to trading out of Barry. It was perhaps not too surprising, then, that he now came forward as the designate Chairman of a new company formally styling itself as The Bristol Channel Passenger Boats, Limited. Easter 1910 had been and gone without the 'Red Funnel Line' fleet having been activated, as had been usual for that holiday period in previous years, and the travelling public may well have wondered what was going on. On Friday 6th May, 1910 this statement appeared in the *Barry Dock News*:

BARRY RED FUNNEL STEAMERS
WILL START RUNNING NEXT WEEK
AND WILL CALL AT CARDIFF, BARRY & PENARTH

The *Gwalia*, one of the steamers of the Barry Red Funnel Line of passenger steamers, having been acquired by the Barrow in Furness Railway Company, the remainder of the fleet, the *Devonia*, *Westonia* and *Barry*, were taken over from the Barry Railway Company, by a syndicate of Cardiff gentlemen on Tuesday last, and the boats will start running from Barry, Cardiff and Penarth next week.

The steamers ran trial trips in the Channel on Wednesday, and were formally taken over by the new proprietary on Thursday. The superintendence of the boats, as last year, will still, we understand, be entrusted to Captain Mackintosh. The prospectus of the new company, the Bristol Channel Steam Boats Ltd [*sic*] will be issued to the public in a day or two, and the nominal capital will be £70,000, of which only £50,000 will at present be raised.

Disregarding goodwill, the Prospectus of the proposed new company of The Bristol Channel Passenger Boats, Limited when it appeared made much of the bargain that was being got by the purchase, for £39,500, of three vessels whose combined purchase cost was said to have amounted to the much greater sum of £66,150. *Westonia*, then 10 years old, was the least valuable of the trio and had the lowest passenger carrying capacity, put at 762 on Class III certificate conditions. *Devonia*, somewhat younger at five years old, could carry 1,015 passengers and the youngest vessel *Barry* from 1907 had a capacity of 816 passengers. Such a fleet doubtless seemed like a bargain at those prices, and the emphasis of the proposed new company's outlook lay in the belief that, unfettered by the 1904 Act which had restricted the earnings of the Barry Railway Company operations, great earnings potential existed in the Bristol Channel generally, and particularly as a result of the privileged access they would have to railway connections at Barry Pier.

To further whet the appetite of the public to take shares in the new company, figures were quoted of the high rate of population growth in Cardiff, Newport and the 'Mining District' since 1891, '. . . from 716,000 in 1891 to 905,000 in 1901. Since the last Census it is well-known the growth has continued at a rapid rate'. Also emphasised were the benefits of the direct linkage with the Barry railway network which would feed traffic into the pier at Barry, and which would continue to feature as a focus for interchange traffic. The Prospectus stated that Barry was excellently situated for catering for '. . . the increasing traffic from the Merthyr, Aberdare and Rhondda, Ely, Llynvi, and other Valleys in possessing direct lines from Pontypridd, Porth and Bridgend right down to the Barry Pier. These routes are much appreciated, and largely patronised by the Mining population for all places in the Bristol Channel, and the Directors propose to continue and develop them'. Elsewhere, and perhaps more importantly, it was stated that the Directors intended to pay particular attention to the services from Cardiff, Penarth and Barry, and the great district served by those ports. Exactly how the gentlemen who had grouped to form the directorship of the new company got together with these common beliefs remains unclear, but there were some familiar names and although the link with the Barry Railway Company might have been formally severed, it appeared that a few of the larger shareholders had confidence that a wholly separate body could make money, in essence by a reversion to plying out of Cardiff.

Whitsuntide 1910

According to Mrs Grundy on Friday 13th May, 1910, *Gwalia* had sailed from Barry Dock for Barrow-in-Furness on the previous day, and she added that 'the daily services of the Red Funnel Fleet will open next Saturday week', i.e. Saturday 21st May, 1910, just after Whitsuntide that year, the Whit Monday falling on 16th May. But there was clearly a sound commercial case for seeking to cash in immediately on the peak Whitsuntide traffic in the Bristol Channel before the regular daily services got underway, and it is notable that the new company had not even been fully constituted at this time! This fact underscores the closeness of the relationship between the new and the old regimes, and that steamers could be prepared for the season, coaled and crewed before the money had even changed hands, so to speak, the official date on the actual Prospectus being 21st May, 1910. Whilst it was very much, of necessity, a new company this kind of co-operation and understanding, plus the fact that there was no change of image or branding, as it would be described today, was remarkable. Apart from the loss of the one-time flagship *Gwalia*, the folk in Barry might have thought very little had changed, as - not surprisingly - the steamers still looked the same, kept their names, and the services that were to be offered by the new company basically replicated those which the railway company had provided up until July 1907, that is, with much less emphasis on sailings from Barry Pier and a return to Cardiff Pier Head.

These services were a daily Cardiff to Weston 'ferry' operation and a daily Cardiff to Ilfracombe service which sailed from Barry at a fixed time, irrespective of tides, and with a train connection from Cardiff Riverside station. It was now only Birnbeck Pier at Weston where the steamers called; the attitude towards the Grand Pier was succinctly expressed in the Campbell Bristol Channel District Guide handbooks of the era, thus:

> . . . the first section with the handsome and commodious pavilion thereon, was opened in the summer of 1904. Although the pier has been carried out a very considerable distance, it is at present useless for any regular steamboat service. Apart from this it forms a most delightful promenade commanding charming views of the town.

Barry Pier would of course be more heavily patronised on those days when there was insufficient water at the Pier Head for the Red Funnel boat to berth there, necessitating all Cardiff passengers to take the Barry Railway Company train from the Riverside station. The Weston and Ilfracombe sailings were normally the preserve of *Westonia* and *Devonia* respectively. The third steamer would enable other excursions to be offered and this extract from the *Western Mail* on Saturday 14th May, 1910 gave further details:

> RED FUNNEL LINE
> SERVICE FROM CARDIFF OPENS TODAY
>
> Today the Red Funnel Line of pleasure steamers commence the season with direct sailings to and from the Pier Head, Cardiff calling at Penarth and Barry, and those who have experienced the luxuriousness of the roomy boats will be glad to hear that all the boats are to form a complete service to the Channel holiday places. At 9.20 this morning the first boat makes a maiden trip to Weston and ten minutes later another boat leaves for Ilfracombe, one of the most popular places on the Channel. An afternoon trip to Ilfracombe will also be made by the favourite steamer *Barry*. Special attention has been given by the company to Whit week and a variety of trips has accordingly been arranged, as can be seen from the advertisement in another column. They include numerous trips to Weston, Minehead, Ilfracombe, Clevedon and Channel cruises. The steamers have recently been overhauled and are spick and span. A new feature has been introduced in the Stewards Department, with catering on the à la carte principal at a moderate tariff. The Chairman of the company is Mr J.B. Ferrier JP, the general manager Captain McIntosh, and the offices are at Stuart Street, Pier Head.

Whitsuntide of 1910 featured the three steamers, under their new management, running the familiar range of Bristol Channel excursions on Whit Monday, 16th May. The advertisements for that day suggest that the 'railway run' boat performed an additional Cardiff-Weston round trip after her arrival back at Cardiff from Ilfracombe in the evening, and that there had been intensive all day 'ferry' services between Cardiff and Weston. Barry Pier was visited from Weston at low-water when the ferry steamer was unable to cross back to Cardiff, and Minehead enjoyed a number of calls too. In describing the Whit Monday trips provided by the fleet of the 'new' Red Funnel Line company, who obviously were seen as very welcome now that they were back at their old berth at Cardiff's Pier Head, the *Western Mail* was just as fulsome in its praise of the newly-rediscovered local operator as were the Ilfracombe papers when waxing lyrical about the P. & A. Campbell Ltd White Funnel steamers:

> Now that the Red Funnel Line of steamers can, under new proprietorship, sail from the Cardiff Pier Head, the public are not slow to take advantage of the facilities offered for

Hillsborough Hill in the background pinpoints this shot, dated 1910, of some of the crew of *Devonia* as having been taken whilst the paddler was alongside at Ilfracombe. The new management of The Bristol Channel Passenger Boats company had taken control from the Barry Railway Company just a few weeks earlier. *Brian Luxton Collection*

over-channel trips. On Whit Monday these steamer excursions were the most popular of outings from the city, and it was quite refreshing to notice how thoroughly the public enjoyed their trips on the Red Funnel steamers, equipped as they are with every convenience for the comfort and pleasure of their patrons. Weston and Minehead were the favourite resorts, the afternoon run to the latter delightful rendezvous being particularly popular. A glance at the advertisement will show that there is an excellent selection of trips provided by the management, and it is not risky to predict that, as the summer advances, the Red Funnel Line will maintain its high reputation as one of the best services for over-channel excursions out of Cardiff. Given good weather conditions a trip to the Somersetshire and Devonshire resorts never fails to please.

For an alternative view of the same Bank Holiday Monday peak traffic levels in 1910, *the Ilfracombe Chronicle* usefully gave some numbers of arrivals by both lines of steamers as well as an indication that the weather was good and played its part in stimulating business, despite the inconvenience of the Bristol Channel tides that day:

This was possibly the most brilliant, as regards weather, of any in the long roll of Ilfracombe holidays. The sunshine record tells of 14.8 hours of unclouded shining, being far beyond that of many other places . . . Visitors were early astir. Some eager ones - about 260 in fact - took boat at Bristol about midnight, and landed from the *Westward Ho* at an hour when most people were in their beds. The passengers had a good opportunity of seeing the comet as they came down Channel, and on arriving set out for the Capstone, Hillsborough and other places, to enjoy a magnificent sunrise. The *Westward Ho* returned at 6.15 am with a handful of passengers, who were spending the day at Cardiff. She returned at 12.30 with 600 passengers, taking nearly half of them to Clovelly for the afternoon. The *Britannia* came from Bristol, landing nearly 500 passengers at 2.30, afterwards taking a good number for a Channel trip to Bideford Bay. The *Devonia* had her full complement of about 1,000 from Cardiff, Barry and Minehead, taking off at the latter place about 400, having landed the same number. She also had a good number for a Channel trip towards Lynmouth . . . taking the steamer business as a whole, there were over 200 more landing at the Pier than on Whit Monday last year . . .

Given that Pockett's *Brighton* also came across from Swansea and deposited 550 passengers at Ilfracombe that morning, and that *Cambria* also came from Cardiff in the afternoon, this was a large volume of traffic to handle and the management of the new Red Funnel Line company would, one assumes, have been encouraged. The process of allottment of shares was taking place at that time, and this is an appropriate point to look more closely at the structure of the new company, and who its main backers were.

The Bristol Channel Passenger Boats, Limited

The purpose of the company was straightforward, and can be summarised as being to manage the business generated by the three steamships acquired from the Barry Railway Company from those places in the Bristol Channel which had been served by the latter company since the 1907 lawsuit, plus Cardiff which now represented the principal traffic-generating target in South Wales. In doing this, Penarth Pier re-appeared properly on the Red Funnel Line map and was to

This Prospectus has been filed with the Registrar of Joint Stock Companies.

The List of Applications will be closed on or before Friday, the 27th day of May, 1910.

THE BRISTOL CHANNEL PASSENGER BOATS, LIMITED.

Incorporated under the Companies (Consolidation) Act, 1908.

RED FUNNEL LINE.

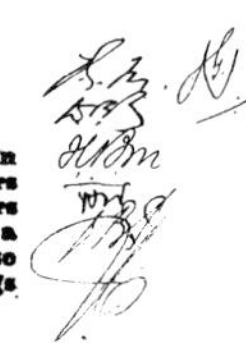

SHARE CAPITAL £70,000

In 70,000 Shares of £1 each.

There are no Founders or Management or Deferred Shares.

ISSUE OF 50,000 ORDINARY SHARES OF £1 EACH.

Payable as to 2/6 per Share on application, 7/6 per share ~~and the balance~~ on Allotment, and the balance on the 30th June 1910

The Articles of Association provide that every Shareholder holding not less than 100 Ordinary Shares in the Capital of the Company, or in the case of joint holders of not less than 100 Ordinary Shares, the joint Shareholder whose name appears first in the register of members in respect of such shares, shall be entitled to a free pass or season ticket entitling him, so long as he shall hold such shares, to travel on any of the Company's Passenger Steamers on ordinary advertised sailings free of charge, except on Good Fridays and Bank Holidays.

DIRECTORS.

JOHN BEST FERRIER, BUTE CRESCENT, CARDIFF (*Chairman*)
Director of Burnyeat Brown & Co, Ltd

DAVID PERCIVAL BARNETT (F. H. LAMBERT, BARNETT & CO., SHIPOWNERS), SHIPOWNER, EXCHANGE, CARDIFF.

JOHN CORY (JOHN CORY & SONS, SHIPOWNERS), SHIPOWNER, MOUNT STUART SQUARE, CARDIFF.
Chairman of the Cardiff Channel Dry Docks and Pontoon Co., Ltd.

JOHN GRIFFITH JONES, CHARTERED ACCOUNTANT, BRYNHYFRYD, PONTYPRIDD.
Director of the Rhondda Valley Breweries Co., Ltd.

HILARY BLONDEL MARQUAND (MARTIN & MARQUAND, SHIPOWNERS), SHIPOWNER, DOCK CHAMBERS, CARDIFF.
Director of Hills Dry Docks and Engineering Co., Ltd.

THOMAS EDWARD MOREL, (MOREL, LIMITED, SHIPOWNERS), SHIPOWNER, STUART STREET, CARDIFF.
Director of the Cardiff Channel Dry Docks and Pontoon Co. Ltd.

HUMPHRY WALLIS (OSBORN & WALLIS, SHIPOWNERS, CARDIFF AND BRISTOL), SHIPOWNER, EXCHANGE, CARDIFF.
Director of the Great Western Colliery Co, Ltd., and Locket's Merthyr Collieries (1894), Ltd.

BANKERS.

LONDON & PROVINCIAL BANK, LIMITED.

REGISTERED 58261 14 MAY 1910

SOLICITORS.

DONALD MACLEAN & HANDCOCK, JAMES STREET, CARDIFF.

BROKERS.

THACKERAY & CO., DOCK CHAMBERS, CARDIFF.

PERCY POWELL, 132, BUTE STREET, CARDIFF.

AUDITORS.

CLARKE, DOVEY & CO., QUEEN STREET, CARDIFF.

SECRETARY & OFFICES.

WILLIAM E. SHIPP, 1, STUART STREET, BUTE DOCKS, CARDIFF.

Presented for filing by

The Prospectus for the new company. *National Archives, Kew*

be served in much the same way as by P. & A. Campbell Ltd on its core Cardiff-Weston 'ferry' services, that is, by practically all sailings in either direction, except when an ebb tide made it prudent to cut the voyage to Cardiff-Weston (or vice versa) direct, to save precious minutes. On occasions a passenger who had gone directly from Penarth to Weston might find that when returning from Weston they might proceed into Cardiff before coming out of there to steam around Penarth Head to get back to Penarth Pier. Penarth would also be served by the 'railway run' boat which now, generally on 11 or 12 days out of 14, dictated by the tidal cycle, reverted to starting at the Pier Head at Cardiff, as it had done during the period 1905-1907. The call at Penarth Pier would take place about 10 minutes after departure from Cardiff, *en route* to Barry Pier, whereupon those who had elected to travel by train to Barry Pier would embark. Penarth Pier would also now see plentiful 'Red Funnel Line' calls by whatever other excursions might happen to be offered from Cardiff, such as those to Mumbles, or to Clevedon and Bristol.

Seven gentlemen put their names forward as Directors of the proposed new company, and the Prospectus stated that the authorised share capital would be £70,000, and that a sum of £50,000 would initially be sought through subscription from the public. According to the Articles of Association, the qualification to be a Director stemmed from having a shareholding of at least £250 nominal value of shares, and at the outset these holdings were stated as being sub-underwritten:

J.B. Ferrier	1,000 shares	H. B. Marquand	1,000 shares
D.P. Barnett	1,500 shares	T. E. Morel	2,500 shares
J. Cory	1,000 shares	H. Wallis	1,000 shares
J. G. Jones	1,000 shares		

Excepting Messrs Ferrier, Barnett and Jones, the other four Directors all had a common professional interest in ship-owning and were well known in Cardiff. The Cory family origins were in Padstow, Cornwall and they had come to Cardiff in 1872 and were heavily involved in shipping and coal-exporting. The Marquand family hailed from Guernsey, and T.E. Morel was the son of Jerseyman Thomas Morel who had first ventured into shipping in the 1860s, carrying new potatoes from the Channel Islands to South Wales. H. Wallis, of the Wallis and Osborn company name, was a Bristolian and the company was associated with Bristol rather than Cardiff, and was Bristol registered.

Some £9,000 of capital was thus underwritten from the outset by these seven gentlemen and this, together with the balance raised through public subscription, was sufficient to enable the steamers to be acquired as planned from Messrs Davies & Hailey, for the sum of £39,500, and all three were duly re-registered in the name of the new company with effect from 21st June, 1910, with J.B. Ferrier designated as the Managing Owner as required under the relevant Board of Trade procedures. The Registered Office of The Bristol Channel Passenger Boats, Ltd was declared as being at 1, Stuart Street, in the City of Cardiff. As an incentive to invest, ownership of 100 ordinary shares would give individuals a free pass for all ordinary advertised sailings, except those on Good Fridays and Bank Holidays.

The Prospectus did not mention any specific agreements between the new company and the Barry Railway Company, but it is evident from later Minute Book extracts that a form of 'user agreement' for Barry Pier had been entered into, albeit without explicit reference to whether charges would be raised for the use of this facility. The railway company still wished to see additional income generated by passengers over its network who were heading for Barry Pier, where if there were no boats there would be no passenger demand. Elsewhere in the Bristol Channel, the 'new' Red Funnel Line was free to agree terms with all of the proprietors of piers and harbours that they wished to use, and at none of these were there any explicit restrictions, and so things were now more evenly matched against the White Funnel Fleet from over the other side. But who would attract the bulk of the Cardiff traffic now that the Barry boats were back?

Prospects for the new company

All this must outwardly have seemed quite promising to the public and to investors; the new company was unrestricted in where it could trade, it had acquired as its fleet vessels which were a known quantity and quite capable of taking on the bigger White Funnel Fleet, and good Whitsuntide carryings would have made a promising start to earnings. What is unclear is whether the launch of shares to the public had actually been as successful as hoped by the new Board. The reason for this doubt can be found in the register of shareholders of The Bristol Channel Passenger Boats, Ltd, which recorded the size of each individual shareholding. Whereas there were a few hundred small holdings, and disregarding the holdings of the seven Directors already mentioned, three names boldly stand out from the rest, as between them almost one-third of the paid-up capital was remarkably accounted for. None other than the Earl of Plymouth had taken 6,000 shares, and David Davies and two sisters of his had each taken 2,000 shares. Some 12,000 shares were thus accounted for by these four individuals, and this poses the obvious question of whether they had somehow been prevailed upon to make up the balance of the required capital (i.e. to generate the cash required to pay off the shipbrokers Davies & Hailey) after a poor public response to the shares being called, or whether their genuine enthusiasm for and belief in the new company prompted them to put up such large sums before the public response was known? The Prospectus stated that a minimum of £31,000 needed to be raised by public subscription before the share issue could proceed to allotment, and this figure can be explained as the difference between that underwritten by the seven Directors' £9,000 and the £40,000 approximately purchase price of the three steamers plus broking commissions. Given the publicly-stated intention to raise £50,000 of the £70,000 mentioned in the Memorandum/Articles, one tends to conclude that the allotment was disappointing, and left the new company rather short of working capital.

Either way, the 1910 season now got underway, and a notable event for the new company now loomed up. Like when Cardiff's new Queen Alexandra Dock had opened in 1907, and the local Barry Railway Company fleet had then been prominent amongst the civic dignitaries, and outshone the Campbell rivals, the local excursion fleet was now again at the forefront. The occasion was the departure of the *Terra Nova* of Scott's expedition to the South Pole from Cardiff, on Wednesday 15th June, 1910. In 1909 Robert Falcon Scott had announced his intention '. . . to reach the South Pole and secure for the British Empire the honour of that achievement' and, to illustrate the scale of interest in this major expedition, some 8,000 men were said to have volunteered to join his party. Ship-owners in Cardiff played a significant role in providing funding to support this captivating venture and *Terra Nova* duly arrived in Cardiff on Friday 10th June, 1910, at the Roath Basin, to make final preparations before the great departure to the South. A reception was held at Cardiff's Royal Hotel the following Monday evening and Scott told those assembled that in recognition of the key part that the Port of Cardiff had played in his party's arrangements, Cardiff would be designated as the port to which *Terra Nova* would return after the expedition.

The Red Funnel Line fleet of steamers were associated in a positive way with this great event, and advertisements in the *Western Mail* on Tuesday 14th June, 1910 showed how special arrangements had been made for the next day:

> Departure of the *Terra Nova*, the Antarctic expedition ship, from Cardiff. The PS *Devonia* will leave the Cardiff Pier Head at 12.45 pm calling at Penarth at 12.55 pm and accompany the *Terra Nova* some distance down channel, returning about 2.30 pm. This trip is under the patronage of the Lord Mayor and Corporation of Cardiff, together with The Chamber of Commerce. The Post Office Band will render musical selections on this trip, and a collection will be made on board in aid of the Cardiff Infirmary.

Also advertised that day were a good range of trips but expediently modifed to incorporate this commitment for *Devonia*, which implied that *Barry* undertook the 'railway run' (with a Minehead call) whilst *Westonia* performed her customary Cardiff-Weston 'ferry' round trips. The White Funnel Fleet offered a comparable trip accompanying *Terra Nova*, but with rather less of the Cardiff civic patronage element, and which was duly undertaken by *Ravenswood*. Numerous tugs had also been chartered to convey parties of well-wishers to view this great occasion and it is quite clear from the Cardiff papers which described the departure - where *Devonia* was on the starboard side of *Terra Nova*, and her White Funnel competitor on her port side, with the crowds cheering themselves hoarse - that all the dignitaries were on the Cardiff ship. The tugs handling *Terra Nova* out of Cardiff were off by Penarth, and then she was away on her journey south.

An interesting aside to this day of altered timetable arrangements for the Red Funnel Line fleet was the way in which, operating with all three vessels, much of the Bristol Channel traffic demand was still provided for in addition to the prestigious Cardiff special excursion. After the expedition ship had left, *Devonia* quickly returned to Cardiff to operate a 2.30 pm sailing to Minehead and Ilfracombe. *Westonia* had already managed four Weston 'ferry' crossings on the morning tide and, on the ebb ran a 4.00 pm sailing to Minehead via Weston, which provided a third call at Minehead after that provided by *Barry* on the morning down 'railway run'. To get the most out of *Barry* that evening, she ran a round trip from Cardiff to Weston and back after completing the return 'railway run', whilst *Westonia* ended the day's proceedings on her last run from Minehead to Cardiff via Weston, making the seventh and last 'ferry' crossing from Weston to Cardiff on that very busy day just before the Midsummer of 1910. For good measure, an opportunity had also been provided for Weston folk to enjoy the spectacle at Cardiff as *Devonia* had been programmed to depart from Weston at 11.00 am for Cardiff - supplementing *Westonia's* ferry runs - prior to taking up the special sailing to see off *Terra Nova*. Down at Ilfracombe the passing of the expedition ship was not overlooked and a special short cruise to view her was offered by *Devonia*, it being reported that *Terra Nova* passed by Ilfracombe at around 6.30 that evening. In this way the maximum yield from the three-strong fleet would have probably been realised on that busy day in 1910.

Competition at Cardiff again

In isolation, one might have thought that a company seeking to run three steamships, in 1910, two of which were capacious and of very recent construction and the third somewhat more utilitarian but still reasonably adequate for short 45-minute, or so, ferry crossings, might easily have found adequate profits there for the taking. There was the particularly convenient operational feature of exclusive access to Barry Pier, the only place in the Bristol Channel where such a purpose-built interchange with rail existed, at any state of the tide. But the passengers were not actually at Barry, and so a reversion to sailings direct from Cardiff, where the populace could easily be found, must have seemed almost guaranteed to succeed. After many years of delay, there was now a tide-free berth at Weston's Birnbeck Pier, achieved after much perseverance on the part of the Weston-super-Mare Pier Company, and the sorry saga of Weston's Grand Pier had already become strictly an irrelevance. From Weston's viewpoint, though, it was Barry that was in the wrong place as Cardiff was the natural destination, not somewhere a few miles out of the way down the coast, even if a train met each arrival at Barry Pier to transport folks to Cardiff Riverside station.

P. & A. Campbell Ltd had of course been engaged in the Bristol Channel excursion business for rather longer than the Red Funnel Line, and by now it had endured five years of unwelcome competition, as the firm saw it, from its Welsh adversaries. The Campbell brothers had been unable to inject any new capital into their own fleet because of depleted takings at lower fares than those they could have charged if left to their own devices. The Red Funnel Line - whether or not in the hands of the Barry Railway Company, or newly-reconstituted as a more direct Cardiff rival - was still a thorn in the flesh. Perhaps a key feature was that the Bristol company was, quite simply, bigger and thus better able to spread its overheads over more vessels, picking up the traffic out of Bristol and Newport as well as at Cardiff. It also had its own workshops in Bristol and had a notably successful engineering record exemplified by its ability to maintain its own fleet each year, and carry out rebuilds locally in Bristol, using either its own labour at the Underfall Yard, or judiciously sending vessels back to the Clyde for heavier work, and using local dry-docking facilities in the City Docks, or at Avonmouth or elsewhere if necessary.

In 1910 the White Funnel Fleet consisted of nine vessels, six of which (*Waverley, Ravenswood, Westward Ho, Cambria, Britannia* and *Albion*) found work in the Bristol Channel. The other three (*Brighton Queen, Bonnie Doon* and *Glen Rosa*) were utilised on the South Coast, berthing and coaling as required at Newhaven, handy for Brighton where much of their traffic was generated. The newest ship of the Bristol Channel fleet was *Britannia* from 1896, and in 1910 it could be said that the Campbell brothers managed a smart, popular fleet which was scarcely overshadowed by any competitors. But being naturally entrepreneurial and ambitious, they must have been frustrated at their inability to fund any new vessels with which to project a more up-to-date image, and be seen to be on more of an even footing with *Devonia* and *Barry*, delivered in 1905 and 1907 respectively. To stress the point about head-to-head competition, a look at the P. & A. Campbell Ltd timetables for that day of 15th June, 1910 when *Terra Nova* sailed for Antarctica is instructive and emphasises that as far as Cardiff was concerned, the two companies were selling to more or less exactly the same market. There were eight P. & A. Campbell Ltd ferry departures to Weston that day, and five minutes after the Barry Red Funnel boat had taken the 'railway run' to Ilfracombe calling at Penarth, Barry, Minehead and Lynmouth a white-funnelled steamer left, at 9.35 am, for Penarth, Minehead, Lynmouth, Ilfracombe and Clovelly. Another P. & A. Campbell Ltd vessel left Cardiff at 11.00 am for Clevedon and Bristol - this was also a Weston sailing, supplementing 'ferry' departures, and would have picked up passengers for Bristol on the English side of the Channel too. Furthermore, another Campbell vessel was advertised to run down-Channel at 2.15 pm from Cardiff and Penarth to Minehead and Ilfracombe.

These were not all the White Funnel offerings that day from Cardiff, yet it will readily be seen that what was being marketed was practically identical to that offered by the new Cardiff company. Given the tidal constraints this was to a great degree inevitable, but it could be argued that whatever passenger demand there was in the Bristol Channel (disregarding the Swansea trade in the hands of Pockett's) was now being catered for by nine vessels (six White Funnel, and three Red Funnel) where for a given volume of demand fewer vessels would doubtless represent greater yields. If one disregards the P. & A. Campbell Ltd presence at Bristol and at Newport, which usually equated to three vessels, then each fleet was fielding three vessels at Cardiff. As fares were the same, it is reasonable to predict that costs would tend to determine which operator was more likely to survive in the longer-term such blatant head-on competition. Just a year before, the Campbell brothers had had the Cardiff traffic all to themselves, and so what was happening in 1910 was now much more fundamental to their future.

A frustration in researching all of this is the absence of any published accounts for the new Cardiff company, but a view of what was happening behind the scenes at least from the perspective of P. & A. Campbell Ltd can be inferred from the latter's official records from the period. Throughout 1909 and into 1910 there are numerous minuted references to the continued necessity for loans and overdraft facilities, and mortgaging the fleet. There is some evidence that P. & A. Campbell Ltd was seeking to get its hands on an additional vessel, although the ship considered was none other than the unsatisfactory *Philomel* then surplus to the requirements of the Furness Railway. As it turned out she was rejected after inspection by Alec Campbell on account of her unsatisfactory boiler condition. This suggests that there was felt to be plenty of demand at Cardiff, and dominance would accrue to the operator that could grab the larger share. The precise circumstances under which P. & A. Campbell Ltd did decide, later in 1910, to proceed and order its first new steamer for 15 years are not wholly clear, but it seems that traffic results were good enough to give the company confidence to take the plunge once the takings were added up and found to be sufficient to enable the bulk of its overdraft to be paid off.

There is evidence that the new company occasionally benefited by charter arrangements and one such was recorded in the *Ilfracombe Weekly News* on Friday 1st July, 1910, leading one to wonder who exactly was the charterer for such an occasion:

> An excursion party of Aberavon Shop Assistants visited the town yesterday. The PS *Devonia* was chartered for the occasion, and it was expected the party would number 1,000, but the somewhat stormy weather reduced the number to 830, who spent an enjoyable day in spite of the roughness of the crossing from Port Talbot.

Meanwhile, there were rumours about that the Red Funnel Line was also doing so well that it was going to purchase a new steamer and Mrs Grundy stated, on Friday 22nd July, 1910, that another vessel of the same type as *Barry* was to be ordered. The report in the *Barry Dock News* of August Bank Holiday traffic volumes painted a very rosy picture:

> BANK HOLIDAY AT BARRY
>
> Favoured with delightful weather, Barry and the different places of holiday attraction in the neighbourhood were crowded with visitors on Monday. It was estimated there were 40,000 people on Barry Island, and immense crowds of pleasure-seekers also thronged to Sully, Porthkerry, Cold Knap, Rhoose, Fontygary and other places in the Vale of Glamorgan. The Red Funnel passenger steamers which called at Barry during the day were filled to overflowing on each occasion, and large crowds of excursionists were carried on the steamers and on the different railway systems without a single mishap.

As if to illustrate how weather conditions could vary considerably up and down the Bristol Channel, the Ilfracombe papers noted that the Bank Holiday had been marred by dull weather, although this had not dampened visitor numbers at the North Devon resort. According to the *Ilfracombe Weekly News Devonia* and *Barry* took 676 and 596 passengers respectively to Ilfracombe on the Saturday (30th July), a very healthy volume, whilst *Cambria, Britannia, Westward Ho* and *Albion* brought 720, 880, 800 and 400 respectively that day. The Saturday sailings probably accounted more for staying passengers than day-trippers than those on Bank Holiday Monday 1st August, 1910, and on that day the Red Funnel Line contented itself with one down-Channel sailing only by *Barry*, which brought 662, after which she took 196 on a Channel cruise. For the White Funnel Fleet, *Britannia* ran down to Ilfracombe twice and *Westward Ho* once, bringing 650 and 821 passengers on the morning runs, and 223 on the second run of *Britannia*. For Channel cruises *Westward Ho* evidently ran three short trips, at 2.30, 5.00 and 6.30 pm, successively taking out 550, 100 and 150 passengers, which figures suggest that perhaps the Cardiff company had miscalculated, or were content for its other two vessels to remain up at Cardiff on intensive ferry crossings.

A slightly different account of the Bank Holiday was given in the *Ilfracombe Chronicle*, which stated that on the Saturday the number of arrivals on the Saturday had exceeded that on any single day of the previous year. It was claimed that many passengers had been left behind at Cardiff, and at Newport. Based on these levels of peak demand one can see how the spectacle of failing to pick up all the traffic that was on offer might have persuaded the Bristol company that the time to expand had finally arrived. But for the new Cardiff company it must have been a matter of frustration that they had been obliged to enter the market with just three vessels and not the four that its predecessors had deployed at peak times.

Another tragedy

Very shortly after this high point of the season, the papers were full of the story of an apparent fatality, which again happened on one of the Red Funnel Line steamers. As Mrs Grundy put it, on Friday 5th August, 1910:

> As the passenger steamer *Barry* was returning up-Channel from a Mumbles and Tenby trip last Thursday, off Porthkerry, a passenger named Chris Fitzgerald, an engine-driver of 119 Moy Road, Cardiff jumped overboard and was drowned. The man had no friends on board, and he was identified by a mackintosh which he left on a seat on deck. Every effort was made by the ship's boats to effect a rescue, but, darkness having set in, unfortunately without avail.

The drama undoubtedly gave the Cardiff company some unwelcome publicity with these sensational headlines the following week, as more details became known:

> MY GRAVE WILL BE SEAWEED
> FATAL LEAP OVERBOARD OFF BARRY
> CARDIFF MAN DEJECTED THROUGH FAILING SIGHT
>
> The deceased, it was reported, had been a Cardiff Railway Company engine-driver who had recently failed an eyesight test, and was depressed. The night was dark, wet and rough, and there were but few people in the after part of the ship. Mr Fitzgerald was quoted as having said 'Tell the Captain I am going: I am ill: I am sorry I have come.' It was clear, the report continued, that the deceased had contemplated suicide, and had left letters. A verdict of 'Suicide whilst in a state of temporary insanity through depression' was recorded.

The routine newspaper reports of the half-yearly Barry Railway Company shareholders' meetings now carried less information of relevance to maritime affairs, and at the meeting held on Friday 5th August, 1910, shortly after the

August Bank Holiday, it was simply noted that the steamers, at an original cost of £104,470 had now all been sold. More to the point, it was noted that there was now an improvement in the dividends to be paid, which would be 7 per cent compared to 6 per cent in the corresponding previous half-year. Little more needed to be said regarding why this was so, but it was also noted that the trend was now moving in the right direction as financial results were improving.

A different aspect of Bristol Channel excursion sailings generally in 1910, following the opening of the new dock at Avomouth the previous year, with its associated facilities to deal with GWR-operated boat-trains from and to London, was the attraction afforded by the new regular ocean-liner sailings of the Royal Canadian Northern Line from Bristol for Canada. Either of two 12,000 ton liners, the *Royal George* and the *Royal Edward* tended to depart at fortnightly intervals from Avonmouth for Quebec and Montreal in the summer, and short evening sailings from Cardiff by both operators to view the departing liners were offered (routinely by P. & A. Campbell Ltd), typically lasting up to to three hours for a fare of one shilling. One cruise by a Red Funnel Line steamer to view the departing *Royal George* was advertised for Thursday 15th September, 1910, on this occasion leaving Barry at 4.10 pm and due to return at 8.00 pm. Such a trip would have provided welcome variety at Barry Pier as so much activity had moved away from there to the Pier Head at Cardiff.

At the longer end of the day-excursions range, it appears that Lundy Island was rarely visited, if at all, by the Red Funnel Line steamers during their period of ownership by The Bristol Channel Passenger Boats, Ltd. But from around 1909 calls to land at Lundy by White Funnel steamer had been initiated although the owners of Lundy were still not then keen to permit more than small numbers of excursions. Otherwise, the practice of the 'railway run' boat extending to Clovelly in high summer was often perpetuated. With runs from Cardiff to Mumbles, Tenby and the Stack Rocks, these represented the outer limits of operations in 1910. Soon enough the season-end came around, and the last mention in the *Barry Dock News* of the Red Funnel Line steamers was to declare that the closing trips would take place at the customary time of the end of September, albeit in this case stretched to the adjacent following Saturday 1st October.

The 1911 season

Much of the rest of this story of the brief life of the Red Funnel Line fleet whilst in the ownership of The Bristol Channel Passenger Boats, Ltd is necessarily derived from surviving official P. & A. Campbell Ltd records, supplemented by occasional newspaper reports of peak holiday carryings. No company records for the 'new' company have been traced, other than those of the Board of Trade dealing with its dissolution. After 1910 the Barry Railway Company records cease to make any mention of the vessels which, in a sense, had become history to them after their books had been adjusted to reflect their sale, with a substantial capital write-down. An allowance should therefore be made for any seeming bias here, as the newspapers in 1911 seem not to have carried any stories of the ailing financial health of the new Cardiff company as a going concern until it was practically all over. The season started normally enough, with *Barry* and *Westonia* commissioned in readiness for the Easter holdays with the customary deployment of the older vessel on the Cardiff-Weston 'ferry' providing three or four round trips daily and *Barry* tending to run down-Channel to Minehead and Ilfracombe. After about a week *Westonia* went back into the Basin at Barry to lay up for a while, leaving *Barry* to sustain all other duties until early in May, when they swapped places. By mid-May both were out again, and after *Devonia* joined the fray on 24th May, 1910 (in time for the Whitsuntide peak) the normal pattern was resumed whereby the biggest vessel, *Devonia*, took charge of the 'railway run'. There was some switching of vessels, and on odd occasions *Westonia* ventured down to Ilfracombe.

An intriguing aspect of the way in which tourists to the Barry area may have viewed passenger steamship services is apparent from the text and advertisements of an *Official Guide to Barry, District and the Vale of Glamorgan* publication issued in 1911 by the Barry Chamber of Trade in conjunction with the Barry Railway Company. There was no mention of the proper name of the Cardiff company and instead the Marine Excursions were described as if to imply they were an integral part of the local railway operation, with emphasis on convenience of interchange:

> . . . there is nothing more exhilarating on a hot summer's day than the delightful sensation of a temperate breeze on one of the magnificent saloon steamers of the Red Funnel Line which call at the Barry Pier. The vessels are equipped in the completest way, and, whilst they are swift, being paddle steamers, they afford an easy passage. The Pontoon Landing Stage, which has been provided by the Barry Company, affords the greatest convenience to passengers embarking and disembarking from the steamers. The trains run alongside the Pontoon within a few yards of the steamers, a provision which is unique in the Bristol Channel . . .

The Whitsuntide weather was favourable, according to the *Ilfracombe Gazette*, and references to record numbers being brought into the town by steamer and train were again made. After running just one steamer from Swansea for many years, Pockett's had decided to augment their *Brighton* with a second vessel *Mavis* acquired from the General Steam Navigation Company, and which had been placed into service by the Whitsuntide of 1911. From this account, the proportion of Ilfracombe traffic which was being handled by the Red Funnel Line during the Bank Holiday period, relative to that which was enjoyed by the P. & A. Campbell Ltd White Funnel Fleet and the newly-enlarged Pockett's fleet can be roughly gauged, starting on Saturday 3rd June, 1911:

> . . . *Brighton* landed 323 passengers, and took on 150 for a trip to Clovelly. On the same day the *Cambria* landed 290; the *Barry* 418; the *Westward Ho* 550; the *Britannia*, 573; *Devonia*, 736; and the *Mavis* 453. [The report continued] . . . on Whit Monday the Pier presented an animated appearance at a very early hour. At half-past six the *Britannia* landed 684 trippers. She took away 96, and at 4.40 in the afternoon again visited Ilfracombe with 820 passengers. The *Brighton* came in with 816 passengers, and took 155 for a trip to the Mumbles. The *Cambria* landed 833 at the Pier, and later took 815 for a cruise to Hartland. The *Westonia* also brought in 640. The same steamer took 176 people

BARRY RAILWAY

— AND —

RED FUNNEL LINE.

QUICKEST ROUTE TO

LYNMOUTH

— AND —

ILFRACOMBE

COMMENCING MAY 29th,

Shortest Sea Passage.	DAILY TIME TABLE SERVICE (SUNDAYS EXCEPTED), *Via* BARRY PIER.	**Trains run alongside Steamers.**

The most convenient route for Passengers and Luggage.

FROM	By Train leaving at	RETURN ARRANGEMENTS.		
	A.M.		During June.	July and August.
			P.M.	P.M.
Porth	9 0			
Pontypridd	9 10			
Treforest	9 15			
Bridgend	8 35	Steamer leaves Ilfracombe	4 0	5 30
Newport, G.W. ..	8 57	,, ,, Off Lynmouth	4 30	6 0
Cardiff (Riverside) ..	9 39			
Barry	9 48	Trains leave Barry Pier on arrival of Steamer.		
Barry Pier Steamer dep. ..	10 5	NOTE.—For Sailings from Thursday, June 22, to Saturday, June 24 inclusive, see special bills.		

☛ **Passengers' Luggage labelled through and transferred from Train to Steamers at Barry Pier free of Charge.**

Cheap Day Trip and Tourist Bookings from all Stations (*see Page 73*), **also from Taff Vale Stations in Rhondda Valleys** *via* **Porth.**

DAY TRIP AND TOURIST TICKETS

Will be issued daily (Sundays excepted) during the Season, to

LYNMOUTH & ILFRACOMBE

ALSO TO

WESTON & MINEHEAD

WHEN STEAMER SAILINGS PERMIT, AS UNDER:—

From \ To	WESTON AND CLEVEDON.				MINEHEAD.		ILFRACOMBE.	
	Via Barry Pier.		*Via* Cardiff (Clarence Road).		*Via* Barry Pier.		*Via* Barry Pier.	
	Day Trip	Tourist	Day Trip	Tourist	Day Trip	Tourist	Day Trip	Tourist
Barry Pier	s. d.	s. d.	s. d.	s. d.	s. d.	s. d.	s. d.	s. d.
Barry Island								
Barry								
Barry Docks					Fore	Cabin.	Fore	Cabin.
Cadoxton	2 0	2 6	2 6	3 6	2 6	3 6	3 0	5 0
Dinas Powis					Saloon.		Saloon.	
Cogan					3 0	4 6	4 0	6 0
Grangetown			—	—				
Cardiff			—	—				
Porth	3 3	4 3	—	—	4 3	6 0	5 0	6 9
Trehafod	3 0	4 3	—	—	4 0	6 0	4 9	6 9
Pontypridd, B.R.	3 0	4 0	3 0	4 0	4 0	5 9	4 9	6 6
Treforest, B.R. ..	2 9	3 9	2 9	3 9	3 9	5 6	4 6	6 3
Efail Isaf ..	2 9	3 9	2 9	3 9	3 9	5 6	4 6	6 3
Creigiau	2 6	3 3	2 6	3 3	3 6	5 3	4 3	6 0
Wenvoe	2 3	2 9	2 9	3 6	3 3	4 9	4 0	6 0
Bridgend	3 3	4 0	—	—	4 0	5 9	4 9	6 9
Southerndown Rd.	3 0	3 9	4 0	4 9	3 9	5 6	4 6	6 6
Llantwit Major ..	2 9	3 6	3 6	4 6	3 6	5 3	4 3	6 3
Gileston	2 6	3 3	3 3	4 3	3 6	5 0	4 3	6 3
Aberthaw ..	2 3	3 0	3 0	4 0	3 0	4 9	4 0	6 0
Rhoose	2 3	3 0	3 0	4 0	3 0	4 9	4 0	6 0

Except where otherwise stated, the Tickets are available Third Class by Rail and Saloon of Steamer.

NOTE.—The Through Bookings may be suspended from certain Stations on Bank Holidays.

Children under 12 years of age, Half-fare. The fare paid does not exempt passengers from the payment of pier dues. Pier dues—Weston, 3d.; Clevedon, 2d.; Minehead, 2d.; Ilfracombe, 2d. Passengers holding Tourist Tickets may return on any day during the Season within two months after date of issue. The Tickets will only be issued after July on the understanding that if not used before the close of the Season, the Companies shall be relieved of all liability. See the Steamboat Companies' Bills for times of sailing.

CLEVEDON.—Passengers holding Tickets to Weston may travel to and from Clevedon without extra charge, but they will not be allowed to break their journey at Weston either on the outward or return trip.

LYNMOUTH.—Ilfracombe Tickets are available to Lynmouth, but landing fees must be paid.

DAY TICKETS TO ILFRACOMBE will be issued by Morning Trains from each of the Stations named, on the dates when the time of sailing will enable passengers to complete the to-and-fro journey the same day.

CLOVELLY.—Passengers holding Ilfracombe Tickets when conveyed in a boat which is running through to Clovelly, may extend their journey to that place on payment of extra fare on board.

LYNMOUTH AND CLOVELLY.—There are no Piers at these places, and no guarantee can be given that passengers desiring to land there will be able to do so.

LUGGAGE.—Passengers holding two-monthly tickets will be allowed, at their own risk, 60-lbs. of personal luggage, which will be transferred free of charge from train to steamer and *vice-versa* at BARRY PIER. For day trips no luggage allowed.

TICKETS ISSUED VIA CARDIFF.—The Cardiff Pier Head is about five minutes' walk from Cardiff (Clarence Road) Station. In the event of passengers returning by boats which do not arrive at Cardiff Docks in time to catch the last train from Clarence Road Station, they may proceed from Riverside Station by a later train; but the transit between the Steamboat and Riverside Station must be at their own risk and expense.

HALF-DAY TICKETS will also be issued via Barry Pier to Weston, Minehead, and Ilfracombe, by specially advertised trips, for particulars of which see Steamboat Company's bills exhibited at Stations.

WEEK-END TICKETS are issued every Saturday from Cardiff to Barry Pier Stations inclusive to Minehead and Ilfracombe via Barry Pier, available to return on following Monday or Tuesday.

CHEAP EXCURSION TICKETS will also be issued to Mumbles and Tenby via Barry Pier by Trips specially advertised from time to time during the Season.

NOTICE.—Through Tickets, available by these Steamboats, are issued by the Company on condition that they are not to be held responsible for any injury, damage, loss, or detention whatever which may occur to Passengers or their luggage during, or in respect of, the journey by Steamboat, or during the transit between the Railway and the Steamboats. The Company do not guarantee that there will be room on the Steamers which are advertised in connection with their trains, and through tickets are issued and must be understood to be accepted subject to this condition.

The links between the Barry Railway Company and the new owners of the Red Funnel Line were such that it was mutually advantageous for joint advertising such as this to be produced, in a 1911 Barry Chamber of Trade *Official Guide to Barry and the Vale of Glamorgan*, emphasising the availability of through fares from stations on the Barry system to Somerset and Devon via Barry Pier. In addition the passenger services operated by the Barry Railway Company to Cardiff (Clarence Road) could also be used in conjunction with Red Funnel Line steamers to Weston from Cardiff Pier Head.

Brian Luxton Collection

for a channel cruise . . . the weather on Whit Monday was very brilliant and warm, and visitors had a very pleasant time. On the Capstone and Hillsborough Hills - the favourite places of resort - the heat of the sun was tempered by a delightfully cooling breeze.

Deciding which vessels to allocate to various duties at peak-times such as this must have been tricky for the Cardiff company with only three ships to juggle between the Cardiff-Weston route and the longer-distance Ilfracombe run, but it seems that on this occasion only a very low proportion of traffic originating at the North Devon resort could be catered for by the Red Funnel Line on the Monday, and none on the Saturday, where the established practice had been for the daily 'railway run' to be augmented. The Bristol Channel tides presented a sort of paradox, in that where the White Funnel vessels' movements were wholly governed by tides, the Red Funnel paddlers aimed to sustain the fixed time 'railway run' from Barry to Ilfracombe regardless. To follow through the Bank Holiday Monday case, high water at Bristol was at 1.27 am and at 2.02 pm on 5th June, 1911. If one allows for excursion steamer passengers being indifferent to sailing overnight, snatching what sleep they could spread out in the saloons, this meant that a White Funnel paddle-steamer could sail to Ilfracombe twice from Bristol in one day (departing at 2.30 am and again at midday). In contrast the Barry 'railway run' boat was locked into a fixed schedule - and thus, put crudely, destined to earn less income under such circumstances. More positively, such a day would have given reasonable Cardiff-Weston ferry potential for both operators, albeit at lower fares. But there was yet another drawback suffered by the Red Funnel Line on such a day, as the 'railway run' boat on its return up-Channel would be too late on the ebb to squeeze in a Cardiff-Weston trip after arrival at the Pier Head from Ilfracombe. For what is was worth, this higher productivity could have been achieved in 1909 by a late-evening Barry-Weston crossing being run after termination of the 'railway run' boat at Barry Pier (but *not* from Cardiff) and exploitation of the low-water pier at Birnbeck - but this is of strictly theoretical interest only!

A major maritime event in 1911 was the Royal Naval Review at Spithead, just after Midsummer, and such was the commercial potential of this event that it was decided to send *Devonia* round to the South Coast. Whether the fact that P. & A. Campbell Ltd was planning to send two of its best vessels, *Westward Ho* and *Britannia*, influenced the Cardiff company is not established, but the advertisements for Thursday 22nd June stated that *Devonia* would leave Barry at 8.30 pm for Southampton, and was due to arrive there at 4.00 pm on Friday 23rd June. On the Saturday she was to leave Southampton Docks at 9.30 am and the Royal Pier at 10.00 am for the Review, spending the whole day viewing the activities. On the Sunday she would leave Southampton at 8.30 pm for Barry and Cardiff, and was due back home on the Monday evening at 7.00. The return fare was three guineas from Cardiff or Barry, not including food or refreshments, nor sleeping accommodation while the boat was at Southampton. This was something of an adventure for *Devonia*, but took place sufficiently early in the season for her absence from mainstream Bristol Channel duties to have been containable. Thursday 22nd June would have been an exceptionally long day for her officers and crew as only a short time was allowed for her to

THE BRISTOL CHANNEL PASSENGER BOATS, LIMITED. (RED FUNNEL LINE.)

SPECIAL TRIPS

(SUNDAYS EXCEPTED), TO

LYNMOUTH AND ILFRACOMBE

FROM BARRY PIER.

By the Magnificent Saloon Steamers "Devonia," "Barry," and "Westonia."

Wind, Weather, and Other Circumstances Permitting.

TRAIN LEAVES DAILY FOR LYNMOUTH AND ILFRACOMBE.

Cogan 9.30, Dynas Powis 9.35, Cadoxton 9.40, Barry Docks 9.44, Barry 9.48, Barry Island, 9.52 a.m. Steamer leaves Barry Pier 10.10 a.m. Returning from Ilfracombe at 6.0, Lynmouth 6.30 p.m. each day.

FRIDAY, AUGUST 19th.

Day Trip and Evening Cruise to Weston.

Trains leave Cogan 7.21 a.m. and 7.54 p.m., Dynas Powis 7.26 a.m. and 7.59 p.m., Cadoxton 7.31 a.m. and 8.4 p m., Barry Docks 7.35 a.m. and 8.8 p.m., Barry 7.39 a.m. and 8.12 p.m., Barry Island 7.43 a.m. and 8.16 p.m. Steamers leave Barry Pier at 7.50 a.m. and 8.25 p.m. Returning from Weston at 9.20 p.m. Fare for Evening Cruise 1/-.

Trip to Weston.

Train leaves Cogan 11.14, Dynas Powis 11.19, Cadoxton 11.24, Barry Docks 11.28, Barry 11.32, Barry Island 11.36 a.m. Steamer leaves Barry Pier 11.45 a.m. Returning from Weston at 9 20 p.m.

Afternoon Trip to Porthcawl.

Train leaves Cogan 2.1, Dynas Powis 2.6, Cadoxton 2.11, Barry Docks 2.15, Barry 2.19, Barry Island 2.22 p.m. Steamer leaves Barry Pier 2.30 p.m. Returning from Porthcawl 6.30 p.m. Fare 2/-.

SATURDAY, AUGUST 20th.

Afternoon Trip to Weston.

Train leaves Cogan 2.1, Dynas Powis 2.6, Cadoxton 2.11, Barry Docks 2.15, Barry 2.19, Barry Island 2.22 p.m. Steamer leaves Barry Pier 2.25 p.m. Returning from Weston 9.40 p.m.

Special Evening Channel Cruise.

Train leaves Cogan 7.54, Dynas Powis 7.59, Cadoxton 8.4, Barry Docks 8.8, Barry 8.12, Barry Island 8.16 p.m. Steamer leaves Barry Pier 8.25 p.m. Returning about 10.0 p.m. Fare 1/-.

WEDNESDAY, AUGUST 24th.

Afternoon Trip to Lynmouth and Ilfracombe.

Train leaves Cogan 2.1, Dynas Powis 2.6, Cadoxton 2.11, Barry Docks 2.15, Barry 2.19, Barry Island 2.22 p.m. Steamer leaves Barry Pier 2.40 p.m. Returning from Ilfracombe (direct) 7.0, Lynmouth 6.30 p.m. Fare—2/6 and 3/6.

THURSDAY, AUGUST 25th.

Afternoon Trip to Weston.

Train leaves Cogan 2.41, Dynas Powis 2.46, Cadoxton 2.51, Barry Docks 2.55, Barry 2.59, Barry Island 3.3 p.m. Steamer leaves Barry Pier 3.10 p.m. Returning from Weston at 9.30 p.m.

D. L. MACINTOSH, General Manager.

Although the ownership of the Red Funnel Line vessels changed in 1910, marketing still referred to that name. This was a typical advertisement for Special Trips from Barry Pier placed in the local Barry newspaper, the *Barry Dock News*, which explains the absence of reference to train times from Cardiff & Grangetown stations. These trips were in addition to the regular daily services provided from Cardiff, and advertised in the *Western Mail* alongside P. & A. Campbell Ltd offerings.

Cardiff Library

load up her overnight passengers for the South Coast and take on bunkers and other essentials after arrival back at Cardiff after that day's 'railway run'.

Perhaps one should not read too much into the delivery to P. & A. Campbell Ltd, in July 1911, of its first newly-built steamer since 1896, *Lady Ismay* from the Troon yard of the Ailsa Shipbuilding Company Limited. Its fleet had remained at the steady size, since the 1903 disposals, of nine vessels and a tenth was now significant inasmuch as the new ship was eminently suitable for economically carrying the crowds on mundane Cardiff to Weston ferry duties, and would also still be suitable for running down to Ilfracombe to relieve or augment the faster 'main-line' fleet of *Westward Ho*, *Cambria* and *Britannia* if required. What did this new vessel mean in terms of a threat to the livelihood of The Bristol Channel Passenger Boats, Ltd? She represented an increase in carrying capacity on the Weston route when thus deployed, and her class IV certificate enabled her to handle 1,020 passengers compared to the 703 that *Waverley* had been able to handle, partnering *Ravenswood* (capacity 819) on the ferry. Just as importantly the oldest Bristol Channel vessel was now displaced and so she could be sent round to the South Coast where she would be seen as an improvement compared to the ageing *Bonnie Doon* (herself duly recalled to Bristol Channel duties) as that vessel approached retirement age.

P. & A. Campbell Ltd was thus making something of a statement at Cardiff, as its newest vessel - consciously registered at the port of Cardiff, rather than at Bristol - was being mainly allocated to the Cardiff traffic, and her comfortable features were naturally presented as a big step forward in this vital part of the White Funnel Fleet business. In 1911 P. & A. Campbell Ltd timetables still tended to deploy two vessels on Cardiff-Weston ferry duties, so as one of them was over 40 per cent bigger than her predecessor, and the Red Funnel Line's capacity remained unaltered, in the shape of the more basic-looking *Westonia* with a class IV capacity of 863 passengers, the market advantage could be expected to move towards the P. & A. Campbell Ltd's undertaking. For Weston-bound passengers walking down from the Bute Street tram terminus to the Pier Head, or across Butetown from Clarence Road station, if confronted with a choice between *Westonia* and the shining new *Lady Ismay*, at very similar fares and times, the choice might very well have been a straightforward one in favour of the newer, bigger and better ship.

The Bristol Channel Passenger Boats, Ltd did its bit for charitable causes, as its predecessors the Barry Railway Company had done, and this statement was made in the *Barry Dock News* on Friday 14th July, 1911, under the heading:

> RED FUNNEL LINE AND THE POOR
>
> Under the auspices of the Slum Workers Brigade Relief Missioners, the Red Funnel Line are giving an all-day boat trip to Minehead to 200 of the poorest old people of Cardiff and Barry on Friday next. The boat will leave Cardiff Pier Head at 9.30 and Barry at 10.10. This is the fifth excursion of the kind organised by the brigade.

It was apparent from the papers after the event that much goodwill had been generated, and seemingly a positive and philanthropic connection was generated by association. P. & A. Campbell Ltd did the same thing too, notably for institutions in Bristol and Ilfracombe, all of which generated good publicity.

Minehead had a pier which was accessible at practically all states of the tide, and formed an important part of the territory of the Red Funnel Line. The Cardiff-Ilfracombe boats would often call in *en route* to collect passengers, as well as which Minehead represented a popular excursion destination in its own right. After it had opened in 1901, additional sheltered accommodation was provided at a later stage. The pier was situated immediately westward of the harbour at Minehead, and was removed during World War II.

Lionel Vaughan Collection

A different aspect of shipping in the summer of 1911, of national significance but with strong local manifestations, was an increasing level of industrial unrest focused on the demands of the National Sailors' and Firemen's Union (NSFU) which included minimum wages, better manning scales for vessels, overtime payments and full union recognition amongst other objectives. By mid-June 1911 there were calls for a national strike, and a degree of campaigning took place, not surprisingly, in Cardiff as a major centre of employment in the industry. For a while dock entrances were heavily picketed, although it is unclear to what extent the Cardiff Pier Head was affected, being more of a public place rather than an embarkation point approached through dock gates. The dispute had escalated into a large-scale withdrawal of labour in Cardiff Docks by mid-July, and one T.E. Morel is recorded as being a major player, through his membership of the Cardiff and Bristol Channel Incorporated Shipowner's Association, an extremely important and influential trade association, in seeking a negotiated solution to get things back to normal. He stated he was not opposed to the principles of trade unions, and after tense talks which involved the Lord Mayor of Cardiff, the union demands were largely met by a settlement being reached on the 3rd of August. The dispute had become increasingly ugly, and cannot have helped traffic levels on excursion sailings as some passengers would probably have opted to avoid getting involved in scenes of unrest. One would guess that overall the Red Funnel Line takings, being based very much on traffic originating at the Port of Cardiff, were hit harder than those of their rivals P. & A. Campbell Ltd, where traffic generated through Bristol (at Hotwells pontoon, quite separate from either the City Docks or the port of Avonmouth) and from Newport (via the Landing Stage in the centre of town, quite apart from the Alexandra Dock) may have been less susceptible to the effects of the industrial unease such as picket lines.

Doubtless some extra advertising efforts were made to get people back on the steamers once the dispute had ended, to restore a sense of normality, and during August some ambitious excursions were offered by Red Funnel Line steamer which suggested a heightened attempt to increase revenue by making more calls on long runs, one example being a trip advertised in the Barry papers to take place on Tuesday 1st August at 10.15 am from Barry Pier to Minehead, Mumbles and Tenby. Whilst more coal would be burned on such a trip by crossing the Channel compared to the more routine direct run along the Glamorgan coast to Mumbles and Tenby, clearly it would be hoped that extra passengers could be taken to and from Minehead, a opportunity to sail from Minehead to Tenby not being common at that time. A few days later, a similar trip was offered for Friday 11th August, this time with departure again from Barry Pier at 10.15 am to Minehead, Tenby and cruise to the Stack Rocks, a splendid long day cruise offering. On both these days the Red Funnel steamers had Tenby and the Pembrokeshire coast to themselves as the White Funnel Fleet chose to offer trips elsewhere rather than compete directly - with convenient tides and at the height of the season trips could be offered to extremes of the Bristol Channel such as Lundy and Chepstow, as well as the more usual fare.

An advertising piece in the *Barry Dock News* on Friday 18th August, 1911 exploited the by now established period of good weather which was being enjoyed, entitled 'Next Week's Channel Trips from Barry':

> With the heat wave still upon us, and yet no sign of its abatement, nothing is more enjoyable than a trip by the Red Funnel Line's fine pleasure steamers. Next week, as in the past, an excellent assortment of these is provided for patrons, and whether one desires a sail merely for the sake of 'the blow', or chiefly to visit some other watering place on the coast, there should be no difficulty in making a choice any day of the week. Weston, Lynmouth & Ilfracombe can be visited daily and at various times, including to Lynmouth and Ilfracombe in the afternoon on Saturday next: today (Friday) a boat goes to the Mumbles: on Monday and Tuesday there are evening cruises to Weston with one to Minehead on Thursday, on which day Clevedon may also be visited with a cruise afterwards to Portishead. Further particulars are in our advertisement columns.

On the face of it all was well, and in the same edition of this newspaper Mrs Grundy went so far as to assert that she had heard '. . . on good authority that next summer will see an addition of one, probably two, new pleasure steamers to the fine passenger fleet of the Red Funnel Line'. This was however merely speculation, although one wonders what had given substance to the rumours.

Log-books of the three Red Funnel Line vessels from 1911 have survived, which give an in-depth insight into the exact workings of the fleet that year, and Donald Anderson wrote in the journal *Ship Ahoy* in 1968 of how the ships interworked, and where they went, in fascinating detail. *Devonia* evidently made further appearances at Port Talbot in July 1911. On 14th August *Devonia* ventured on one of the regular high-season cruises from Cardiff to Tenby, which after arrival at the Pembrokeshire pier went on to offer a short cruise down the coast to the Stack Rocks. Another ambitious high-season excursion advertised in Barry was for Monday 28th August, with a 7.50 am departure for Lynmouth, Ilfracombe and Clovelly, and thence a cruise to Tintagel Head, for a fare of six shillings.

All may have seemed to be going well but on 1st September disaster struck on another of these longer trips, when a crank-pin broke on *Devonia* and the engines were unable to be turned. All passengers were put ashore at Tenby, and tugs were called from Cardiff, which arrived early the next day. Arriving back at Barry under tow at 7 pm on 2nd September, the season ended prematurely for *Devonia,* and this event may well have been the turning-point for the management as a combination of paying the costs of transporting her passengers home, the fees for tugs, and then probably two weeks loss of earnings at what was still a busy part of the season, must have been a huge drain on cash resources.

What turned out to be the final advertisement for The Bristol Channel Passenger Boats, Ltd in the *Barry Dock News* was that placed on Friday 29th September, 1911, and Mrs Grundy was now ominously silent on the season end and was to remain so for the next few weeks, almost certainly unaware of discussions of a serious nature taking place behind closed doors.

Collapse of The Bristol Channel Passenger Boats Ltd

For the other two ships, the season closed at the end of September, and my guess is that when all three ships were safely laid up in the Basin at Barry, their crews paid off and a full reckoning of the season's takings was assembled, some unpleasant conclusions were drawn. The management had, in effect, run all the services they could have done around the Bristol Channel, and suffered the misfortune of a loss of earnings after the breakdown of *Devonia*. Now a decision had to be made regarding the cost of repairs to that ship, against an uncertain climate where they could scarcely avoid noting that their Bristol competitors had been able to expand in 1911, seemingly successfully. A look at the sequence of recorded Minutes of the meetings of the P. & A. Campbell Ltd Directors at this time makes particularly fascinating reading, as by 18th September, 1911 the decision had been taken to procure another new steamer (i.e. for the 1912 season), broadly similar to *Lady Ismay*. Less than a fortnight later they reconvened to consider a letter received from a Mr Hailey of Cardiff, proposing an amalgamation between the Red Funnel Line and P. & A. Campbell Ltd where, for a consideration of £45,000, the latter were offered the three ships and the goodwill associated with a going concern. Imagine their reaction! After six years of competition here was an offer they may have perhaps expected, but the recorded decision was decisively to reject any notion of a proposed amalgamation - at that price - and as well as hastening to affirm their next new steamer order on Alec Campbell's strong recommendation not to delay, to respond to Mr Hailey and counter-offer £30,000.

This must have come as a bitter blow to the Cardiff company, which by now was effectively defeated through this exchange. Mr Hailey (as a shipbroker acting on behalf of The Bristol Channel Passenger Boats, Ltd) responded by rejecting the £30,000 offered by P. & A. Campbell Ltd but suggested that taking £2,000 off the originally sought £45,000 would be acceptable to his clients. Again, this was rejected. Matters dragged on, and by 13th November, 1911 a fresh offer to sell to P. & A. Campbell Ltd at £35,000 was made, and again this was rejected. Alec Campbell counter-offered £32,000, and one can see why as by now his company was in the driving-seat, and arguably did not actually need what was being offered for sale, unless at a giveaway price. Purchase would however eliminate the irritant of direct competition. Mrs Grundy had by now got wind of what was going on and, on Friday 17th November, made the following statement, albeit putting a brave face on matters by implying some sort of equal terms rather than outright failure of the local company: 'It is rumoured that a fusion will take place between the Red Funnel and the White Funnel Fleets of passenger steamers'.

There was a sense of victory in the air in Bristol's Britannia Buildings by the Cumberland Basin, home to the company headquarters of P. & A. Campbell Ltd. By 22nd November, 1911, an agreement was finally reached that the Cardiff company would settle for £34,000, and Mr Hailey was invited over to Bristol to draw up the Heads of Terms for the sale. It seemed that the battle was now over - the Red Funnel Fleet would disappear from the Bristol Channel in that guise, and a completely different phase of existence would now ensue for the trio of ships. It was rumoured that Alec Campbell had said, when the Clydebank-built ships appeared in the Bristol Channel, particularly the more economical *Barry*, that he himself would have been happy to have been their owner, and finally it seemed that they were coming his way. Upholding local pride to the end Mrs Grundy's final pronouncement should therefore, perhaps, be taken with a pinch of salt:

> Negotiations for the fusion of the Red and White Funnel lines of steamers are, it is understood, almost completed, and it is probable that the transfer will be sanctioned by the shareholders this week. The directorate will comprise mainly Cardiff gentlemen, but two Directors of the Red Funnel Line will be elected to the board.

There was no 'fusion' of course, certainly from the Bristol perspective. All that remained, procedurally, was for the defeated Cardiff company to be liquidated once the sale was completed. The Campbell brothers had won but only after many years of prolonged fighting. They were poised to preside over the period before the Great War when almost unprecedented expansion of their fleet, from nine vessels to 14, now put them at their greatest strength ever - this was to be truly the heyday of P. & A. Campbell Ltd, Passenger Steamship Owners, as its letterheads proudly proclaimed.

Chapter Five

Barry Pier in the White Funnel Era

'Year by year the Bristol Channel, with its wealth of scenic beauty, attracts visitors in ever-increasing numbers, and the district is becoming more and more the Holiday-Ground of England. How much this is due to the magnificient service of steamers of P. & A. Campbell Ltd, it is not for us to say, but the enormous numbers of passengers carried last season may be considered sufficient commentary . . . this year P. & A. Campbell Ltd have acquired the Red Funnel fleet of steamers, which will henceforth bear the familiar 'White Funnel', the amalgamation creating the largest flotilla of pleasure steamers sailing under one flag in the United Kingdom.'

Preface to the *Bristol Channel District Guide*, 1912 (34th edition)

Under new management

Strictly, the story of the Barry Red Funnel Line steamers - either when operated by the Barry Railway Company between 1905 and 1909, or by the successor body in 1910 and 1911 - effectively ended once the take-over of the surviving fleet of three paddle-steamers *Devonia, Barry* and *Westonia* by P. & A. Campbell Ltd was agreed prior to the commencement of the 1912 season. The one-time Red Funnel Line vessels came under a very different new management, and the Bristol company could well now afford to be gracious in victory. The short-lived concern 'The Bristol Channel Passenger Boats, Ltd' was wholly out of the picture once it was resolved, on 15th January, 1912, that the company be wound up. Board of Trade files record that a formal winding-up meeting subsequently took place on 17th October, 1912, and that truly was it for the challengers at Barry and, latterly, Cardiff.

Yet an odd effect of the decision, back in the 1890s, to build a railway to Barry Island and then extend it to the new Barry Pier, and subsequently build a fine fleet of paddle-steamers, was that the assets created ashore and afloat through this speculation went on to earn more income afterwards, and for rather longer under P. & A. Campbell Ltd control, than when under local South Walian management. Barry Pier itself, and its associated railway connection, went on to outlive the former Barry fleet. It was undoubtedly a useful facility, and played its part in the network of piers and harbours dotted around the Bristol Channel from which P. & A. Campbell Ltd had already been conducting its business since the 1880s. This last part of the story of the Barry Railway Steamers therefore addresses the afterlife of both the fleet and the pier which had together been created to fulfil a grandiose vision, but which can with hindsight be seen to have only achieved very limited commercial success for the original promoters, under challenging market and trading conditions.

Until the Great War in 1914 not much really changed at Barry Pier, and the services which had been developed by the railway company continued but with certain subtle changes, although of course the white funnel now prevailed. The least successful member of the Barry fleet, *Westonia*, underwent significant rebuilding for her 1912 season as a White Funnel Fleet steamer renamed as

Tintern, and the other two vessels *Devonia* and *Barry* initially kept their names in the expanded P. & A. Campbell Ltd fleet. By an odd twist of events, the one-time Barry flagship *Gwalia* - which had been sold in 1910 to the Furness Railway and renamed *Lady Moyra* - was to re-appear in her native Bristol Channel territory after the Great War. This was initially under the guise of the Tucker's 'Yellow Funnel Fleet' which briefly competed against P. & A. Campbell Ltd between 1919-1921, but then succumbed. Acquired by P. & A. Campbell Ltd in readiness for the 1923 season, it was thus the case that all three purpose-built Barry Railway Company vessels were eventually re-united, in the colours of the Bristol company. Like her former fleetmates, she was not destined to survive after World War II.

Three vessels join the White Funnel Fleet: 1912 to 1914

P. & A. Campbell Ltd had, at the beginning of 1912, good reason to feel relieved that the competetive pressure that had been coming from its challengers in South Wales had finally been dealt with to its advantage. Things had started to turn around after a good 1910 season, when it eventually became feasible to go for its own first new-building for many years - *Lady Ismay* - for the 1911 season, and thereafter buy up the opposition on more or less its own terms. Its confidence - before seeing the Cardiff-based Bristol Channel Passenger Boats, Ltd undertaking finally falter after the 1911 season - had been such that it had been able to order a second new ship in anticipation of the 1912 season. This duly entered the fleet as *Glen Avon*, and essentially represented a repeat order of *Lady Ismay*, albeit slightly beefed-up in terms of dimensions and power. Having made these two key investment decisions, then buying up three more vessels was clearly going to stretch company finances much further, and arguably gave Campbells a rather bigger fleet than was actually needed to handle Bristol Channel traffic. Doubtless this was felt preferable to seeing them slip into the hands of another competitor. Company Minute Book references at this time only enable a sketchy analysis of P. & A. Campbell Ltd thinking to be made, but it does seem that whilst the company was building new ships it was nonetheless open to suitable offers for a part of the fleet, as the key issue of the competitors had been adroitly dealt with. No light can be shed on exactly why *Westonia* was selected for reconstruction, given her track record, but once Barry Pier and its traffic requirements came into the P. & A. Campbell Ltd portfolio in 1912, it was fairly clear that only two ships were going to be needed - one for Weston ferry services, and one for the 'railway run' - rather than the three which had actually been acquired.

For the 1912 season it appears that no radical attempt was made to change things as regards the running of the former Barry operations, but it was notable that when regular down-Channel sailings got underway at Whitsuntide it was recorded in Ilfracombe that a P. & A. Campbell Ltd ship, *Cambria*, commenced the Barry run, rather than a former Barry vessel. Little change was made to overall 'main-line' service provision in 1912 after takeover of the Barry traffic, with one vessel carrying out daily 'railway run' duties (between the customary start and end dates in May and September respectively). In a sort of reversion

BARRY RAILWAY and P. & A. Campbell, Ltd.

Daily Time Table Service (Sundays excepted) to (off) **Lynmouth** and **Ilfracombe** and to § **Minehead** on dates shown below, *via* Barry Pier.

JULY. FROM	By Train leaving at	*FARES—Rail and Boat* ILFRACOMBE Single	Day	Tourist	Week End	§ MINEHEAD Single	Day	Tourist	Week End
	a m								
Newport, G.W. ..	9 0	..	4 6	6 6	5 6	..	..	..	..
Cardiff (Riverside) ..	9 39								
Grangetown	9 24								
Cogan	9 29								
Dinas Powis	9 34	3 6	4 0	6 0	5 0	2 6	3 0	4 6	4 0
Cadoxton	9 39								
Barry Dock	9 42								
Barry	9 46								
Barry Island	9 50								
Porth .. .. *	9 0	..	5 3	7 3	..	..	4 3	6 3	..
Trehafod .. .. *	9 4	..	5 0	7 3	..	..	4 0	6 3	..
Pontypridd, B.R. .. *	9 10	..	5 0	7 0	..	..	4 0	6 0	..
Treforest B.R. .. *	9 15	..	4 9	6 9	..	..	3 9	5 9	..
Efail Isaf .. .. *	9 21	..	4 9	6 9	..	..	3 9	5 6	..
Creigiau .. .. *	9 26	..	4 6	6 6	..	..	3 6	5 3	..
Wenvoe .. .. *	9 37	..	4 3	6 3	..	..	3 6	4 9	..
Bridgend	8 35	4 10	5 0	7 0	6 3	4 0	4 3	6 0	..
Southerndown Road ..	8 44	4 6	4 9	6 9	..	3 9	4 0	5 6	..
Llantwit Major ..	8 55	4 3	4 6	6 6	5 9	3 3	3 9	5 3	..
Gileston	9 2	4 0	4 6	6 6	..	3 0	3 6	5 0	..
Aberthaw	9 6	4 0	4 3	6 3	..	2 9	3 3	4 9	..
Rhoose	9 12	3 9	3 4	6 3	..	2 9	3 3	4 9	..
Barry Pier steamer dep.	10 15								

* No through bookings on August 5 and 6 from these stations.

§ Steamer calls at MINEHEAD except on July 11, 12, 13, 15, 16, 26, 27, 29 and 30 returning from MINEHEAD at **7-30** pm.

Return Times from ILFRACOMBE calling off LYNMOUTH 35 minutes later—

July 13, 24, 25 .. .. **5-45** pm. | July 29 .. **6-15** pm.
July 1 to 12, 17 to 23, 26, 27, 31 **6-0** pm. | July 15, 16, 30 **6-30** pm.

Children under 12 years of age Half Fare. The fare does not exempt passengers from the payment of pier dues, viz. 2d at Minehead and Ilfracombe. Passengers holding Tourist tickets may return on any day during the season within two months after the day of issue. The Tickets will only be issued after July on the understanding that if not used before the close of the season the Companies shall be relieved of all liability.

LYNMOUTH.—Ilfracombe tickets are available to Lynmouth, but landing fees must be paid.

DAY TICKETS to ILFRACOMBE will be issued by Morning trains from each of the stations named on the dates when the time of sailing will enable passengers to complete the to-and-fro journey same day.

CLOVELLY.—Passengers holding Ilfracombe tickets when conveyed in a boat which is running through to Clovelly, may extend their journey to that place on payment of extra fare on board.

LYNMOUTH AND CLOVELLY.—There are no Piers at these places and no guarantee can be given that Passengers desiring to land there will be able to do so.

LUGGAGE.—Passengers holding two-monthly tickets will be allowed at their own risk, 60-lbs. of personal luggage, which will be transferred free of charge from train to steamer and *vice versa* at BARRY PIER. For day trips no luggage allowed.

HALF-DAY TICKETS will also be issued *via* Barry Pier to Minehead and Ilfracombe, by specially advertised trips, for particulars of which see Steamboat Company's bills exhibited at stations.

WEEK END TICKETS are issued every Saturday from Cardiff to Barry Pier Stations inclusive to Minehead and Ilfracombe *via* Barry Pier, available to return on following Monday or Tuesday.

CHEAP EXCURSION TICKETS will also be issued to Mumbles and Tenby *via* Barry Pier by trips specially advertised from time to time during the Season.

NOTICE.—Through tickets, available by these Steamboats, are issued by the Company on condition that they are not to be held responsible for any injury, damage, loss, or detention whatever which may occur to Passengers or their luggage during, or in respect of, the journey by Steamboat, or during the transit between the Railway and the Steamboats. The Company do not guarantee that there will be room on the Steamers which are advertised in connection with their trains, and through tickets are issued and must be understood to be accepted subject to this condition.

BARRY RAILWAY and P. & A. Campbell, Ltd.

Regular Daily Service (Sundays excepted) to **Weston**

JULY.

FROM	*via* Barry Pier Train Times					Boat leaves Weston	*FARES* Single	Day Trip	Tourist	Rail and Boat Times see Companies Time Tables	*via* Cardiff Clarence Rd Day Trip	Tourist
	a m	p m	p m	p m	p m		s d	s d	s d		s d	s d
Cardiff (Riverside)	9 30	12 5	2 32	5 48	a7 45							
Grangetown	9 24	12 9	2 36	5 52	a7 49							
Cogan ..	9 29	12 14	2 41	5 57	a7 54							
Dinas Powis	9 34	12 19	2 46	6 2	a7 59	11.10	1 6	2 0	2 6		2 6	3 6
Cadoxton ..	9 39	12 24	2 51	6 7	a8 4							
Barry Dock ..	9 42	12 28	2 55	6 11	a8 8							
Barry ..	9 46	12 32	2 59	6 15	a8 12	am.						
Barry Island	9 50	12 36	3 3	6 19	a8 16							
Porth .. *	9 0	..	1 37	3 20	..		..	3 3	4 3		..	..
Trehafod .. *	9 4	..	1 41	3 24	..	2.10	..	3 0	4 3		..	..
Pontypridd, B.R. *	9 10	..	1 48	3 30	..		..	3 0	4 0		3 0	4 0
Treforest B.R. *	9 15	..	1 52	3 34	..		..	2 9	3 9		2 9	3 9
Efail Isaf .. *	9 21	..	1 58	3 40	..	4.10	..	2 9	3 9		2 9	3 9
Creigiau .. *	9 26	..	2 4	3 46	..		..	2 6	3 3		2 6	3 3
Wenvoe .. *	9 37	..	2 16	3 58	..	7.20	..	2 3	2 9		2 9	3 6
Bridgend ..	8 35	11 12	1 42	4 32	..		2 10	3 3	4 0		..	..
Southerndown Road	8 44	11 20	1 51	4 41	..	a9.20	2 7	3 0	3 9		4 0	4 9
Llantwit Major	8 55	11 30	2 2	5 34	..		2 1	2 9	3 6		3 6	4 6
Gileston ..	9 2	11 37	2 9	5 41	..		1 10	2 6	3 3		3 3	4 3
Aberthaw ..	9 6	11 41	2 13	5 46	..	pm.	1 9	2 3	3 0		3 0	4 0
Rhoose ..	9 12	11 47	2 19	5 52	..		1 7	2 3	3 0		3 0	4 0
Barry Pier depart	10 15	12 50	3 15	6 30	a8 30							

*No Through Bookings on August 5th and 6th from these Stations.
a Not on Tuesdays and Fridays.

NOTE—The Through Bookings will be suspended on Bank Holidays.

Children under 12 years of age, Half-fare. The fare paid does not exempt passengers from the payment of pier dues. Pier dues—Weston 3d, Clevedon 2d, Minehead 2d, Ilfracombe 2d. Passengers holding Tourist Tickets may return on any day during the Season within two months after date of issue. The Tickets will only be issued after July on the understanding that if not used before the close of the Season, the Companies shall be relieved of all liability. See the Steamboat Companies' Bills for times of special sailings.

CLEVEDON—When Steamer is proceeding to Clevedon, passengers holding Tickets to Weston may travel to and from Clevedon without extra charge, but they will not be allowed to break their journey at Weston either on the outward or return trip.

TICKETS ISSUED VIA CARDIFF—The Cardiff Pier Head is about five minutes' walk from Cardiff (Clarence Road) Station. In the event of passengers returning by boats which do not arrive at Cardiff Docks in time to catch the last train from Clarence Road Station, they may proceed from Riverside Station by a later train; but the transit between he Steamboat and Riverside Station must be at their own risk and expense.

In the first year after the takeover, the services provided by P. & A. Campbell Ltd at Barry Pier in 1912 were little changed from what had operated in Barry Railway Company days, after its forced withdrawal from Cardiff. These two pages were added to the weekly timetable booklets published by the Bristol company, and set out details of the regular Barry-Ilfracombe 'Railway Run' service, as well as a revived Barry-Weston 'ferry' service, operated by a Barry-based vessel, generally with four round trips daily at fixed times irrespective of the tides, all rail-connected. The Cardiff pages would list those days when the 'railway run' would now actually start at Cardiff and call at Penarth before picking up the fixed 10.15 Barry departure time. *Author's Collection* to 1908/09 season arrangements (i.e. after the Barry Railway Company had had to withdraw from Cardiff Pier Head), it was decided to run one vessel on Barry-Weston 'ferry' duties, typically four round trips per day that year, all rail-connected from and to Cardiff Riverside in the established manner. As the season progressed the introduction of the new-building *Glen Avon* was a notable event, and it was inevitable that purpose-built tonnage would call into question the retention of inherited or older and less attractive vessels. It should be mentioned here that, unusually, four vessels were able to be deployed on high-season South Coast duties in 1912 once *Albion* was superseded by the new *Glen Avon* on the Newport station.

It can be assumed that *Westonia* was still deemed to be unsatisfactory after the 1912 season despite her reconstruction as *Tintern*, but it does appear that an offer for £10,000 from a Glasgow broker to purchase her on behalf of a foreign client came at a time when the cash from that transaction was very welcome to reduce the mortgage and bank overdraft payments then being incurred. Somewhat cryptically the Board noted on 15th April, 1913 that it was 'desirable that the steamer should be sold' and left the matter to Captains Peter & Alec to deal with as they thought fit. By May her disposal to the Portuguese State Railway was agreed, and the White Funnel Fleet duly reduced its size by one vessel. The new name for the steamer which had already carried five names in her varied 13-year career - successively *Tantallon Castle, Sussex Belle, Rhos Colwyn, Westonia* and finally *Tintern* - was to be *Alentejo*. Shortly after this the Board also agreed that *Bonnie Doon* would no longer be used, and she went for scrap later in the year.

Close scrutiny of 1913 season schedules suggests that one fewer vessel was deployed in the Bristol Channel that year in regard to Barry traffic requirements, and on many days a 'dedicated' vessel would not have been necessary. A less rigorous adherence to set times for provision of the Barry-Weston ferry services was evident, and fewer round trips were provided. On some occasions, more use might be made of the Newport boat, which was less productive than the others. This was because only one journey per tide could generally be got out of a vessel which was obliged to await the flood tide on the River Usk each morning before making a single departure from the town's Landing Stage, usually across to Weston but sometimes elsewhere. A paddle-steamer leaving Newport for Weston in the morning could, if so required afterwards, quite easily make a journey between Weston and Barry, and return, in between the afternoon tide, and thence a return voyage from Weston to Newport. This pattern exploited the tide-free advantage of Barry Pier quite neatly, but of course had never been an option open to the Barry Railway Company when confined to the home port. Thus, the reduced fleet strength compared to 1912 was not a problem, as better utilisation meant that Barry Pier was still being served as the new operator saw fit, through what would now be described as economies of scale through interworking.

During the 1913 August Bank Holiday period the Ilfracombe newspapers continued to record ever-growing numbers of visitors arriving by steamer in this halcyon pre-war heyday, and on Saturday 2nd August *Devonia* brought down an astonishing 986 passengers on her first run from Cardiff, and another 806 on a

Pleasure Sailings

(Weather and other circumstances permitting), from

ILFRACOMBE AND LYNMOUTH, TO

Bristol, Cardiff,

PENARTH, SHARPNESS,
NEWPORT, MINEHEAD,
WESTON, CHEPSTOW.
CLEVEDON,

CLOVELLY, TENBY, NEWQUAY, &c.,

By the Magnificent Saloon Steamers of

P. & A. CAMPBELL, Ltd.,

THE . . .

WHITE Funnel Fleet

(Fastest and Best Passenger Steamers in the Bristol Channel),

Britannia, Cambria, Westward Ho! Albion, Ravenswood, Waverley, &c.

For Bills of Sailings, and all particulars, apply to the Agent, **F. W. BIRMINGHAM,** Steamship Chambers, Quay, Ilfracombe; or P. and A. CAMPBELL, Ltd., Cumberland Basin, Bristol.

BOOK YOUR TICKETS AT

P. & A. CAMPBELL'S (Ltd) OFFICE, QUAY;
WHITE BOX OFFICE, PIER

Perhaps they were a little slow to catch on down in Ilfracombe that the composition of the White Funnel Fleet changed considerably in the years preceding the Great War! This advertisement in the *Ilfracombe Gazette* for 2nd August, 1912 emphasises the necessity to choose a WHITE Funnel Fleet steamer (after the Red Funnel Line ships had been eliminated) but wholly fails to mention that the new *Lady Ismay* and *Glen Avon* had joined the fleet, as well as *Devonia, Barry* and *Tintern.*
Ilfracombe Museum

Tintern, ex-*Westonia*, berthed at the Hotwells pontoon, with *Westward Ho* nearby, in 1912.
Richard Clammer Collection

second run, whilst 830 came on *Westward Ho* from Bristol and Cardiff, and 400 from Newport and Weston on *Glen Avon*. *Britannia* brought another 300 from Bristol, whilst *Brighton* made two runs from Swansea carrying 833 and 813 respectively. On Monday 4th August, 1913 thousands more flooded in as *Devonia* brought 800 from Bristol and Cardiff, *Britannia* brought 854 from Bristol and *Cambria* 690 from Cardiff. Over a thousand took excursions out of Ilfracombe that day, *Devonia* taking 394 to Clovelly, *Britannia* 372 on a cruise to Bideford Bay and *Cambria* 400 to Lynmouth. A little later that year, it fell to 'the magnificent saloon steamer *Barry*' to be placed at the disposal of the Ilfracombe Holiday Saturday Committee for a fund-raising excursion, and that body chose to run a special afternoon cruise on Monday 1st September at 3.00 pm from Ilfracombe to Porthcawl, returning at 7.15. The Committee kept the entire proceeds of ticket sales at 1*s*. 6*d*. per adult, from around 450 passengers, whilst P. & A. Campbell Ltd shouldered the expenses of providing the ship - this continued a philanthropic tradition which went back to the very beginnings of the Campbell steamers at Ilfracombe.

The pattern of services at Barry Pier in 1914 was broadly similar to that established in 1913, and it is reasonable to assume that due to P. & A. Campbell Ltd's flexible deployment of its ships these were not solely the preserve of *Devonia* and *Barry*. The prospering affairs of the company were such that a third new paddle-steamer joined the White Funnel Fleet in 1914, *Glen Usk*, which closely followed the style of *Lady Ismay* and *Glen Avon*. This put the fleet at a remarkable strength of 13 vessels, with 10 deployed in the Bristol Channel that year and three on the South Coast. One interesting development of services in 1914 was the inauguration of a new excursion from Ilfracombe to Bideford, the first of which was taken by *Barry* on Thursday 23rd July, and the Ilfracombe newspapers stated that a cruise out of Bideford, to Morte Bay, would also be offered before the return voyage to Ilfracombe. It was said that such excursions would be repeated as tides and circumstances permitted.

Barry kept her name after absorption into the White Funnel Fleet in 1912, and looked very spruce in this 'official' view. *Lionel Vaughan Collection*

Devonia also kept her name after absorption into the White Funnel Fleet in 1912, and almost looked like she had been designed to wear the Campbell colours in this 'official' view. *Lionel Vaughan Collection*

On the final August Bank Holiday weekend before the Great War heavy numbers again featured on the steamers coming into Ilfracombe, *Devonia* running two trips down-Channel on Saturday 1st August, 1914. On the Monday she brought 500, and we are left with a vision of her running a cruise out to Lundy that day, with 320 passengers on board. Normality was to end shortly after this, and along with the majority of their P. & A. Campbell Ltd fleetmates the former Barry Railway Company Red Funnel Line steamers *Devonia* and *Barry* were duly called up for wartime duties. Minesweeping and other duties during hostilities for British excursion paddle-steamers have been very thoroughly dealt with elsewhere, and readers are referred particularly to the works of Chris Collard for further details of these wartime activities.

After the declaration of war in August 1914 the former Barry flagship *Gwalia,* acquired by the Furness Railway Company in 1910 and renamed *Lady Moyra,* took up minesweeping duties, which she survived. Likewise her sister *Devonia* left Bristol in September 1914, and was not returned to P. & A. Campbell Ltd until May 1919, staying out of service that season pending reconditioning. The third Barry vessel, *Barry,* had a rather different wartime experience. She was used to transport prisoners of war in late 1914, and after visiting Dublin returned to Bristol still wearing her peacetime colours in the remainder of that year, being laid-up over the winter. In July 1915 she left Bristol for transport duties linked to the Gallipoli campaign, and a flavour of these is best gained from reproducing (*below*) some of what was published in most inter-war years' editions of the P. & A. Campbell Ltd *Bristol Channel District Guide* handbooks, which described the remarkable service she rendered. She was not returned to P. & A. Campbell Ltd until September 1919.

> . . . she sailed from Bristol Floating Harbour on July 24th, 1915, and later put in at Ilfracombe for the last time for many a long and anxious day. On the following day she left the popular North Devon resort, and headed Westward Ho! under seated orders, but, when these were opened, her head was turned eastward, and she arrived at Mudros Harbour on August 8th. In the morning she received orders from HMS *Europa,* the flagship, and shipped ammunition and troops for Suvla Bay. There she received her baptism of fire, as troops and ammunition came over and dropped bombs, and though missiles fell on both sides, the *Barry* was never once hit . . . for six weeks the plucky Bristol paddle-steamer carried on her work, visiting Anzac as well as Suvla Bay, usually doing two journeys a day . . . she was constantly under fire . . . each trip from the torpedo nets at Mudros to Suvla was something like 60 miles, and had to be done on a set course, because of the minefields in the Aegean Sea. The *Barry* carried on until the latter end of November, when she encountered a heavy blizzard . . . when the storm had blown itself out the *Barry* went to Suvla Beach to take off cases of frost-bitten British soldiers. Both officers and men of the *Barry* did all they possibly could for our stricken heroes. Three or four times the *Barry* put off with something like 750 sufferers aboard on each trip and discharged them into hospital lighters and hospital ships for Mudros. She afterwards carried on her duties till the evacuation . . . Next the *Barry* was on duty at Salonika, and carried troops, stores, guns and ammunitions to Katrina, in the Gulf of Salonika, which landed under Mount Olympus. She was often bombed by aeroplanes while on this duty. After a week or two here, once again she worked the Imbros-Mudros ferry.

After the Great War the Pockett steamers had effectively ceased operations out of Swansea, and in 1920 P. & A. Campbell Ltd decided to operate there. *Barry* was utilised on occasions as the Swansea steamer, and is seen here with a good crowd on board. *H.A. Allen Collection*

After 1923 services between Brighton, Eastbourne, Hastings and Boulogne were reinstated by P. & A. Campbell Ltd, in which *Devonia* featured prominently. *Lionel Vaughan Collection*

Relief Party Arrives

In June of 1917, a relief crew of the Mercantile Marine Reserve arrived for the *Barry*, and the crew, who for over two years had faced the dangers from land, sea and air in the Dardanelles, were shipped aboard the *Implacable*, for 'Blighty'. The battleship proceeded to Devonport, and thence to Portsmouth, where the *Barry's* gallant band were paid off and discharged. The paddles of the *Barry*, however, still continued to churn the waters of the Mediterranean, though her name was altered to *Barryfield*, as a destroyer bearing the same name as the Bristol steamer was attached to the naval force. Until the end of hostilities the staunch vessel, which was built for pleasure and not for the game of war, stayed out East.

After the Great War

The Great War affected the fortunes of the excursion-steamer industry, and after cessation of hostilities in 1918 the P. & A. Campbell Ltd fleet was greatly depleted and services, when resumed in 1919, ran on a rather restricted basis. Calls did not resume at Barry Pier until 1922. Before this, however, the former Barry vessel *Gwalia* that had sailed away from the Bristol Channel to strengthen the Furness Railway fleet in 1910, to become their *Lady Moyra*, found herself as one of the first paddlers to reinstate post-war excursion sailings in her home waters, albeit not yet as a white-funnelled steamer. The Cardiff company Tucker's saw an opportunity to enter the excursions market in 1919, having purchased *Lady Moyra* and a smaller vessel *Lady Evelyn* from the Furness Railway which had decided not to reinstate its own sailings between Barrow and Fleetwood. The Tucker vessels were promoted as The Yellow Funnel Fleet, and in the early summer of 1919 newspapers began to announce the imminent resumption of Bristol Channel excursion sailings. P. & A. Campbell Ltd did not have either *Devonia* or *Barry* available to them for the 1919 season, and after their own *Glen Avon* reinstated the White Funnel Fleet presence down-Channel on the Ilfracombe run on Monday 14th July, 1919, it fell to the other original Clydebank-built Barry vessel *Gwalia* as *Lady Moyra* to initiate an alternative Yellow Funnel Fleet presence a few days later, on Friday 25th July, 1919. The competition lasted for three seasons, 1919-21 inclusive, but in 1920 the Campbell brothers were in a position to run eight steamers in the Bristol Channel, rather than just make do with four as they had been obliged to do in 1919. *Devonia* and *Barry* were now back and, after 1921 the Yellow Funnel Fleet steamers were obliged to retire, defeated, into lay-up. After almost a year of disuse, the Campbell brothers decided to acquire both *Lady Moyra* and *Lady Evelyn* in 1922 in readiness for them to greatly expand their operations in 1923 with a return to the South Coast station at Brighton, which had not enjoyed White Funnel Fleet steamer services since 1914.

In this endeavour the former Barry vessels were to play a major part in the between-the-war years, as *Devonia* was selected to become the prime South Coast vessel which would run the French day-excursion services until 1932. Her first Boulogne sailing took place on Tuesday 19th May, 1923. In that initial season of reinstated South Coast services *Devonia* was supported by *Ravenswood* and *Brighton Belle* (the former *Lady Evelyn*, rebuilt). *Barry* remained in the Bristol Channel in 1923, and was duly joined by *Lady Moyra*, the three ex-Barry vessels

BARRY RAILWAY.

Rich in Picturesque Scenery and Historical Associations, the Vale of Glamorgan affords a Holiday ground of exceptional interest to the worker seeking rest and relaxation, as well as to lovers of Nature.

Traversed by the Vale of Glamorgan Line from Barry to Bridgend, it is easily accessible by means of the excellent Train service and cheap travelling facilities provided by the Barry Railway Co.

PLACES OF INTEREST IN THE VICINITY OF:—

RHOOSE	Fontigary Bay: a spot unsurpassed for Picnics. Delightful cliff walks.
ABERTHAW ..	Quaint Village and Fonmon Castle.
GILESTON	St. Athan and Gileston Villages, The Leys, Excellent Golf Links.
LLANTWIT MAJOR	Town of antiquarian interest, ancient Town Hall, Church, and other Historical Buildings, Boverton Castle, St. Donat's Castle, Nash Lighthouses, Beach, etc., etc.
SOUTHERNDOWN	Bracing Health Resort, with extensive views of Bristol Channel, etc., Dunraven Castle, Splendid Golf Links.

BARRY ISLAND.

BATHING.
BOATING.
AMUSEMENTS.
INVIGORATING CLIMATE.

FREQUENT TRAIN SERVICE.
IDEAL CENTRE FOR VISITING THE VALE OF GLAMORGAN.

Whitmore Bay, Barry Island, with its wide and magnificent expanse of sand, is one of the greatest natural assets of Wales. A fine promenade surrounds the bay and connects the two prominent headlands which run far into the sea on the East and the West.

W. WADDELL,
General Manager.

The Barry Railway Company lost its independence at the Grouping, joining the Great Western Railway as a constituent company. This advertisement for the charms of the Vale of Glamorgan district served by the Barry Railway Company appeared in 1922 in the 40th edition of the P. & A. Campbell Ltd. Bristol Channel District Guide. Its context was to publicise those attractions to folk choosing to travel to Barry from, say, Bristol by steamer, as well as to underline the perhaps more popular attractions of Barry Island. *Author's Collection* thus being re-united in one fleet. The next change of note took place before the 1925 season, when the old name *Waverley* was bestowed upon *Barry*, which continued for that season in the Bristol Channel. The following year, 1926, she too went south to join *Devonia* whilst *Lady Moyra* spent the year in lay-up on account of the coal strike. The pattern of three vessels on the South Coast station, sailing principally from Brighton, Eastbourne and Hastings, persisted into the 1930s but another major change took place in readiness for the 1933 season, when it was decided to revive the old favourite name of *Brighton Queen* and bestow this upon *Lady Moyra*. Thereafter the newly-renamed ex-Barry vessel switched places with *Devonia*, which returned to Bristol Channel duties.

The late H.G. Owen made his first voyages on *Lady Moyra* and *Devonia* in 1927, and recalled that the windows in the deckhouses of *Lady Moyra* still had the Furness Railway device, the Cavendish coat-of-arms, which carried their motto *Cavendo Tutus*. She still had her open engine-room. During the summer of 1930 *Lady Moyra* had the large saloon windows aft smashed on two occasions while crossing from Swansea to Ilfracombe, and during the winter of 1930/31 these were replaced with small rectangular ports the same as forward, and the engine-room was cased in with windows, Campbell-fashion. He also recalled that *Devonia* had her large after saloon windows altered to rectangular ports when she was reconditioned in 1919-1920. It is unclear whether her engine-room was cased-in in 1912 when she first became a Campbell vessel, or whether this was done in 1919-20. In 1912 *Devonia* had been sent up to the Inglis yard in Glasgow, where her sponsons were reduced in width and she had been given new paddle wheels with eight floats instead of seven.

When Barry Pier re-opened in 1922 it was principally for the 'railway run' services, as after the Great War no 'dedicated' rail-connected Barry-Weston 'ferry' service *per se* was resumed. Thus, a normal day at Barry might see a morning departure down-Channel to Ilfracombe, possibly calling at Minehead in addition to the call off Lynmouth, after the connecting train from Cardiff Riverside had arrived. The afternoon run back up-Channel still tended to leave Ilfracombe at the usual time, with a Clovelly extension in high summer. If tides were adverse, the 'railway run' would commence at Barry and all Cardiff passengers would travel down to Barry Pier station by train when there was no water at the Pier Head at Cardiff. The other calls at Barry Pier would be principally those made by vessels mainly working the Cardiff-Weston 'ferry', at times of low-water which made it impossible to get back to Cardiff from Birnbeck Pier. After crossing from Weston to Barry, there might on occasions be a Welsh Coast cruise operated, or a cruise around the Holm Islands. An interesting feature of the 1922 *Bradshaw* railway timetable, after the Barry Railway Company had become a constituent of the Great Western Railway, was that the train times over the Barry main line showed that the boat-trains to and from Barry Pier station were booked to take the longer route over the former Taff Vale Railway line from Cogan through Penarth and Lavernock before rejoining the Barry line at Cadoxton. This made sense, certainly for Penarth passengers on those days when the 'railway run' boat was actually scheduled to commence its run at Barry Pier.

Barry Railways

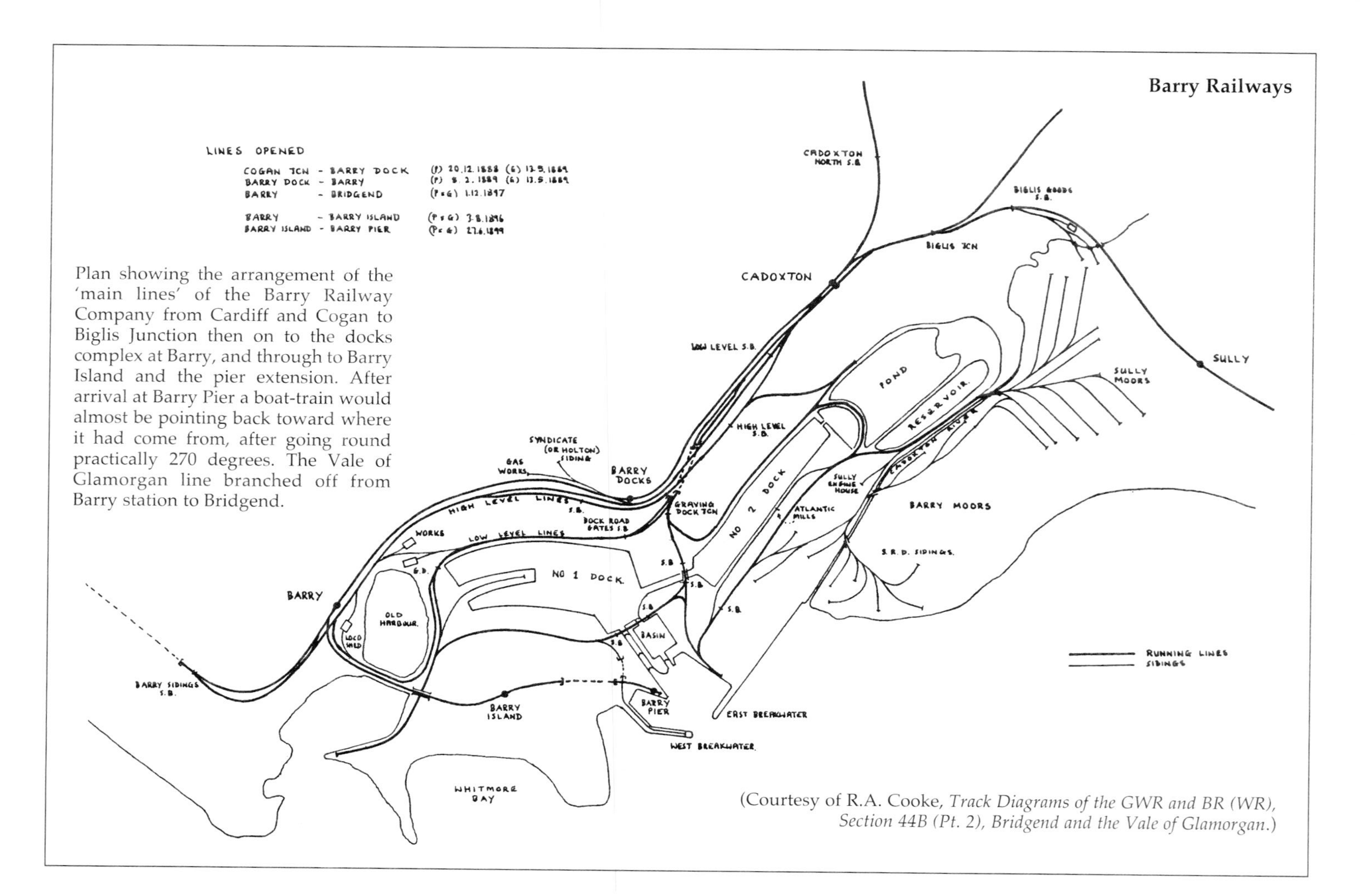

Plan showing the arrangement of the 'main lines' of the Barry Railway Company from Cardiff and Cogan to Biglis Junction then on to the docks complex at Barry, and through to Barry Island and the pier extension. After arrival at Barry Pier a boat-train would almost be pointing back toward where it had come from, after going round practically 270 degrees. The Vale of Glamorgan line branched off from Barry station to Bridgend.

(Courtesy of R.A. Cooke, *Track Diagrams of the GWR and BR (WR), Section 44B (Pt. 2), Bridgend and the Vale of Glamorgan.*)

Alterations to the Barry Pier branch

Little changed in terms of the track arrangements of the Barry Pier railway branch line after the opening in 1899 of the Pier extension, which was double track, from Barry Island station through the tunnel. The overall length of the extension was rather less than half a mile, from a mileage of 8 m. 76 ch. at Barry Island station to 9 m. 34 ch. at the stop-block at Barry Pier. Of this, 208 yards were in tunnel. Considerable rationalisation occurred in 1929 when the signal box at Barry Pier was taken out of use, and the line through the tunnel was reduced to a single track. Whilst both platforms at Barry Pier remained in use from a ground-frame connection just inside the tunnel, and a run-round facility remained for locomotives arriving on the pontoon side of the station, the occasions when two passenger trains were required together at Barry Pier were now far fewer than in the early days and, conversely, other alterations at Barry Island effected during the same overall rationalisation of facilities by the GWR amounted to an upgrade, as more stabling sidings for excursion trains were installed. These arrangements lasted until well into the 1960s.

The former Barry steamers in the 1930s

Seventy years on, capturing first-hand memories of what the former Barry vessels were doing in the White Funnel Fleet in the 1930s seems rather a challenge. It was the author's good fortune to be given access to the diaries of Sid Robinson of Newport, who was born in 1914 and pursued a career in the shipbuilding and repairing industry in South Wales and Bristol before and after World War II. Sid's professional role carried on right into the 1990s, well after conventional retirement age, and in more recent years he acted as an adviser to Waverley Steam Navigation Ltd when the preserved paddler had a major rebuild, including new wheels, at Avonmouth. This specialist role involved the preparation of tender documentation, as well as drawings and dimension details, maintaining progressive cost records and generally overseeing on behalf of the owners the work carried out.

As a 16-year-old who had started working at Newport in the drawing office of the engineering and ironfounding business of W. A. Baker and Co. Ltd, Sid's introduction to the first of the one-time Barry vessels *Gwalia*, then *Lady Moyra* in the P. & A. Campbell Ltd fleet, took place in 1931. Sid was well aware then of the history and different background of the trio *Lady Moyra*, *Devonia* and *Waverley* (formerly *Barry*) and I have attempted here to put his memories alongside the advertised schedules of the period to try and give a flavour of the way the Clydebank-built ships were used in the White Funnel Fleet and how they appeared to passengers. The trio was, in the 1930s, in a sense outnumbered by the original vessels built at other yards to the P. & A. Campbell Ltd specification. In no way, though, did the former Barry vessels appear to be of secondary status, but the relatively heavy coal consumption of the two faster earlier vessels did influence the way in which their owners tended to deploy them. They would either bring them out for a short Bristol Channel high-

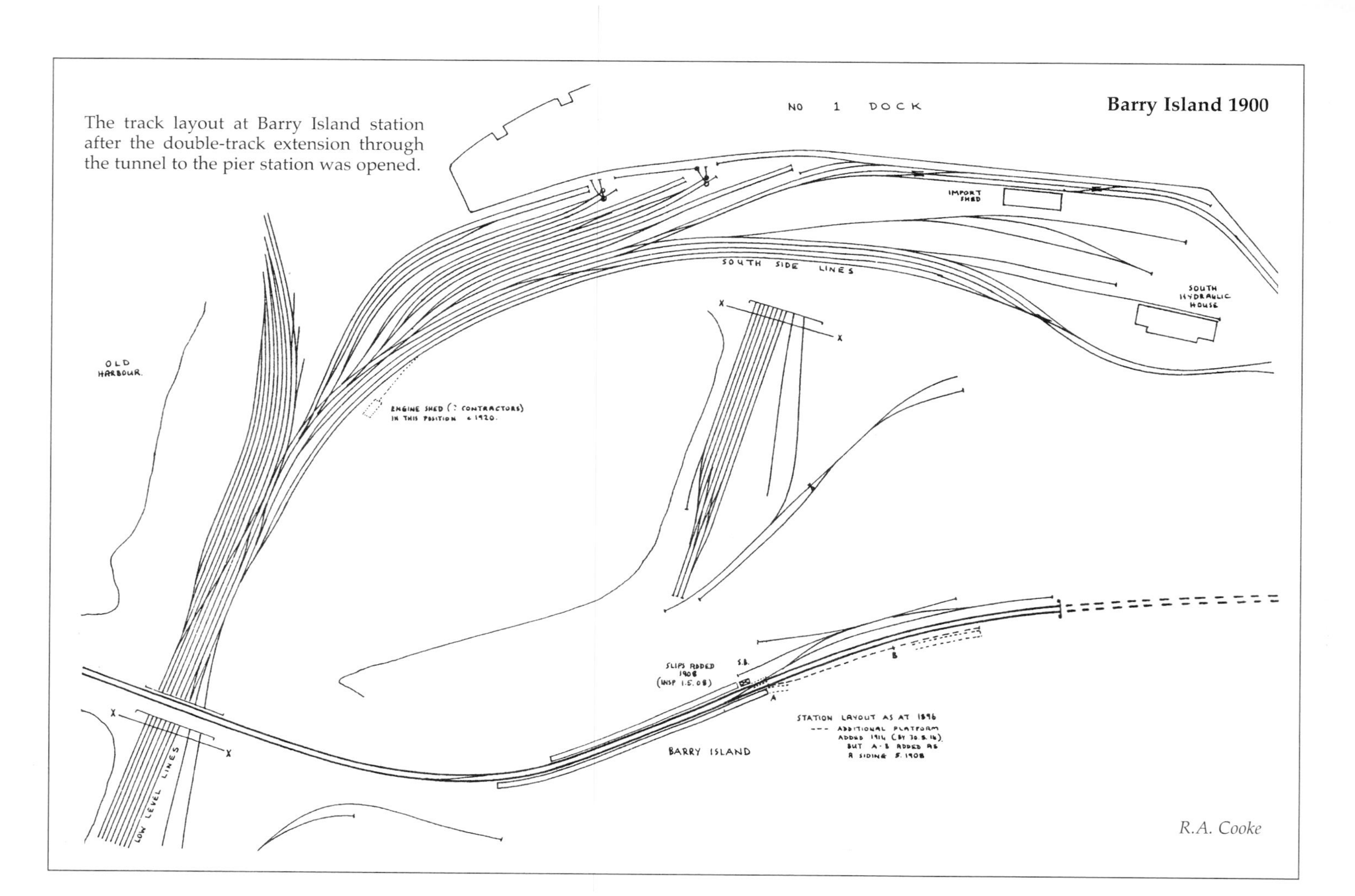

The track layout at Barry Island station after the double-track extension through the tunnel to the pier station was opened.

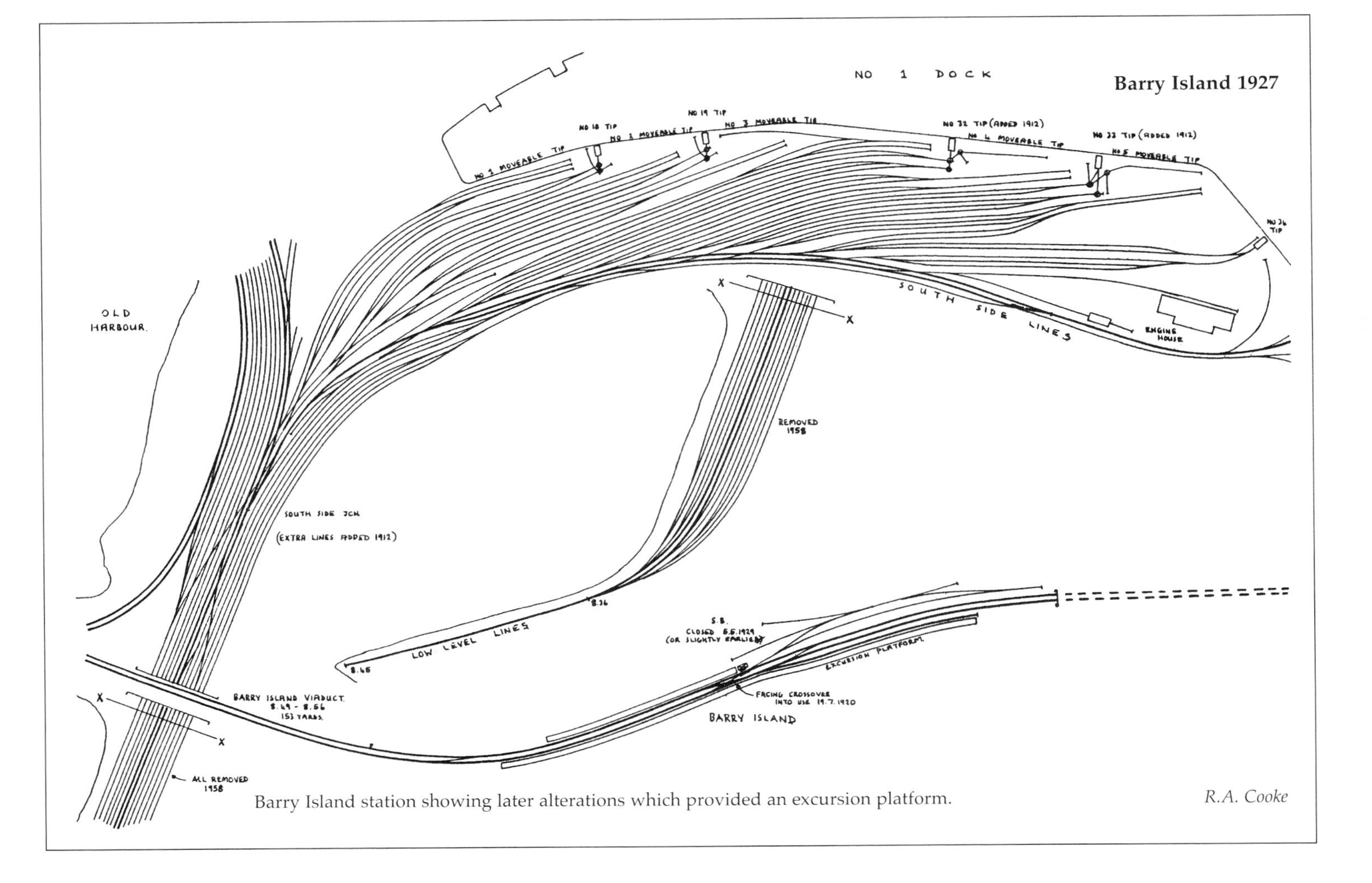

Barry Island station showing later alterations which provided an excursion platform.

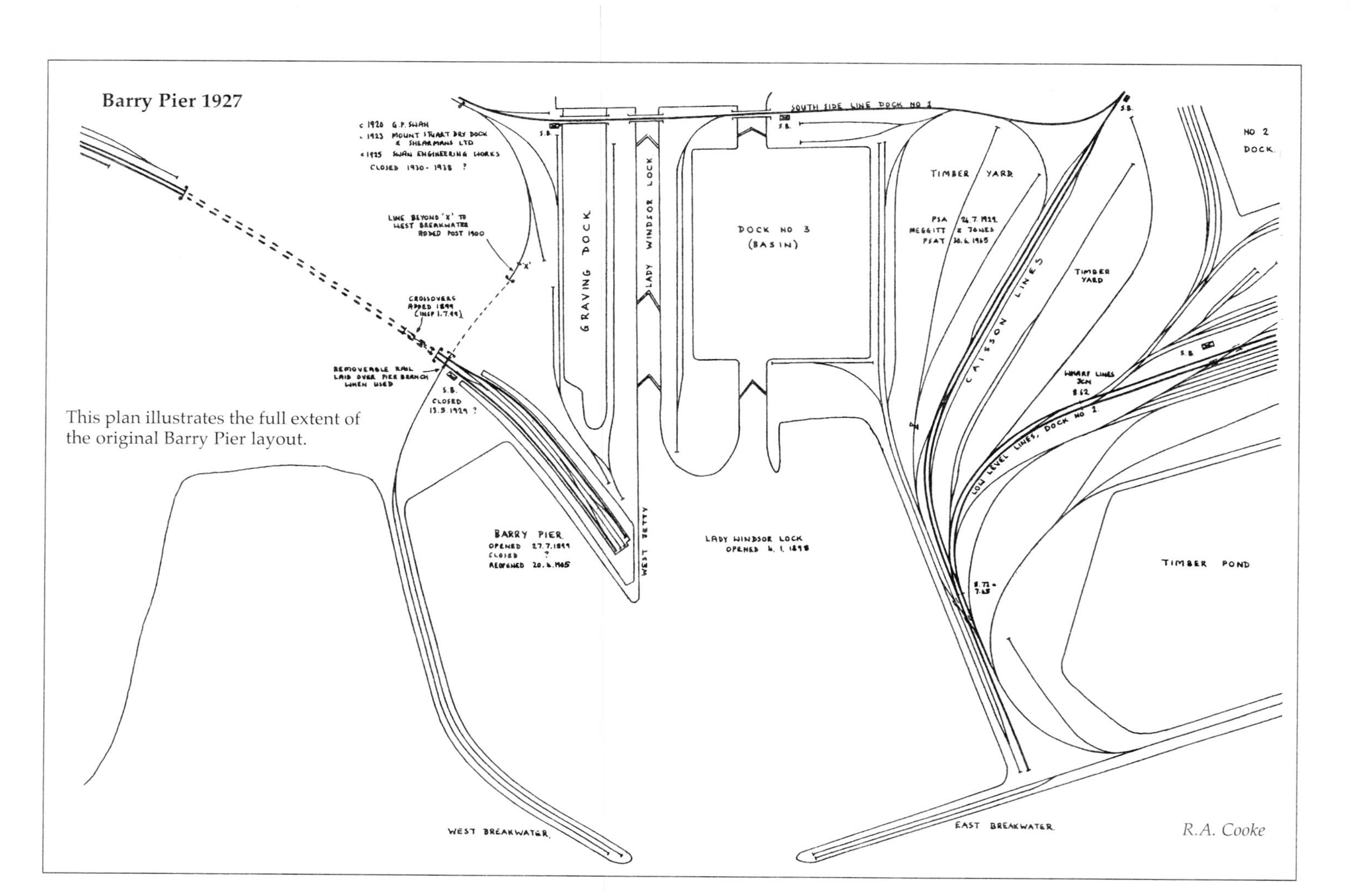

This plan illustrates the full extent of the original Barry Pier layout.

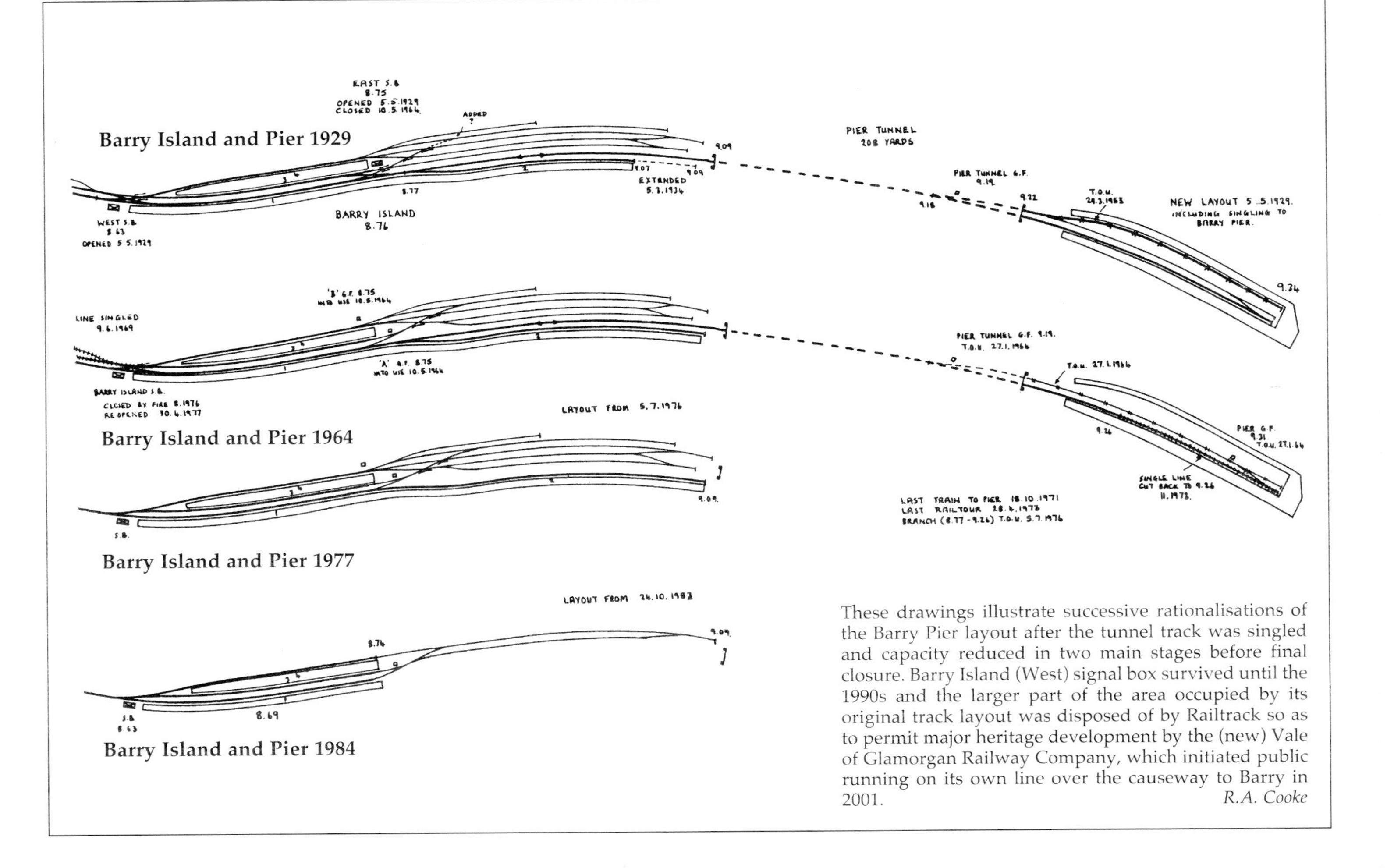

These drawings illustrate successive rationalisations of the Barry Pier layout after the tunnel track was singled and capacity reduced in two main stages before final closure. Barry Island (West) signal box survived until the 1990s and the larger part of the area occupied by its original track layout was disposed of by Railtrack so as to permit major heritage development by the (new) Vale of Glamorgan Railway Company, which initiated public running on its own line over the causeway to Barry in 2001. *R.A. Cooke*

Devonia, at Bristol in June 1934. *Richard Clammer Collection*

Passengers on a day-excursion to Barry Island would also be seeking sustenance and this Ice Cream Parlour formed an attraction in the 1930s, as advertised in the 1933 Edition of the P. & A. Campbell Ltd *Bristol Channel District Guide.* *Author's Collection*

FORTE'S

BRITAIN'S PREMIER ICES

Are delicious, nutritious, very rich in Vitamins and a great Table Sweet Favourite

Ice Cream Parlor

BARRY ISLAND

summer period, or - where the good turn of speed was required, despite the expense of coal - use them to maintain an adequate time ashore in France, when on the Brighton station, to get to Boulogne or Calais or other French ports and back in acceptable timings, as well as on the longer coastal runs to Margate and Bournemouth. This coal consumption factor was critical in their utilisation - the 1905-built pair were reckoned to consume 35 tons per day on a full schedule, whereas original P. & A. Campbell Ltd vessels such as *Britannia* and *Westward Ho* consumed less coal per day, and the later-built vessels such as *Glen Usk* were even more economical in fuel consumption.

Whilst Sid took advantage of the opportunities for short trips from the Landing Stage at Newport which were offered typically by *Ravenswood* in those days which were affordable, ranging between 6*d*. and two shillings a time, these were clearly somewhat less exciting than going 'deep sea' beyond the outer limits of the Bristol Channel. An eight-hour cycle-ride on a newly-purchased Rudge-Whitworth bicycle from Newport to Swansea on Bank Holiday Monday 3rd August, 1931, and thence a tram-journey to Mumbles on the then newly-electrified Swansea & Mumbles Railway, enabled Sid to make his first voyage on *Lady Moyra*, on a one-hour cruise around Swansea Bay. The schedule that day (for the one-time *Gwalia*) was unusual and somewhat hectic but reflected the likely demand of the crowds for some sea air on a peak Bank Holiday Monday, which started with a crossing at 8.45 am from Swansea and Mumbles to Ilfracombe and immediate return, after which no fewer than five short trips were advertised. These were at 1.00 pm from Swansea and 1.15 pm from Mumbles along the Gower Coast, returning to Mumbles only. Then there were four 'Channel trips' from Mumbles at 12.45, 4.00, 5.15 and 6.30 pm, each at a fare of 1*s*. 6*d*. After these cruises, *Lady Moyra* returned to Ilfracombe at 7.30 pm from Mumbles to pick up the passengers who would have had about 10½ hours ashore in North Devon, and would have got back to Swansea around 11.15 that night. Sid stayed the night at the Vivian public house near the old Guildhall in Swansea, for the sum of four shillings bed and breakfast.

By 1932 Sid had started work in an administrative role for the Newport Shipowners' Association, which looked after - *inter alia* - the organisation of some 400 coal trimmers at Newport Docks. That year, Sid went for another cruise on *Lady Moyra*, but this time rather further afield. Making an early start at 7.15 am on Sunday 28th August, 1932 on the connecting steamer *Glen Usk* from Cardiff to Ilfracombe, *Lady Moyra* was booked to leave there at 10.15 am for a 'Special Excursion to the Old World Town of Padstow' with over two hours ashore, and would have started at Swansea that day. Whilst Sid was enjoying the delights of North Cornwall, the paddler offered a cruise from Padstow down the Cornish Coast, passing Trevose Head, to off Newquay, after which the departure from Padstow to Ilfracombe was advertised at 4.15 pm, arriving back at about 8.30 pm. For the hardy souls who had come across from South Wales in the morning, Barry Pier now came into its own as there would be no water at Cardiff for the connecting 9.00 pm return sailing up-Channel from Ilfracombe that night by *Glen Usk*, and so Sid travelled home very late from Barry Pier to Newport by connecting train. He recorded the weather that day as being warm and sunny.

It was decided to revive the popular name of the paddle-steamer *Waverley* and this was bestowed upon the one-time *Barry* in 1925. She was deployed both in the Bristol Channel and on South Coast duties after the name change. *Richard Clammer Collection*

Paddlebox details of *Waverley*, formerly *Barry* (compare this picture with that of *Gwalia*: even in Campbell ownership, the crest of the railway company was retained into the 1930s). *H.A. Allen Collection*

The next year saw Sid again out and about in pursuit of one of the other ex-Barry steamers. On Sunday 18th June, 1933 he joined *Glen Usk* for an 7.00 am departure from Cardiff to Ilfracombe where he intended to join *Devonia* for the round trip to Padstow. However, the weather conditions were dreadful and after encountering heavy seas and gale force conditions, *Glen Usk* turned back off the Foreland and deposited a disappointed Sid back at Cardiff at 12.30 pm. He had also seen *Waverley* leave Cardiff that morning, only to sail out to anchor in Cardiff Roads. Her Bristol Channel sojourn would have been of only a fleeting nature in 1933 as she was scheduled to leave Cardiff for Brighton on Wednesday 21st June. Sid became aware later that day that *Devonia*, then in her first year as the Swansea steamer after replacing *Lady Moyra*, never made it across the Channel either and had to put back into Swansea as Ilfracombe harbour was unable to accept ships. At this stage *Lady Moyra* had become the second *Brighton Queen*, and would have already gone south for her new role as the principal ship at Brighton.

Another career change by 1934 saw Sid more involved directly in shipbuilding and ship repairing as he had then joined the purchasing department in the Mounstuart Dry Dock company at Cardiff. Clearly impressed by the magnificent scenery on the Padstow run in 1932 and frustrated at not getting there again the subsequent year, Sid now had another go. This time he set off on Sunday 24th June, 1934, leaving home at 5.45 am for a special train at 6.45 from Newport to Cardiff and Barry Pier to catch *Westward Ho* from there to Ilfracombe. Through bookings were offered from Newport on this combined rail & steamer excursion, at a fare of 12*s*. 6*d*. One would have needed to save up for a big day-out such as this. This time Sid had better luck and enjoyed his very first sailing on board *Devonia* at 10.15 am from Ilfracombe to Padstow, and thus made his acquaintance with the second of the three former Barry vessels. He recorded that a large crowd watched the arrival of the paddler at the Cornish port, after which she took a cruise down the River Camel, before returning at 4.45 pm from Padstow for Ilfracombe. An uneventful run back up Channel on *Westward Ho* took passengers back to Barry Pier by about 11.30 pm, and Sid got home by 1.15 the next morning by special train from Barry Pier to Cardiff and Newport, in the rain. Sid noted that Captain Bill Riddell was master of *Devonia* in 1934, and had also been the master of *Lady Moyra* before *Devonia* had been transferred to the Swansea station.

A long-distance paddle-steamer excursion was a major undertaking for a young man with limited spare time and finances in the 1930s, but Sid was keen to sample the third of the Barry trio, the one-time *Barry*, latterly *Waverley*, which had eluded him in previous years by being away on South Coast duties. An opportunity arose in 1935 as *Waverley* had returned to Bristol Channel duties that season, and on Sunday 11th August, after rising at 4.30, another early morning train journey at 6.30 from Newport to Barry enabled Sid to board *Waverley* to travel down at 7.45 from Barry Pier to Ilfracombe, calling *en route* at Lynmouth and arriving at 10.00 am. *Devonia* again ran from Ilfracombe to Padstow, having come across from Swansea, and on this occasion Sid noted that there was a large swell on the outwards voyage around Hartland Point and down the Cornish coast, there being 324 passengers on board. Arrival at Padstow was at 2.15 pm, with good time ashore before the return departure from there at 4.45 pm. As on the previous years voyage, the return up-Channel

Another name-change took place in the 1930s when *Lady Moyra* (built for the Barry Railway Company as *Gwalia*) took the popular name of *Brighton Queen*, after which she spent most of her time as the principal steamer at Brighton. Her handsome profile was unchanged and she looked just as good carrying white funnels as in her youth as a Red Funnel Line vessel. This was an 'official' P. & A. Campbell Ltd postcard, possibly issued shortly after her introduction to her new role in the South. *Richard Clammer Collection*

Waverley (formerly *Barry*, built in 1907) depicted in August 1934. *Richard Clammer Collection*

from Ilfracombe (at 8.50 pm, on *Waverley*) was to Barry Pier, arriving at 11.45 pm. The connecting train left there at 12.05 am Monday getting back to Newport at 1.00 am, giving another very long but satisfying Bristol Channel day-out.

This still left the dual challenge of sailing in different waters on the former *Lady Moyra* which had undergone a facelift before being renamed *Brighton Queen*. Aged 21 in 1935, he now took the plunge to make his first White Funnel Fleet Sussex Coast trip, setting off for Brighton by train, and thence by tram to the Palace Pier, to embark upon *Brighton Queen* on Friday 30th August, 1935. This was to enjoy the classic run to Boulogne, calling *en route* at Eastbourne and Hastings, with around 300 other passengers on board. In rather rough conditions the little *Brighton Belle* was passed off Eastbourne, and the Dutch liner *Amsterdam* was also passed that morning. At this time one could travel on these day-excursions to France without a full passport, and Sid recalled collecting a 'day passport' from the booking-office on the Palace Pier with his travel ticket. French customs officers travelled on *Brighton Queen*, and inspected and stamped this passport on the outwards journey, enabling Sid to have a leisurely few hours seeing Boulogne for the first time. Conditions worsened during the day, and the Sussex piers were closed to *Brighton Queen* in the evening as she made her way back from France, so a contingency plan was applied, whereby she put into Newhaven, not arriving there until 12.10 the next morning. Arrival back at Brighton by special bus was at 1.30 am, after which Sid passed a few hours in an all-night cafe before catching the first train of the morning back to London on the way home to Wales.

Over a period of five seasons, 1931-1935 inclusive, Sid had now sampled all the ex-Barry fleet, one of which had changed its identity to become a 'dedicated' South Coast vessel. There was still another challenge, that of sailing on one of the celebrated trips around Land's End when a Bristol-based ship would set out - carrying passengers for the 24 hours-plus sailing - on a positioning voyage from Bristol or Cardiff, or both, to Brighton at the commencement of the season, or the homeward voyage when the season had ended. He decided to sail from Brighton to Bristol on *Waverley* on Monday 28th September, 1936. This involved an overnight journey from Newport to London setting off on the Sunday, and catching an early morning train from London Victoria to Brighton, in order to be able to board *Waverley* for her 11.15 am departure for Ryde, Ilfracombe, Cardiff and Bristol. The sea was particularly calm, and after passing the German liner *Bremen* off Spithead and sailing past Weymouth and Portland, darkness fell about half-way across Lyme Bay. The lights of Torquay and Brixham could be seen in the distance before *Waverley* rounded the Lizard at about 1.00 am and Land's End at about 3.00 am. The entrance to the River Camel was seen at about 7.00 am, and Sid enjoyed lunchtime ashore in Ilfracombe between 11.00 am and 1.30 pm whilst the turn of the tide was awaited. *Waverley* then proceeded to Cardiff, calling in at 4.15 pm. Rather than disembark then and go home to Newport to catch up on some sleep, Sid chose to do things properly by completing the full trip to Bristol and arrived at the Hotwells Landing Stage at 6.30 pm, whence *Waverley* proceeded straightaway into the Cumberland Basin, her season ended on Tuesday 29th September, 1936. Sid then walked up to Temple Meads station and caught a train at 8.25 pm home to Newport, very satisfied after a most successful first 'round trip'.

Another 'official' P. & A. Campbell Ltd postcard view, this time of *Devonia*, probably during her period back in the Bristol Channel in the late-1930s. She was not commissioned for the 1939 season. *Richard Clammer Collection*

Devonia at Porthcawl, 1930s. The Swansea steamer often called in at Porthcawl harbour if the tides permitted, and on occasions Porthcawl might be included on a Cardiff to Mumbles & Tenby excursion. *H.A. Allen Collection*

In this manner Sid travelled on the entire surviving Barry fleet over six seasons using the limited opportunities open to him, and exploring much of the outer reaches of the territories of the White Funnel Fleet, both at home in the Bristol Channel and away on the South Coast. To broaden his range, in 1937 he ventured westward on *Devonia* along the coast of West Wales, again with an early start by train at 5.24 am on Sunday 8th August, 1937 from Newport to Swansea. She left Pockett's Wharf (as it was still known locally) for a cruise to Mumbles, Tenby and the Stack Rocks, giving just an hour ashore at Tenby - and this only took place after a quick return trip (at 8.15 am) from Swansea to Porthcawl beforehand! Such mileages were extreme, but by no means odd, as the big ships needed to earn every possible penny during the relatively short but intensive summer seasons. The two-funnelled 1905-built vessels impressed him greatly, with their own distinctive style, and the equally well-found 1907-built single-funnelled paddler was a great favourite too. The Campbell brothers had, after years of tough competition from their adversaries at Barry, ended up acquiring three fine ships at a good price, which went on to earn their keep.

Sid made another trip on *Devonia*, from Mumbles to Ilfracombe, on Wednesday 17th August, 1938, not realising at the time that this was to be his last trip on that vessel, as she was destined not to be re-commissioned for passenger use the following season. His work took him to Avonmouth in 1939, which necessitated a change of abode, and he spent the war years there immersed in the vital business of ship repairing. He recalled that *Devonia* had proceeded from Bristol, at the start of the 1939 season, to Avonmouth for dry-docking, where he saw her on Saturday 15th July, 1939, ostensibly before commencing her normal summer season duties. Around a month later, by 13th August, 1939, she had been moved to the repair jetty at Avonmouth Old Dock, but never actually entered passenger service that year. She finally sailed from Bristol for Milford Haven on Wednesday 13th September, 1939 for a new, wartime role.

Time was running out for the former Barry vessels after the final 1939 season, and all three were to be lost in the World War II. Again, the research carried out by Chris Collard should be referred to for the full story. The first to be lost were the 1905-built original pair *Brighton Queen* (formerly *Gwalia*) and *Devonia*, at Dunkirk in 1940, within days of one another. *Waverley*, formerly *Barry*, which had acquired the new name of *Snaefell*, was lost on minesweeping duties off the north-east coast during the following year, 1941. But in the peacetime years that had passed since the Barry fleet had been built, in 1905 and in 1907, leading up to World War II it was notable that all three vessels had now spent longer wearing the white funnel than they had the red funnels for their first proud owner, the Barry Railway Company, which had itself passed into history after 1922.

A busy day at Barry Pier, Sunday 5th June, 1938

The year 1938 was the last one before World War II in which the complete 11-strong White Funnel Fleet was operated, and which still included the three former Barry vessels. By Whitsuntide the three vessels detailed for South Coast duties (*Brighton Queen*, formerly *Gwalia*/*Lady Moyra*, *Waverley* formerly *Barry*, and the

The usefulness of the pontoon berth at Barry Pier at low tide is well illustrated in this view of *Ravenswood*, which had doubtless just come across from Weston-super-Mare. The island of Steep Holm is clearly visible between the breakwaters. *H.A. Allen Collection*

Scarcely any room is left on deck in this view of a crowded *Waverley*, from an 'official' P. & A. Campbell Ltd postcard. *Richard Clammer Collection*

newest Campbell ship built in 1922, *Glen Gower*) would have taken up their station, leaving the other eight in the Bristol Channel. The third ex-Barry vessel *Devonia* had, since 1933, usually been the Swansea-based steamer in each high-summer period, and tended not to be commissioned until July on account of her higher fuel consumption. As a result, the more economical *Glen Usk* usually acted as the early-season Swansea steamer. The Swansea-based steamer had little to do with Barry, generally providing a frequent link between Swansea, Mumbles and Ilfracombe as well as forays to Porthcawl and Tenby, and various cruise destinations out of Ilfracombe. With this fleet disposition, the connection of the former Barry Railway Company paddlers with their 'home port' had therefore all but ended, but Barry Pier itself continued to play a key role in the operations of the Bristol Channel-based fleet generally. The year 1938 is a good one to study operations in the Bristol Channel generally, and more particularly at Barry Pier, to see how the existence of this tidally-unconstrained facility influenced programming of the paddlers to their respective stations of Bristol, Newport, Cardiff and Swansea. If the 1912-1914 period had been the heyday of the White Funnel Fleet, then 1938 was arguably a second high point in the history of the P. & A. Campbell Ltd business.

Only seven of the eight Bristol Channel paddlers had been commissioned by early-summer 1938, with *Devonia* not making a first appearance until well into July. Timetables for the day in question, Whit Sunday 5th June, 1938, are particularly interesting as this day was a comparatively rare one when there was a departure from Barry Pier all the way to Lundy Island, to land. This is how the steamers were timetabled at Barry Pier that day, in simplified form, it being notable that there was by now no set 'railway run' departure down-Channel, nor any particular pattern of Barry-Weston-super-Mare 'ferry' services as in the days before the Great War. Nevertheless, four connecting trains were provided for the outgoing steamers that day, by way of extending Barry Island trains for a further three or four minutes, which could easily be managed without disrupting basic services between Cardiff and Barry.

Vessel from	*Dep. Barry Pier*		*Destination*
10.30 am ex-Cardiff & Penarth	11.15 *am*	(*a*)	Minehead, Lynmouth, Ilfracombe & Lundy
11.00 am ex-Bristol & Clevedon	2.00 *pm*	(*b*)	Lynmouth & Ilfracombe
4.00 pm ex-Weston	(5.00)		(*lay-over*)
2.30 pm ex-Bristol	5.15	(*c*)	cruise to Porlock Bay
(from lay-over)	7.45	(*d*)	Weston
6.00 pm ex-Ilfracombe	8.20		Weston and Newport
(from Porlock Bay cruise)	8.30		(*finish*)
6.10 pm ex-Ilfracombe	8.35		Weston, Clevedon and Bristol
6.00 pm ex-Lundy & Ilfracombe	10.15		Penarth and Cardiff

Notes

(*a*) Depart Cardiff (General) 10.12 am, call Grangetown, Cadoxton, Barry Dock, Barry and Barry Island.

(*b*) Depart Cardiff (General) 1.10 pm, call Grangetown, Cogan, Dinas Powis, Cadoxton, Barry Dock, Barry and Barry Island.

(*c*) Depart Cogan 4.34 pm, call Dinas Powis, Cadoxton, Barry Dock, Barry and Barry Island.

(*d*) Depart Cardiff (General) 7.03 pm, call Grangetown, Cogan, Dinas Powis, Cadoxton, Barry Dock, Barry and Barry Island. (Passengers return to Barry via boat Weston to Cardiff, thence any train.)

Waverley became HMS *Snaefell*, and is seen here at Milford Haven in December 1939.
Mitchell Library

Devonia, beached, pictured here on a French/Belgian postcard. *Mitchell Library*

It can thus be seen that the main Cardiff boat called in at Barry Pier, and that one of two vessels deployed on Cardiff-Weston 'ferry' duties called in during the afternoon. The call at Barry Pier by a boat from Bristol heading for Ilfracombe was notable, as this gave the opportunity for folk from Bristol and Clevedon to spend a day at Barry Island. For good measure, the later departure from Barry Pier of a second sailing which had come from Bristol offered, unusually, a Porlock Bay cruise. After tea-time, things started to move in the opposite direction, as it were, there being no less than three vessels returning up-Channel from Ilfracombe that evening which were all scheduled to put in at Barry Pier, whilst there were also three crossings from Barry back to Weston.

The Loss of the Brighton Queen

The loss of *Brighton Queen* occurred in the frightening circumstances of the Dunkerque evacuation, and the stirring story of what happened was described by Captain Watson who spoke to a *Western Daily Press* reporter days after he returned home to Bristol after the ordeal. This item was published on Wednesday 12th June, 1940.

Last Fight of the *Brighton Queen*

Bristol Captain's Story of 'Real Good Day'

The story of the last gallant fight of the *Brighton Queen*, former Bristol pleasure steamer, in the heroic evacuation from Dunkirk, was told to a *Western Daily Press* and *Bristol Mirror* representative yesterday.

On her first visit to Dunkirk, Messrs P. & A. Campbell's well-known steamer found a motor-vessel hard ashore with 500 troops aboard. With ropes and wires passed over her stern the *Brighton Queen* succeeded in towing her off, and having filled herself up with weary warriors, made a successful run to England. The motor-vessel was towed astern all the time until near the English coast when she proceeded under her own engines which had been repaired on the voyage.

Having landed her complement of soldiers, the *Brighton Queen* received orders to return to Dunkirk. This time the Germans gave her a warm welcome, and for half an hour she was subject to incessant bombing attacks, the planes coming over in waves. At one period 60 bombs, including several 500-pounders, were dropped round her in a quarter of an hour. Dunkirk was, however, reached successfully in spite of the number of ships which had been bombed and sunk round the entrance to the breakwater. Berthed near the breakwater, the *Brighton Queen* in a quarter of an hour embarked several hundred French troops.

Dash for Open Sea

She then made a dash for the open sea, and for thirty minutes was left unattacked. After she had rounded the fairway buoy to set a course for home, the Germans appeared in mass formation. Flying over the steamer, they returned again from south-east and west, making a concentrated attack, which only succeeded after three formations had power-dived. All the time the men of the *Brighton Queen* kept up an intense fire with Lewis and Bren guns, while the crew of the 12-pounder did excellent work in continuous rapid fire. After the third formation had power-dived, the last plane succeeded in registering a direct hit.

CAMPBELL'S SAILINGS

(Weather and Circumstances Permitting)

Monday, September 3rd to Friday, September 14th, 1951

From BARRY PIER

MONDAY, SEPTEMBER 3rd.

Lynmouth and Ilfracombe Leave Barry 10.15 and 11.50 a.m. Leave Ilfracombe 5.0 p.m. Lynmouth 5.30 p.m. direct to Barry ; or Leave Ilfracombe 6.0 p.m. Lynmouth 6.30 p.m. for Barry (via Minehead).
Single Trip to Weston, Clevedon and Bristol Leave Barry 7.0 p.m.
Note.—Steamer leaves Bristol 9.15 a.m., Clevedon 10.20 a.m., Weston 11.0 a.m. for Barry.
Steamer leaves Minehead 7.45 p.m. for Barry.

TUESDAY, SEPTEMBER 4th.

Lynmouth and Ilfracombe Leave Barry 10.15 a.m. Leave Ilfracombe 6.0 p.m. Lynmouth 6.30 p.m. for Barry (via Minehead) ; or Leave Ilfracombe 5.30 p.m. Lynmouth 6.0 p.m. direct to Barry.
Lynmouth, Ilfracombe and Cruise to Porlock Bay Leave Barry 12.0 noon Leave Ilfracombe 6.0 p.m. Lynmouth 6.30 p.m. for Barry (via Minehead) ; or Leave Ilfracombe 5.30 p.m. Lynmouth 6.0 p.m. direct to Barry. Fare, to include Cruise 17s.
Single Trip to Weston, Clevedon and Bristol Leave Barry 7.30 p.m.
Note.—Steamer leaves Bristol 9.15 a.m., Clevedon 10.30 a.m., Weston 11.10 a.m. for Barry.
Steamer leaves Minehead 7.45 p.m. for Barry.

WEDNESDAY, SEPTEMBER 5th.

Lynmouth, Ilfracombe and Cruise to off Clovelly Leave Barry 12.15 p.m. Leave Ilfracombe 6.0 p.m. Lynmouth 6.30 p.m. for Barry. Fare to include Cruise, 17s.6d.
Afternoon Cruise to off Minehead Leave Barry 2.30 p.m. Back about 5.15 p.m. Fare 4s.6d.
Single Trip to Weston and Clevedon Leave Barry 5.30 p.m.
Single Trip to Minehead Leave Barry 7.15 p.m.
Single Trip to Clevedon and Bristol Leave Barry 8.0 p.m.
Note.—Steamer leaves Bristol 9.15 a.m., Clevedon 10.35 a.m. for Barry.
Steamer leaves Weston 11.45 a.m. for Barry.

THURSDAY, SEPTEMBER 6th.

Minehead. Leave Barry 8.45 a.m. Leave Minehead 9.10 p.m. for Barry.
Lynmouth, Ilfracombe and Lundy Island (to land) Leave Barry 10.0 a.m. Leave Lundy 5.15 p.m. Ilfracombe 6.45 p.m. Lynmouth 7.15 p.m. for Barry. Return Fare to Lundy Island 18s.6d.
Single Trip to Weston Leave Barry 5.45 p.m.
Evening Cruise calling at Minehead Leave Barry 7.45 p.m. Leave Minehead 9.10 p.m. for Barry. Fare 5s.6d.
Note.—Steamer leaves Weston 11.0 a.m. for Barry.
Steamer leaves Minehead 10.0 a.m. for Barry.

FRIDAY, SEPTEMBER 7th.

Lynmouth and Ilfracombe Leave Barry 12.15 p.m. Leave Ilfracombe 5.45 p.m. Lynmouth 6.15 p.m. for Barry.
Single Trip to Weston Leave Barry 6.0 p.m.
Single Trip to Clevedon and Bristol Leave Barry 7.45 p.m.
Note.—Steamer leaves Weston 2.45 p.m. for Barry.
Steamer leaves Bristol 9.15 a.m., Clevedon 10.35 a.m. for Barry.

SATURDAY, SEPTEMBER 8th.

Lynmouth and Ilfracombe Leave Barry 10.0 a.m. and 12.30 p.m. Leave Ilfracombe 6.0 and 6.15 p.m. Lynmouth 6.30 and 6.45 p.m. for Barry.
Single Trip to Minehead Leave Barry 10.0 a.m.
Afternoon Cruise along the Welsh Coast Leave Barry 4.0 p.m. Back about 6.15 p.m. Fare 4s.
Single Trip to Weston Leave Barry 6.30 p.m.
Single Trip to Clevedon and Bristol Leave Barry 7.0 p.m.
Single Trip to Weston, Clevedon and Bristol Leave Barry 8.0 p.m.
Note.—Steamers leave Weston 11.40 a.m. and 3.0 p.m. for Barry.
Steamer leaves Bristol 11.30 a.m., Clevedon 12.45 p.m. for Barry.

SUNDAY, SEPTEMBER 9th.

Lynmouth, Ilfracombe and Lundy Island (to land) Leave Barry 9.45 a.m. Leave Lundy 5.0 p.m. Ilfracombe 6.45 p.m. Lynmouth 7.15 p.m. for Barry. Return Fare to Lundy Island 18s.6d.
Lynmouth and Ilfracombe Leave Barry 1.30 p.m. Leave Ilfracombe 6.30 p.m. Lynmouth 7.0 p.m. for Barry. Return Fare (this trip only) 10s.
Afternoon Cruise to off Minehead Leave Barry 4.15 p.m. Back about 7.0 p.m. Fare, 4s.6d.
Single Trip to Weston Leave Barry 7.15 p.m.
Single Trip to Weston, Clevedon and Bristol Leave Barry 8.35 p.m.
Note.—Steamers leave Weston 12.30 p.m. and 3.15 p.m. for Barry.

MONDAY, SEPTEMBER 10th.

Ilfracombe and Lundy Island (to land) Leave Barry 10.15 a.m. Leave Lundy 5.15 p.m. Leave Ilfracombe 7.30 p.m. for Barry.
Afternoon Trip to Ilfracombe Leave Barry 3.5 p.m. Leave Ifracombe 7.30 p.m. for Barry. Return Fare (this trip only) 10s.0d.
Single Trips to Lynmouth Leave Barry 10.15 a.m. and 3.5 p.m.

TUESDAY, SEPTEMBER 11th.

Evening Cruise calling at Ilfracombe. Leave Barry 6.15 p.m. Leave Ilfracombe 9.0 for Barry. Fare 8s.6d.
Single Trip to Lynmouth. Leave Barry 6.15 p.m.
Note.—Steamer leaves Ilfracombe 10.30 a.m. Lynmouth 10.30 a.m. for Barry. Steamer leaves Weston 7.30 p.m. for Barry.

WEDNESDAY, SEPTEMBER 12th.

Single Trip to Weston Leave Barry 7.30 a.m.
Lynmouth and Ilfracombe Leave Barry 8.45 a.m. Leave Ilfracombe 4.15 p.m. Lynmouth 4.45 p.m. for Barry.
Afternoon Trip to Minehead Leave Barry 2.50 p.m. Leave Minehead 5.50 p.m. for Barry. Return Fare 6s.

THURSDAY, SEPTEMBER 13th.

Lynmouth and Ilfracombe Leave Barry 9.45 a.m. Leave Ilfracombe 2.15 p.m. Lynmouth 2.45 p.m. for Barry.
Afternoon Trip to Minehead Leave Barry 3.50 p.m. Leave Minehead 7.0 p.m. for Barry. Return Fare 6s.

FRIDAY, SEPTEMBER 14th.

Lynmouth and Ilfracombe Leave Barry 10.45 a.m. Leave Ilfracombe 2.45 p.m. Lynmouth 3.15 p.m. for Barry.
Single Trip to Weston Leave Barry 2.30 p.m.
Single Trip to Clevedon and Bristol Leave Barry 4.45 p.m.
Note.—Steamer leaves Weston 10.0 a.m. for Barry.
Steamer leaves Bristol 8.0 a.m., Clevedon 9.5 a.m. for Barry.

FARES from BARRY PIER

	SINGLE	DAY RETURN	MONTHLY RETURN
WESTON	5s. 6d.	7s. 6d.	
MINEHEAD	6s. 6d.	8s. 6d.	11s. 6d.
LYNMOUTH or ILFRACOMBE	10s. 0d.	13s. 6d.	17s. 0d.

	SINGLE
CLEVEDON ...	6s. 0d.
BRISTOL ...	7s. 0d

Passengers booking Monthly Tickets for Minehead must acquaint themselves that there is a convenient return sailing.

A P. & A. Campbell Ltd handbill advertising sailings from Barry Pier in the 1951 season, where a fair amount of choice of trips was still on offer. *Author's Collection*

The order was given to abandon ship. All on board who could, took to the water and swam around, some clinging to the little wreckage there was left. Fortunately, the sea was smooth, for the life-saving apparatus, with the exception of two rafts, had either been lost or smashed. Small craft and a sloop nearby took prompt action and rescued as many as possible.

Gunned in the Sea

Then the Germans returned and, after dropping more bombs, dived and machine-gunned the survivors struggling in the water. This attack lasted about a quarter of an hour.

About two hours after the steamer had been sunk, all that could be rescued had been picked up, and a course was set by the other vessels for England. On the way over the enemy again appeared and dropped several more salvos of bombs but without effect.

Capt. Watson was in the water something like two hours before he was picked up, and was about the last to leave the ship. 'But', he added to our representative, 'it was a real good day. For it was something attempted, something done'. Dunkirk, he described as an inferno. A pall of black smoke hung everywhere, pierced continually by leaping red tongues of flame. There was not a whole building in the place. Those which had not been demolished were burning fiercely. It was a tragic picture of destruction.

Capt. Watson, who for the two seasons before this war, was in command of *Ravenswood*, took over the *Brighton Queen* at the outbreak of hostilities, when she left Bristol to be fitted for her hazardous war work.

Post-war years

After the end of the war in 1945 the story was much the same for excursion steamer operators as it had been in 1919, with depleted fleets and difficulties in getting vessels back into service. An additional difficulty was presented by the reduced numbers of places at which calls could be made after the destruction of, or damage sustained by, seaside piers. Minehead Pier had actually disappeared during World War II, having being deemed by an Army officer to be in the way of a gun mounted on the old harbour, looking down-Channel! Thus in April 1946, when an initial resumption of Bristol Channel excursion activity from Bristol by *Ravenswood* became possible, there were only a few places she could actually go until the piers at Clevedon, Penarth, Weston, Mumbles and Ilfracombe later came back into use. But the pontoon-berths at Bristol, Newport, Cardiff and Barry were still available, and thus Barry Pier saw its first post-war steamer call advertised to take place on Good Friday 19th April, 1946.

As the White Funnel Fleet gradually regained some of its pre-war strength in the years until the early-1950s, Barry Pier continued to receive its share of calls, albeit with no recognisable traces of the regular service patterns of the early days. During the 1950s the fortunes of P. & A. Campbell Ltd waned as demand for excursion sailings declined, and by 1959 the fleet was down to just two vessels. Some serious questions had to be asked in 1960 by the then owners, the British Transport Commission, about whether funding could be justified for repairs to the structures at Barry Pier, and, after some negotiations, P. & A. Campbell Ltd agreed to contribute to remedial works which were undertaken in 1961/62. This bought time for Barry Pier for the remainder of that decade

Passenger facilities at Barry Pier station were only of a basic character and this picture of an auto-train on an SLS Railtour dates from Saturday 13th July, 1957, after much of the track at the Pier station had been removed, and only the platform nearest to the pontoon was still in use. As can be seen from the railtour details on the special tickets printed for the occasion, Barry Pier was one of a wide variety of locations visited that day, most of the routes traversed having been subsequently closed in the 1960s and 1970s. A significant portion of the original Barry Railway Company network however, between Cogan and Barry Island, remains in use.
Howard Jones Collection

Diagram illustrating proximity of the embarkation point of Barry Pier relative to the main attractions of Barry Island and its railway station. The pier was out of sight to anybody in Whitmore Bay but a brisk walk up to Redbrink Crescent gave access to the footpath down past Jackson's Bay and on to the pier, as an alternative to catching the train. Butlins Holiday Camp took shape in the early-1960s.
Author's Collection

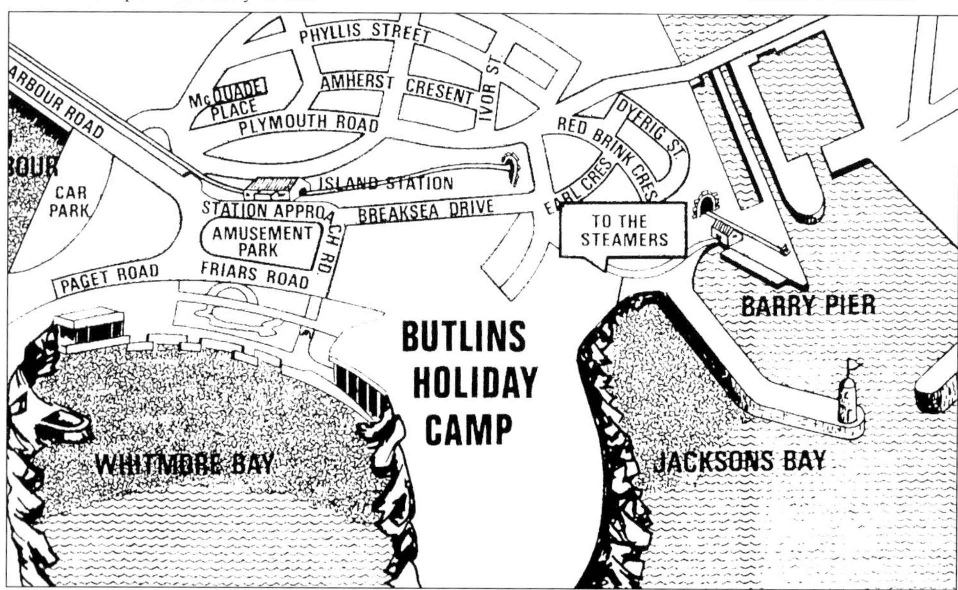

when motorships started to replace the paddlers, until the time was reached towards the end of the 1971 season when it was decided to withdraw from the old-established Cardiff-Weston 'ferry' operation and just operate *Balmoral*, the sole survivor of the White Funnel Fleet on down-Channel services mainly out of Swansea. It was stated in October 1971 that 'the pontoons at Cardiff and Barry have been condemned and will not be used after this season', but in fact occasional steamer calls at Barry did continue throughout 1972 and 1973 even though connecting train services were no longer provided.

Barry Pier sustained gale damage during the winter of 1973/74. Although a very small number of services still made use of the facility during the 1974 season, confirmation came from P. & A. Campbell Ltd in January 1975 that the end had now come, and that calls at Barry Pier would cease completely. Shortly after this the pontoon was removed and, apart from very occasional calls made at the main Barry dock entrance lock by *Balmoral* in the last years of the White Funnel Fleet up until 1980, that really was the end of the Barry Railway Company connection in any tangible sense. In a final reckoning the three purpose-built Red Funnel Line paddle-steamers had each managed about 35 years, and the pier almost three-quarters of a century. The sheer scale of the works of the Barry Railway Company can still be seen at Barry Dock and thereabouts, and it takes little imagination today to envisage a paddle-steamer sailing, well-laden with excited passengers, from this evocative corner of industrial South Wales out into the waters of the Bristol Channel, where the established order of the P.& A. Campbell Ltd empire was once so fiercely challenged.

Balmoral joined the White Funnel Fleet in 1969, when Barry Pier was still in regular use, and is seen here after arrival from Weymouth on 17th May of that year. Seen from the camera of a passenger on board *Westward Ho.* *Pat Murrell Collection*

Barry Pier remained in regular use for a couple more seasons, and *Balmoral* is seen here arriving on a sunny day in August 1971 to collect a few more passengers. The last trains to Barry Pier ran in October of that year after P. & A. Campbell Ltd cut back upper Bristol Channel services after the demise of the motorship *Westward Ho.* *Stan Basnett*

Around Barry Pier today (I): the pontoon has gone, and the Flat Holm boat *Lewis Alexander* is berthed on the corner of the structure to which the pontoon lay adjacent. The pilot station sits on the site of Barry Pier station, the Barry lifeboat awaits a call to duty, and the Lady Windsor entrance-lock is 'behind' in this view, looking up-Channel towards Sully: 2nd August, 2002. *Author*

Postscript: Steamers at Barry after the end of the White Funnel Fleet era

Regarding excursion steamers, Barry could be said to have slumbered in the 1980s after the withdrawal of *Balmoral* as a P. & A. Campbell Ltd-owned vessel. Without Barry Pier, it seemed as though an era had irrevocably ended, as there was seemingly nowhere suitable for an excursion vessel such as *Waverley*, which visited the Bristol Channel annually after her return to service in the late-1970s, to tie up. Nearby Penarth Pier played a key role in the development of the services provided by Waverley Excursions Ltd and the remarkable return to service of *Balmoral* in 1986 as consort to the world's last sea-going paddle-steamer, as *Waverley* was promoted, was an event few predicted.

Back in the 1890s Treharne Pier at Barry Island provided a calling-point for early excursion steamers such as the paddle-tugs operated by Edwards, Robertson, about whom we heard at the beginning of this story. As a result of some persistence by Barry-born Terry Sylvester, then a Director of Waverley Excursions Ltd (WEL) and a key influence in the success of the preservation movement, the South Glamorgan local authority was persuaded to tidy up the access through the coach-park along the breakwater to what became known as Barry Old Harbour, where mooring bollards were erected a stone's throw away from where Treharne Pier had once stood a century before. In the mid-1990s a small number of calls were made by both *Waverley* and *Balmoral* at this location, when tides permitted. The author made one trip from Barry Old Harbour to Penarth on the paddler when she called in on her return up-Channel on an evening cruise which had called at Minehead. On another occasion, *Balmoral* called in whilst on passage on a big morning tide, from Penarth to Porthcawl, and berthing there was an operation calling for all the skill and local knowledge that her Captain had.

A number of key WEL personnel have a strong Barry connection, notably Captain Steve Colledge (master of *Waverley*) and WEL Chairman and one-time Superintendent Engineer Ian MacMillan, who has overseen the recent refits of both classic vessels. In 2003 former *Balmoral* Second Engineer from P. & A. Campbell Ltd days, Ken Angel of Barry, still helped out as required, and a new development in June 2004 was a special sailing from Barry No. 1 Dock (now referred to as Barry Waterfront) by *Waverley* to Penarth and Clevedon, in connection with the Barry Festival of Transport to promote the growing Vale of Glamorgan heritage railway which links Barry Island with the newly-built Hood Road station just along from No. 1 Dock. An aim of this concern is to reinstate a train-service through the former Barry Railway Company tunnel from Barry Island station to the site of the former Barry Pier.

The maritime link of the Bristol Channel island of Flat Holm is with Barry, and although the pontoon has long gone the small vessel *Lewis Alexander* provides scheduled sailings from her berth at the corner of the Barry Pier & Barry Dock Entrance Lock structure. Continued regeneration efforts by the Vale of Glamorgan Council make it likely that things will continue to develop around Barry Dock . . .

Around Barry Pier today (II): the tunnel mouth of the line from Barry Island station has been bricked up for many years since closure in 1971; 2nd August, 2002. *Author*

Around Barry Pier today (III): the other end of the tunnel can just be discerned in this view taken from the footbridge at Barry Island station. The Vale of Glamorgan Railway Company project had started to take shape from its new base at Plymouth Road: 2nd August, 2002. *Author*

Author's Notes

As will have been gathered from the text, the precise ownership and identity of the Barry paddle steamers was rather convoluted. Despite that which is stated on the caption of the colour picture (page 148), there never was a legally-constituted 'Barry and Bristol Channel Steamship Company', and the postcard from which it was taken, based on a Clyde trials photograph, appears to have been retouched to simulate (faked) red funnels instead of the buff funnels with which *Gwalia* is documented to have been delivered. The first change of colour scheme which *Gwalia* and *Devonia* underwent (around May-June 1905) was similar to that used by the fleet of the Glasgow & South Western Railway, defined by Alan Paterson thus: 'Above a red underbody, the hull was painted dove grey with white saloons, sponson houses and paddle boxes, while the funnel was scarlet with black top. Deckhouses were the usual varnished teak, and lifeboats white'. The second change of colour scheme, thought to have taken place before the 1906 season, although some commentators have opined 1907, was to a black hull-colour, still with red funnels, and which with minor detail variants continued throughout the era of ownership by the successor to the Barry Railway Company for 1910 and 1911, The Bristol Channel Passenger Boats Ltd.

The title of the Chairman of the Barry Railway Company was Lord Windsor, in the earlier part of the story, and he is referred to in the text as such. From December 1905 he became the Earl of Plymouth (the first), and which title is thus referred to in the text after that time. He was Chairman of the Barry Railway Company throughout its life.

Although this can only be conjecture, I think the principal underlying spirit of the Barry Railway Company from its infancy, and which perhaps guided the diversification into passenger shipping, can possibly be gleaned from this part of the speech made by David Davies, the Deputy Chairman of the company. He rose to speak at the luncheon given on 18th July, 1889 to commemorate the opening of Barry Dock and, after proposing the toast 'Success to the Barry Dock and Railways', and describing the background to the new undertaking and the belief that it had been vitally necessary to develop commerce, he uttered these remarks:

> It is not our object in providing these works, nor has it been from the beginning of our great enterprise, to create an undue competition, but to provide ample accommodation for the rapid and unfettered expansion of the various trades of the district, and so facilitate their development for the general benefit of the whole community . . . I have no hesitation in stating my firm belief that we shall be the means of further increasing the trade to such a degree by the favourable position and great extent of our works, the safety they afford, as well as by the numerous and various facilities provided . . . such that there need be no excessive competition for it, but only such healthy rivalry as will result in the the ultimate advantage of all.

The paddle-steamer *Waverley* made a special call at Barry No. 1 Dock, now known as the Waterfront, in June 2004, and berthed not far from the former Barry (low-level) goods shed which has since become a feature of the Hood Road platform used by the Vale of Glamorgan Railway.
Author

Acknowledgements

A large number of people, either knowingly or unwittingly, have helped in the gathering together of information about the Barry steamers over the last few years, to the extent that I eventually felt there was enough to pull the story together in a reasonably complete manner. As stated in the Introduction, I owe a great debt to the late George (H.G.) Owen of Swansea who carried out his own original research into the operations of the Barry steamers, three of which he had travelled on himself in the 1920s and 1930s in Campbell days. It was most satisfying to share the information with George that I gathered from different sources to those which he had tapped into to build up a picture of how the Barry Railway Company Directors at first worked with, and then turned against the Campbell interests in Bristol. Dr David Jenkins of the National Museums and Galleries of Wales provided research help, and much encouragement from Terry Sylvester, formerly the Chairman of Waverley organisation and himself a scion of Barry, was also received.

Many friends and acquaintances within the Paddle Steamer Preservation Society have added other pieces of information, notably Sid Robinson with his memories and diaries of travel in the 1930s, and Donald Anderson who edited the excellent journal *Ship Ahoy* and himself researched aspects of the short-lived Bristol Channel Passenger Boats Ltd and the Tuckers 'Yellow Funnel Fleet' concerns. John Spears provided help with company records data, and Howard Jones with some 1950s memorabilia. Others have greatly assisted with illustrative material, and it is doubtful if this book would have been possible without the unrestricted access I had to the photographic and postcard collection of Lionel Vaughan, well known in Bristol Channel circles for his genial personality aboard the preserved vessels *Waverley* and *Balmoral* which keep alive the traditions at Barry and elsewhere.

Access to old copies of local newspapers at the remarkable Ilfracombe Museum has been invaluable, for which I thank Sue Pullen and her colleagues. My trips to the Glasgow University Business Archive and the National Archives at Kew to check on resources connected with the Barry story were also pleasurable, and the help of George Gardiner at Glasgow in extracting copies of shipbuilders plans for the Clyde-built Barry fleet and other data was greatly appreciated. Enquiries at both the Maritime Coastguard Agency and Glamorgan County Record Office in Cardiff regarding ships registry details also met with great help and courtesy. The photographic and timetable collections of the late H.A. Allen have been an important aspect in understanding what went on at Barry Pier before and during the P. & A. Campbell Ltd era, for which I thank the trustees of the collection. Ken Jenkins of Bristol kindly made available previously unseen photographs of the Barry steamers. Other information came from Brian Luxton of Barry, whose own pictorial books on Barry and the surrounding region make fascinating reading, and Tony Cooke made available his very detailed railway line diagrams of the Barry area, from his own much wider Great Western Railway researches.

I should also thank Colin Chapman for his advice on Barry Railway Company affairs, including maritime references, and finally Richard Clammer for proof-reading and continuing moral support.

Sources

Custom House Registers for the Port of Cardiff (older volumes for Cardiff are held at the Glamorgan Record Office, at Cardiff). More recent volumes are held by the Maritime & Coastguard Agency at Ty Glas, Cardiff.

Minute Books of the Barry Railway Company, Press Cuttings volumes (held at National Archives, Kew).

Minute Books of P. & A. Campbell Ltd (held at Bristol City Archive).

Board of Trade records of dissolved companies (held at National Archives, Kew).

Records of John Brown & Company, Ltd (latterly Upper Clyde Shipbuilders), held at University of Glasgow, Archive Services.

Parliamentary records

Barry Railway (Steam Vessels) Act, 1904

Midland Railway Act 1905,

Pier & Harbour Order Confirmation (No. 3) Act, 1906 (relating to Burnham, in the County of Somerset)

The Burnham (Somerset) Pier Act 1907

Newspapers and Periodicals

Barry Dock News

Bristol Times & Mirror

Ilfracombe Chronicle

Ilfracombe Gazette and Observer

North Devon Journal

South Wales Argus

Western Daily Press

Western Mail

Weston Mercury & Somersetshire Herald

Journals/Magazines

Clyde River Steamer Club annual magazines, in particular Edn 34/Summer 1998, article by J.A. Innes, 'The Clydebank Paddlers'.

Cruising Monthly, 1960s-date

Paddle Wheels, quarterly journal of the Paddle Steamer Preservation Society

Ship Ahoy, published 1955-69 by the South Wales Branch of the World Ship Society, in particular:

Autumn 1957, 'The Barry Railway', by H.G. Owen

Spring 1962, 'The Pockett Packets', by H.G. Owen,

Spring 1968, 'Scrapbook for 1911', by D.J. Anderson

The Railway Magazine, two items: (1) October 1906, Illustrated interview with Edward Lake, General Manager, Barry Railway; (2) April 1918, 'The Barry Railway: Its Characteristics, Engines and Traffic' by M.L. Hopwood. Also, *Track Layout Diagrams of the GWR and BR(WR) Vol. 44B Pt. 2, Barry & the Vale of Glamorgan* by R.A. Cooke, 1987

NB *Best of Ship Ahoy;* a compilation of articles from *Ship Ahoy* was published April 1999 by the Bristol Channel Branch of the Paddle Steamer Preservation Society, including the two stated above from 1962 and 1968.

Bibliography

Athill, R., *The Somerset and Dorset Railway* (David & Charles, 1967)

Ballinger, J., *Guide to Cardiff, City and Port* (National Union of Conservative & Constitution Associations, 1908)

Barrie, D.S.M., *The Barry Railway* (The Oakwood Press, 1962)

Brodie, I., *Steamers of the Forth* (David & Charles, 1976)

Burtt, F., *Cross-Channel & Coastal Paddle Steamers* (Richard Tilling, 1937)

Campbell, Ltd P. & A., *The Bristol Channel District Guide*, various editions (F.G. Warne for P. & A. Campbell)

Chapman, C., *The Vale of Glamorgan Railway* (The Oakwood Press, 1998)

Chappell, E.L., *History of the Port of Cardiff*, 1939 (Second Edition 1994, Priory Press, Cardiff)

Collard, C., *A Dangerous Occupation* (Wheelhouse Books, 1999)

Collard, C., *On Admiralty Service* (Tempus Publishing, 2003)

Collard, C., *Special Excursions* (Wheelhouse Books, 1998)

Coombes, N., *Passenger Steamers of the Bristol Channel* (Twelveheads Press, 1990)

Coombes, N., *White Funnel Magic* (Twelveheads Press, 1995)

Cumbrian Railways Association, *Furness Railway 150* (Cumbrian Railways Association, 1996)

Davis, G.M., *The loss of HMS Montagu, Lundy 1906* (G.M. & R.C. Davis - privately published, 1981)

Duckworth, C.L.D., and Langmuir, G.E., *West Coast Steamers* (Stephenson, 1966)

Farr, G., *West Country Passenger Steamers* (Stephenson, 1967)

Handley, C., *Maritime Activities of the Somerset & Dorset Railway* (Millstream Books, 2001)

Hope, Iain, *The Campbells of Kilmun* (Aggregate Publications, Johnstone, 1981)

Jenkins, Dr D., *Shipowners of Cardiff: A Class by Themselves* (University of Wales, 1997)

Luxton, B.C., *Old Barry in photographs, Vols 1, 2, 3,* (Stewart Williams, Barry, 1977/78/90)

McQueen, Andrew, *Clyde River Steamers 1872-1922* (The Strong Oak Press, 1990)

Miller, B.J., *Rails to Prosperity - the Barry & After* (Regional Publications (Bristol) Ltd, 1984)

Moore, Donald (Ed.), *Barry - The Centenary Book,* (Barry Centenary Book Committee Ltd, 1984)

Paterson, A.J.S., *The Golden Years of the Clyde Steamers 1889-1914* (David & Charles, 1969)

Paterson, A.J.S., *Classic Scottish Paddle Steamers* (David & Charles, 1982)

Poole, S., *Weston-super-Mare, a Pictorial History* (Phillimore, 1995)

Rhys, E., *The South Wales Coast* (T. Fisher Unwin, 1911)

Thomas, I., *Top Sawyer* (Longmans, Green & Co. Ltd, 1938, reprinted 1988)

Thornley, F.C., *Steamers of North Wales* (Stephenson, 1952)

Thornton, E.C.B., *South Coast Pleasure Steamers - new edition* (Stephenson, 1969)

Wall, R., *Bristol Channel Pleasure Steamers* (David & Charles, 1973)

Waters, B., *The Bristol Channel* (J.M. Dent & Sons, 1955)

Wilson, R., *Passenger Steamers of the G&SW* (Twelveheads, 1991)

Other sources

Ward Lock, various 'Red' guides

Index